BRING BACK
THE BUFFALO!

BRING BACK THE BUFFALO!

A Sustainable Future for America's Great Plains

Ernest Callenbach

ISLAND PRESS
Washington, D.C. • Covelo, California

LIBRARY OF CONGRESS CATALOGING-IN-PUBLICATION DATA

Callenbach, Ernest.
Bring back the buffalo! : a sustainable future for America's Great
Plains / Ernest Callenbach.
p. cm.
Includes bibliographical references and index.
ISBN 1-55963-440-5 (cloth)
1. American bison— Great Plains.   I. Title.
SF401.A45C34 1996
333.95′9—dc20   95-4864
CIP

Printed on recycled, acid-free paper ✪
Manufactured in the United States of America

10 9 8 7 6 5 4 3 2 1

FOR CHRISTINE
As always, beloved instigator and collaborator

And in memory of all those who
saved the buffalo from extinction, including

SAMUEL WALKING COYOTE

CHARLES ALLARD

MICHAEL PABLO

C. J. "BUFFALO" JONES

CHARLES GOODNIGHT

CAPTAIN MOSES HARRIS

SCOTTY PHILIP

Contents

Part I: BISON PAST   *1*
Chapter One: The Bison Heartland   *9*
Chapter Two: The Managed Land   *37*

Part II: BISON PRESENT   *59*
Chapter Three: Bison on Indian Reservations   *65*
Chapter Four: Bison on Public Lands   *87*
Chapter Five: Bison on Ranches   *115*

Part III: BISON FUTURE   *145*
Chapter Six: Bison Country   *149*
Chapter Seven: Real Productivity   *171*
Chapter Eight: Bison as a Food Source   *185*
Chapter Nine: A Buffalo Commons   *199*
Chapter Ten: Bison and Wind Power   *221*
Chapter Eleven: Bison Politics and Cowboy Culture   *241*

CONCLUSION: They Will Come   *261*

Notes   *263*
Recipes   *272*
Acknowledgments   *274*
Index   *275*

Part I Bison Past

Many fine books look back with painful nostalgia to the days when 60 million buffalo roamed the grasslands of America and tell of how they fell tragic victims to human greed. This book instead looks forward with high hopes to a future when these legendary beasts will again grace the American landscape in vast numbers—providing permanent sustenance to the rural inhabitants of the Great Plains and playing a key role in the balance of nature on the Plains.

Buffalo are coming back, even though some Americans may think they are extinct. Some 200,000 buffalo, in fact, are alive on the North American continent now. These magnificent animals have already regained a place among us. In the future, if we give them room, they can roam again over much of their former range, and their presence can help us to restore it to permanent productivity. Indeed, the fate of the bison may well prove emblematic of the future of our nation.

The Plains are bison country. Bison have successfully inhabited the region for ten thousand years, since the last ice age, and their bigger and wider-horned progenitor species were here for hundreds of thousands of years before that. Bison fit the western landscape, with its sweeping expanses, its pitiless winters, its austere beauty. In their powerful, shaggy profile, in their ability to forage over limitless areas, find food under the snow, and endure blizzards, bison have always belonged in the West. Bringing them back to a significant portion of their native home will heal a painful gap in our national memory.

Only a hundred and fifty years ago, the Great Plains were invaded by Euro-Americans intent on reproducing in these new territories the agriculture of northern Europe, based on grains, sheep, and cattle. The livestock they relied on had been bred over the centuries to stolid timidity in the hedged pastures and mild climate of Europe and England; they could survive on the Plains only with extensive human help. To make room for them, and for fields created by breaking the prairie sod, the newcomers reduced the proud and innumerable bison to a remnant species on the verge of extinction, and decimated the bison-hunting Indian tribes along with them.

But history takes curious turns. Now, throughout the country, bison are coming back. There are twenty bison herds in the mountain valleys of my home state of Pennsylvania, and herds exist in all fifty states of the union. There are large commercial bison ranches operating in many Plains states; the fact that bison are a source of nutritious, low-fat meat makes them attractive to ranchers, restaurateurs, and people watching their diets—all of whom would benefit if bison became a part of the national meat supply. To Indians, bison are a basic link to the spiritual energy of the universe, and many tribes are actively restoring bison to reservation lands. To ecologists, bison are a key element in the complex ecosystem of the Plains, and public herds in Yellowstone National Park and other parks have multiplied greatly.

No one can now doubt that bison again have a future in their own land. But what kind of future will it be? Bison are alert, independent, robust animals, with all the dignity of the wild. We are considering here a species that deserves to be our official national animal—a memorable symbol of fierce American pride in survival with freedom, as is the bald eagle, our national bird. Strength, endurance, adaptability, and cooperation in the face of danger make the bison a striking emblem of America. In the last chapter, I will outline several measures that Congress should enact to ensure the survival of bison in the wild; the first should be to give it official national animal status. This action would celebrate the fact that bison have been brought back from near extinction—perhaps our most dramatic environmental success story.

This book focuses on an often ignored region, the Great Plains, which extends through ten states and occupies a high, dry grassland region where Euro-American plow agriculture and, to a lesser degree, cattle ranching, have been in steep decline since the 1920s. It is a spacious, captivating, and starkly beautiful area, but its limited rainfall and recurrent droughts impose inescapable limits on farming. More than a hundred Plains counties, the equivalent of several whole states, are now emptier of people than the level once considered to define the American frontier—a mere two persons per square mile—and more counties are joining the list.

Thus, in some ways the Plains might appear to be an unpromising part of the nation. But the Plains are the only region in the country—and perhaps in the world—where there is a real chance of achieving, within the lifetimes of present generations, a way of living on the land that will be sustainable for centuries to come. On the Plains we can transform current petroleum-based farming and ranching into an enduring, self-reliant system resting on the perennial resources of the region: sun, grass, and wind. On the Plains, a deep planetary challenge of long-term human survival waits to be met.

"Bison" or "buffalo"? They are the same animal and should properly be called bison. "Buffalo" may derive from an early French explorer's phrase, since boeuf *in French refers to cattle. The term should really be reserved for the Cape buffalo of South Africa and the water buffalo of Asia, which both have wide, curved horns.*

For more than ten thousand years, this region was a rich wonderland of endless grasslands—prime habitat for bison. It still is, despite the tracery of railroads, fences, roads, and power lines laid across it in the past hundred and fifty years and the sometimes thriving county seats and other towns that dot the landscape. The fading of Euro-American farms from the Plains is often lamented, but from a biological point of view it represents a process of reestablishment of a rural population level that the land can support. And that level, it is becoming clear, can be maintained indefinitely through two fundamental changes that lie ahead for the Plains: first, the restoration of the great grazing herds of bison and the smaller numbers of pronghorn, deer, and elk that naturally accompany them, and second, the widespread development of wind power.

We can envision the future Plains as vibrantly sustainable, preserving traditional American values in small towns scattered through the region.

A bull's mighty shoulders and horns, combined with two thousand pounds of bone and muscle, make him fearless. Thick hair—up to six inches thick on the "cape"—protects him against cold. Bison have ranged from the far north to Mexico. Photo: Michael H. Francis.

These towns will draw their strength from some continued farming, from surrounding herds of bison providing a healthy, low-fat alternative to beef, and from "wind farms" with turbine towers sprinkled along the rises and ridges. The beauty, grandeur, and dignity of the land will be restored and preserved. The towns will much resemble those towns remaining vigorous today—in some cases, with such innovations as stout fencing around them to keep bison out. The soil and its grasses, for reasons we will examine later, will be healthier than at present. Many fences and small county roads will no longer be needed. Thus, in large areas, aside from an occasional highway or power line, the grasses will again blow endlessly in the Plains winds, a splendid playground supporting humans and grazing herds alike.

"Sustainable," a basic ecological term, is applied to an ecosystem that can endure stably over a long period. (An ecosystem is a community of living organisms, usually including human beings, linked in complex relations of interdependence.) For ecologists as for the ecosystems they study, the long term is much longer than for politicians or corporate officials, who normally look ahead only to the next election or the next quarterly financial report. When ecologically oriented people ask for sustainability, they are asking for arrangements that will work dependably until the next ice age comes—probably several thousand years in the future.

Sustainability will, I believe, become the dominant idea of the twenty-first century, displacing the ideology of unlimited growth that we inherited from the era of industrial expansion. Even with "merely" 5.5 billion people on earth, roughly half living barely above a subsistence level and thus capable of only local damage, we are pressing severely against the limits our planet sets for human extraction and utilization of materials and energy. Alarm bells keep going off: ozone thinning, expected climate change, a drop in per capita grain supplies, unpredictable waves of migration. Further major disruptions of the natural order would ensue if most of the earth's population attained even the consumption levels of, say, the United States in 1965—about half of what Americans now consume. Ecological catastrophes also seem inevitable if the now rich nations merely continue their present consumption patterns, the biological impacts of which are distributed all over the planet. Social-ecological disasters are already well under way, of course, in Africa and Latin America.

Amid this ongoing and deepening global crisis, the opportunity the Plains offer for "sustainable shrinkage" is unique and remarkable. The Plains provide a laboratory in which shrinkage in rural population and in agricultural activity is already taking place. The question of whether this shrinkage can lead to a transition to sustainability is thus of far more than regional or national interest. On the Plains we might be able to read lessons for the fate of the earth and of our species.

The possibilities are inspiring. We inherit in the Plains a spacious landscape that once functioned beautifully and productively, its many plant and animal inhabitants (including humans) living in balance for the more than ten millennia from the last glacial age until the massive ecological transformation brought by Euro-American settlement. Can this now troubled land be restored to its natural functioning? Although the challenge may seem massive, it is actually far less daunting than was the attempt by Euro-American settlers to turn a third of a nation from grasslands into farms—with a speed and on a scale for which there were no precedents in all of human history. The replacement of native grazing animals by imported livestock, the displacement of native grasses by European ones, the extermination of the predators who once performed crucial roles at the top of the Plains food chains—these changes represented the most stupendous transformation of a landscape that human beings have ever attempted. Now that this imported economy of cows and plows has run its course, we must seize the opportunity to restore the age-old natural balance. And in this great story, bison have a central role to play.

Bison are indomitable, unpredictable, and powerful; they demand respect from humans. As they return to the landscape in large numbers, we will have to explore a new kind of relationship between our species and theirs. Still, any danger bison may pose to humans is infrequent, mostly accidental, and generally avoidable by using ordinary common sense—that is, respecting them and keeping a safe distance.

The ecological virtues of bison are exceptional. They digest grasses and other plants more efficiently than do livestock, and "harvesting" of bison, if such a term can be used, would utilize that basic, renewable, solar-driven process with maximum efficiency. They do less ecological damage to the land than livestock do, especially in waterside areas. Their presence on the Plains would be sustainable for as long as we can see ahead.

It is sometimes thought visionary to imagine a coming solar age, in which not only our food but also our energy supplies derive from the sunlight that will impinge on our planet for millions of years to come—our only truly permanent supply of energy. Throughout history, however, humans have *always* lived in solar ages. First, as gatherers and hunters harvesting edible plants and killing animals, we directly captured the photosynthetic productivity of plants and the animals that lived on them. Then, as we began to develop the crafts of town and city living, we utilized the solar energy stored in the timber of forests that still surrounded early cities—to bake our clay pots, cook our food, hold up our roofs, warm our houses.

When all the easily accessible wood was gone, we turned to fossil fuels laid down by solar-driven biological activity hundreds of millions of years ago: initially coal and, more recently, oil and gas. On the earth's limited store of fossil fuels, and the myriad advanced technologies of agriculture and industry dependent on them, we have built a human population approaching 6 billion and a complex infrastructure of physical facilities for transporting, housing, and employing ourselves.

Individuals can sometimes display foresight and responsibility within the brief time scale of human lives. However, there is little reason to believe that humans as a species have thus far given any more real thought to the long-term future than have butterflies. The naturalist Edward O. Wilson observes, "Ecological and evolutionary time, spanning centuries and millennia, can be conceived in an intellectual mode but has no immediate emotional impact." Only very recently have we begun to have at least a glimmering of what we must do to better our chances of fruitful and long-term occupancy of the planet. But as a result, evolutionary changes are afoot in the ways we manage our grasslands, agricultural lands, forests, and fisheries. These changes affect land owners, workers in the various industries involved, government agencies, and members of the public—both as consumers and as citizens—and engender lawsuits, political campaigns, new regulations, and new attitudes.

The buffalo nickel, first minted in 1913, bore an Indian head on the reverse side. At that time, many Americans were under the impression that both Indians and bison had vanished from the Plains. The nickel, designed by James Earle Fraser, was criticized for the unrealistic position of the buffalo head, but the image remains a classic American icon.

Strenuous argument is always inevitable and necessary as old ideas give way to new. This book attempts to make a constructive contribution to one aspect of a great debate that will continue beyond our lifetimes. Some of the information presented will be generally familiar to readers who have followed scientific and environmental thinking during the past several decades. But it is my hope that the book will also appeal to many readers who are simply interested in the future of our country—for its people and its nonhuman inhabitants alike. I have attempted to lay out clearly the basic issues we must resolve to find solutions that will serve the planet, the nation, and the responsible earth citizens we should aspire to be.

Chapter One
The Bison Heartland

For more than ten centuries the bison, elk, deer, and pronghorn played in grasslands that covered what we now label as a dozen states, over which they ranged freely as forage and browse and water sources drew them. They were kept from overrunning their food resources by two major kinds of predator, human hunters and disease organisms, though wolves and bears had some effect too. The sun-powered productivity of the continent's sea of grass was shared with millions of prairie dogs, with ferrets and badgers and hawks that preyed on the prairie dogs, and with billions of tiny decomposers that consumed dead organic material and sent it on its next life cycle. Thick, rich soils were held in place against the fierce Plains winds and the scouring Plains rainstorms by a deep, tough network of perennial roots; thus, erosion was minimized and streams ran clear. The bounty of the landscape seemed immeasurable and eternal, with bison as its dominant feature.

Bison are quintessentially American animals: stalwart, noble symbols of wildness, freedom, and self-sufficiency. In their heyday, when 30 to 60 million bison roamed North America, they were the most numerous grazing animals on earth, far surpassing even the great African wildebeest herds.

The largest and most powerful animals on the continent, bison have a special claim on our attention. They are intimately tied to the history of America, as well as to the ecology of our grasslands. And, as we shall see, they have a place in our future as well.

The breathtaking splendor of the bison herds of three hundred years ago was almost indescribable to the first European observers. Today, when our cattle stand meekly behind fences and bawl for their dinner, those thundering wild herds are beyond our imagining. Then, bison were a standard part of the American landscape across half the continent, as omnipresent as cars are today. The random bounty they represented was incalculable, like that of falling fruit from tropical trees—they were simply *there*, part of the endless plenty offered by the original garden of the continent.

In several prehistoric forms, bison had endured in North America for hundreds of thousands of years. Indeed, it may well have been in pursuing bison that hunters first crossed the Bering land bridge and populated the Western Hemisphere. During the long centuries of Native American occupation of the continent, bison provided the Plains dwellers with food, shelter, clothing, fuel, and artifacts. Later, during settlement of the Midwest and Plains, bison furnished the Euro-American immigrants with food, warm robes and coats, and clean-burning dung chips for their cooking fires—an essential in largely treeless regions. Although later whites showed little compunction about wiping out the bison, America could not have become what it is if bison had not provided a living bridge across the Plains.

The first Spaniards who spotted bison understandably called them *vacas*, cows. But bison only superficially resemble cattle. For one thing, bison are surprisingly agile and fast: they can spin instantly on front or rear legs and can outrun the fastest horse over a five-mile chase. Bison are magnificent, muscular beasts: bulls weigh as much as a ton; cows, more than half that. Their stampedes literally make the earth tremble. They are eye-catching in their unique humped profile and shaggy coats; resourceful in finding grass, whether in dry seasons or in the teeth of blizzards; cooperative and resolute against predators.

As early observers learned, bison are wary of humans. People sometimes tame newborn bison calves, but not for long. Today's wild bison, such as those on the National Bison Range in Montana, can be herded by expert riders into enclosures for annual culling and vaccination, though a few recalcitrant bulls always elude the herders. Once driven into the corrals and chutes, many bison get hurt trying to kick or butt their way out even through 4-inch-thick timbers. The implicit motto of the bison rings with a determination we remember well from our history: Live Free or Die!

Their dominance of the American landscape rested on the fact that bison were perfectly adapted to life on the enormous grasslands of the continent. Bison are ruminants, with multipart stomachs that maintain a resident population of microbes to ferment chewed grass and render it capable of absorption. A typical bison day, whether over the long centuries or now, begins with a predawn grazing period, followed by alternating periods of regurgitating and chewing their cud and more grazing. This process enables bison to digest cellulose, the principal solid component of plants, and explains why they could be so numerous over such an extensive range.

A basic bison group numbers twenty to fifty animals; the endless herds described in frontier tales gathered only during migration. It was once believed that bison migrated seasonally over long distances from north to south and back, but it is now thought that their migrations covered only a few hundred miles and were generally directed toward better grazing land or water. Bison also move around because of weather, as has been observed in Yellowstone National Park and historically; fierce bliz-

Grazing bison move steadily over the grasslands, traveling almost as fast as a person walks. Photo: South Dakota Department of Tourism.

zards drive them toward rougher or timbered country, where they can shelter from the wind and snow. A bison group will sometimes cross long stretches of dry country. Bison tend to visit water at least once a day, though they can, if necessary, go several days without water—far longer than cattle can. Movement over the land is led by mature females, who are widely thought to be more intelligent than males and have an excellent memory for seasonal and spatial patterns of grass availability and locations of water sources. Nobody now alive has seen a really large migrating bison herd, but historical accounts describe, with perhaps some exaggeration, herds stretching as far as the eye can see, estimated to be as much as a hundred miles in length.

A drawing of a bison by a Jesuit missionary explorer, Father Hennepin, about 1680. Many early attempts to catch the proper head position, hump outline, and sloping back were less successful.

For bison, grazing involves movement while eating, over distances ranging from a quarter mile to three miles, followed by a brief resting period—not the relatively stationary grazing of cattle. Grazing bison may appear from a distance to be moving slowly, but they often travel at a good walking pace for a human. Due to their different anatomical structure, the gait of bison is not exactly like that of cattle.

In the wild, bison live for an average of twelve to fifteen years, though some individuals may live to forty. They are fearsome in defending themselves against predators. Predators, of course, are essential to every healthy ecosystem as regulators of population balances. Since the 1930s, scientists have known that predator control harms rather than helps bison and other large wild species, for steady predation is necessary to weed out weaker animals and thus keep the herd as a whole strong. In Canada, wolves have been observed hunting bison successfully—though they prefer to go after the relatively solitary moose—but careful observation in Yellowstone has revealed that severe winter weather kills far more bison than do predators of any kind. Native American hunters also played a crucial role as predators on bison before the European period. Their hunting impacts did not become ecologically unbalancing until whites brought them firearms and provided markets for hides and tongues.

The condition of a bison's fur varies from the deep, thick, warm coat of late fall and winter through the ragged-looking coat of spring and summer when the heavy fur is being shed in patches. Because bison eyes are set farther out on the sides of the head than those of cattle, they have practically 360-degree vision. They can detect very distant movements that are almost imperceptible to humans. However, at closer ranges they rely more on their excellent senses of smell and hearing. Like other social animals, they remain acutely aware of the locations and dispositions of nearby herd-mates, on whom their welfare and sometimes their safety depend—but who in return demand unceasing attention to dominance-submission relationships.

Whether on the move or loafing around, a bison herd is surprisingly noisy. Groups of cows and their calves, either newly born or yearlings, tend to stick fairly close together and engage in steady interchanges through re-assuring grunts—not the mooing many people expect. Attention is secured and deference demanded through a variety of sounds ranging from snorts to growls, often accompanied by attitude-adjustment butting. Occasion-ally bison will utter a sonorous snort that bears some resemblance to sounds made by their distant mammalian relatives, humpback whales. Bulls have a wide repertoire of threatening noises, from an early-warning low rumble with extended, whitish tongue to terrifying bellows and roars, which become so loud in the mating season that they can be heard as much as three miles away.

Like other animals, including humans, bison also signal their inten-tions by body postures. They maintain firm and stable dominance orders, among females as well as males; moreover, a dominant cow can intimidate a subdominant bull. Rank-indicating gestures with head and horns are very common, especially among the top animals. The bison tail is also very expressive. As Milo J. Schult and Arnold O. Haugen, experienced observers of contemporary bison under all imaginable conditions, put it:

An observer can get some idea of a buffalo's state of mind by looking at the position of the tail. When undisturbed, the buffalo's tail hangs down or flicks back and forth occasionally to get rid of a pesky fly. When mildly excited, the tail is raised somewhat; the greater the degree of excitement, the higher and more rigid the tail posture. Such excitement is frequently accompanied by defecation. Finally, when fully aroused and combative, the tail is held in a rigid, upright position. It is at this time that the observer should be most wary.

The fly-whisk function is important; like other large grazers, bison are bothered by a variety of flies.

Considering their size and weight, bison are remarkably light on their hooves. They can scramble up steep slopes quickly, and it is frequently said that they can jump over a six-foot fence from a standing start. They can scratch their shoulders or face by delicately bringing a rear foot forward. They enjoy licking and grooming themselves and other bison. And they love to frolic; young animals especially often simply run about aimlessly, mock-mating, play-fighting, and even play-stampeding.

For most of the year, bulls live on the fringes of groups of cows and calves. Individual bulls may wander deep into woodsy canyons, enjoying patches of grass too small to interest the whole herd. Only during the rutting season, in midsummer, do bulls mingle with the cows. The bison mating season is a time of much bellowing, challenging, threatening, and head-to-head butting contests between dominant bulls. Bison skulls are remarkably thick in the forehead area, which is covered with a heavy pad of fur, and the horns are curved in such a way that frontal butting does not usually involve goring. A fight normally ends with the weaker bull backing away and trotting off. Here nature seems to be aiming for genetic sorting but not death; a few dominant bulls, who intimidate all the others, mate with the cows. Only in captivity, where one bull can get cornered, do fatal fights seem to be common.

A bull who has just been dominated by another bull seems to "work off his frustration" by roaring, pawing the ground or even goring it, and wallowing—lying down and rolling back and forth vigorously, often in a dusty depression that is also used for insect-control wallowing. A dominant bull patiently "tends" a cow in whom he is interested, staying close behind or alongside her for many hours, or sometimes even several days if necessary.

During this time he fends off the approaches of other bulls, occasionally rests his chin on her rump, does a certain amount of sniffing and licking, and waits until she is ready to be mounted. In this process, he smirks at her in a stylized, neck-extended grimace called the lip curl, the precise function of which nobody—except, presumably, the bison themselves—really knows.

Most calves are born in late April to mid-May following a nine-and-a-half-month gestation period. Whereas the coats of adult bison are varying shades of dark brown, the calves are bright orange-rust and remain so for about three months. Initially, they have no humps. They weigh between thirty and seventy pounds at birth and are extremely winsome. A bison cow is ferociously protective and allows nothing and nobody to get between herself and her calf.

Our Lost Companions

Among the Indians, bison and many other animals were treated in stories and in life as beings who spoke, felt, and thought much as humans do. They were an equal part of the universe, deserving of careful attention, respect, and love; they were spoken of in the same terms as were family or clan members. And animals were to be seen everywhere—close outside the villages or camps, just over the hills, coming down to drink at the streams. (Bison wore deep trails leading to riverbanks.) Not a day passed without important interactions between humans and other species. This constant contact is hard for moderns to imagine. For most of us, animals are merely an industrial resource. Cattle and poultry are produced out of our daily sight, and we consume them in processed forms that are carefully rendered unrecognizable; to acknowledge that our steaks or drumsticks come from fellow beings would be too painful.

We are distantly aware of wild creatures inhabiting landscapes we seldom visit—parks and wilderness areas, where deer and bears and eagles may occasionally be seen—but these creatures do not qualify as part of our "real," everyday lives. We count ourselves lucky to experience them through nature programs on television.

Thus we modern human beings live in a landscape that is, by the standards of our long history as a species on earth, deprived of our large animal companions. Yet we evolved to what we are in close conjunction with these animals, over millions of years. On some deep level we must miss them, for they gave the human world spiritual meaning as well as sustenance. When we came to dominate them almost completely, and subsequently wiped many of them off the planet, we lost essential evolutionary partners, and we are the lonelier for it. Their absence is our loss, psychologically, spiritually, and morally, and it is felt by many besides Indians and poets. If you go to a zoo—a melancholy experience in the eyes of many—and watch the human animals there, especially the children, you may see in their eyes some recognition of our fundamental comradeship with wild animals.

There are people, and I am one of them, who believe that the natural landscape with its full range of inhabitants can be restored in protected areas. There we can bring back in meaningful numbers the great carnivores who evolved with humans as the top predators in North America: grizzly bears, wolves, mountain lions. Through the devoted efforts of conservation biologists and their allies we may yet manage to preserve large enough wild areas to guarantee the survival of small remnants of these magnificent species—like us, predators who occupy the tops of complex food chains.

But in realistic terms, the bison is the only large wild animal with whom there is any prospect of sustained coexistence on mass terms. (With bison would naturally come smaller numbers of the other species that share grassland habitats with them, chiefly pronghorn, elk, mountain sheep, and deer.) Bison do not fear humans, and a modest level of human activity does not make an area uninhabitable for bison, as even very limited road-building, mining, or timber cutting do for bears. We can, therefore, share land with bison in a way we could not with most other large animals. The possibility of our coexisting with bison opens up some novel and exciting prospects for conservation biology (the new field which applies biological science to species preservation), for land management, and for ranching. It also challenges us, as we will see later, to imagine new relations between ourselves and wild nature.

In about a quarter of what is now the contiguous United States, bison prevailed as the most numerous, the most impressive, and also the most useful members of the animal kingdom. We will not see huge migrating herds, but it is reasonable to predict that in fifty or a hundred years, a mere moment in the bison species lifetime, there will be millions of these mighty lords of grass again. A large ecological detour will have been completed, and one part of the United States, at least, will have been restored to a naturally sustainable state.

Land, Rivers, and Climate

"In the long run, land determines."

—*Wes Jackson, paraphrasing John Wesley Powell*

Bison once ranged over a much larger territory than the Great Plains, which many still think of as bison's sole ancestral home. All the tallgrass prairies just to the east, with better soil and more rain, were bison territory too, and the richer forage of this region must have supported the densest herds. (The general quality and particularly the protein content of grass depends directly on rains, especially spring rains.) But bison also inhabited areas where forests were dominant, since they can browse on leaves as well as graze on grass. There were bison as far east as the Appalachians, where I grew up; perhaps out of some deep folk memory, my hometown baseball

After a bout of grazing, bison loaf, often lying down to chew their cuds and rest.

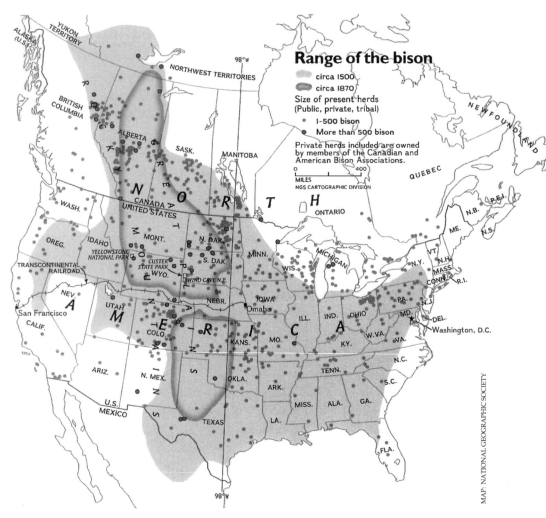

MAP: NATIONAL GEOGRAPHIC SOCIETY

Range of the bison

circa 1500

circa 1870

Size of present herds
(Public, private, tribal)

• 1–500 bison

● More than 500 bison

Private herds included are owned
by members of the Canadian and
American Bison Associations.

0 ——— 400
MILES
NGS CARTOGRAPHIC DIVISION

team in central Pennsylvania was called the Boalsburg Bisons. When English settlers first arrived in Georgia, they encountered "innumerable" bison. There were bison in Mexico, in Texas, and on up through Canada to the Yukon. There were bison in the Rockies, as there still are—in Yellowstone National Park; at the National Bison Range in Moiese, Montana; in Grand Teton National Park; and on the Flying D Ranch in Montana, owned by media magnate Ted Turner. However, they never spread in significant numbers through the dry and inhospitable Great Basin into the lusher country along the West Coast.

Nowadays, you can find small, thriving ranched herds of bison everywhere in the country. But their heartland remains the Great Plains, and that is where we are likely to see, in coming decades, the greatest resurgence of bison herds. There land is cheap; most of it is unrewarding for farming. But it was home to the bison, and it will be again. The Plains are high, dry, gently rolling country, and until white occupation they were entirely covered with mixed native grasses, including the grama grasses which were the main sustenance for the bison. Originally the Plains were treeless except for cottonwoods and willows along the streams. In some sections, like the Sand Hills of Nebraska, the predominant impression of the region as you move through it is rather like being at sea; you think that once you crest the next rise you will gain a view of a broad vista and get your bearings, but in reality all you see from the rise is a new series of rises. In the absence of mountains or other massive landmarks, early white arrivals, like the Indians before them, relied on the rivers for orientation; without them, they would have needed to use compass and sextant, like seaborne navigators.

It is easy to confuse the Plains with the neighboring prairies to the east. The two domains do not divide sharply along some boundary line; nor is their topography uniformly different. They are defined by rainfall and soil types, both of which have local variations. In a general way, we could say that the prairies extend through the great, mostly flat central valley that occupies the middle of the country to the edge of the eastern woodlands, which in historical times covered much of the country east of the Mississippi River. Westward, the prairies extend at least through the first tier of states west of the Mississippi and give way to the drier, sparser Plains in the Dakotas, Nebraska, Kansas, Oklahoma, and Texas. From there, the Plains run to the Rockies, and within the Rockies there are basins that have a predominantly Plains character. On both Plains and prairies, local differences in landforms, stream patterns, soil and vegetation, and temperature made life easier or more difficult for bison. But throughout this vast area, bison roamed free, occupying what ecologists call their niche—their special place in the great panorama of life.

The Soil and Under the Soil

To people who think that grass is just grass, the Plains and the prairies offer an unknown new universe. Short (six to twelve inches tall) buffalo grass, hairy grama, and blue grama grow on the driest, short-grass Plains. On the rainier eastern prairies, Indian grass, big bluestem, and switchgrass reach heights of six to twelve feet. The mixed prairie in between has western wheatgrass, little bluestem, and sideoats grama. All these grasses intermix to some extent, depending on local conditions of soil and moisture, so there is no rigid division of grass types. An undisturbed grassland is a thing of underappreciated beauty. As Lynn Jacobs writes,

> *Prairie grassland usually contains an average of 125–150 plant species and numerous animal species. Here one finds many different grasses and flowering plants. Perennial forbs [nonwoody but nongrass plants] are widespread, especially members of the sunflower and legume families. Annuals typically comprise less than 5 percent of plant species. Thick stands of bushes and trees commonly line drainages. . . . While generally less biotically diverse than the bunchgrass community, prairie grassland usually has many more individuals and a much greater biomass per unit of area. . . . Indeed, grassland generally has the deepest, most fertile and productive soil, highest erosion resistance and water retention, and greatest biomass of animals of all the major bioregions.*

Plains and prairie soil, like soil everywhere on the planet except in the driest deserts, is home to countless small organisms whose total subsurface mass is much greater, for any given natural area, than that of the more visibly imposing large mammals aboveground. Studies carried out on the prairies have counted nematodes, which are small roundworms with teeth, and found that they number a half million per square foot; they consume more of the region's basic biological productivity than do the cows or bison that tramp over them. (Subsoil life thrives better, research shows, when the grasses are grazed.) But even these amazing numbers are dwarfed by the numbers of microorganisms. A pinch of fertile agricultural soil weighing one gram may contain more than 2.5 billion bacteria; 400,000 fungi; 50,000 algae; and 30,000 protozoa. It is these microscopic beings that convert nitrogen, phosphorus, and sulfur in the soil into forms that higher plants such as grasses can utilize. Thus, without these microorganisms there could be no plants, no bison, and no humans. Moreover, they decompose organic matter such as dead grass leaves and stems and animal droppings, releasing carbon dioxide and water into the soil and leaving a residue of fine particles that we call humus, the buildup of which has, in fact, created the deep prairie soils. Thus, in a full biological perspective, life under the soil surface is more critical, complex, and massive than is the life visible to us. This is particularly true of Plains and prairie native grasses, which have larger parts underground than aboveground.

Buffalo Grass*

Once the bed of an inland sea, the Plains owe their basic slope and elevation to sediments washed down from the Rocky Mountains. Their nearest counterpart is the Russian steppes. Rainfall is skimpy and erratic, averaging around 20 inches or less per year; in recent years it has averaged 13 inches in northwestern Montana, 16 inches in west-central North Dakota, 17 inches in southwestern South Dakota, and 19 inches in Oklahoma. But multiyear droughts are the norm, and attempts to plow the land, which was originally protected by a thick cover of remarkably deep-rooted, dense grasses, have sooner or later led many farmers to disaster. The soil itself is fertile, and wheat is still a major crop, along with a drought-resistant sorghum called milo; indeed, the Plains still produce most of America's wheat exports. But plow agriculture using annual monocrops like wheat and corn leaves the soil between plants unprotected and is a permanent invitation to erosion.

Throughout the world, erosion by wind and water has been dangerously depleting overgrazed grasslands, causing desertification and lower productivity for human purposes. In America, just as in less-developed countries, we "mine" soil by letting it wash downstream to the oceans. This erosion process is far advanced everywhere in the country, including the deep-topsoil area of the Midwest. It is also severe on the dry, windblown

*This and the similar grass drawings that follow are reprinted from *North American Range Plants*, 4th edition, by James Stubbendieck, Stephan L. Hatch, and Charles H. Butterfield, by permission of the University of Nebraska Press. Copyright © 1981, 1982, 1986, 1992 by the University of Nebraska Press.

Plains grasslands. Even in those extensive Plains areas that have hardly been plowed, where most of the grasslands are used for cattle raising, degradation due to overgrazing is depleting the land. As we will see, bison are part of the solution to erosion problems.

Bison and Grassland Ecology

"Grazing large herds of bison in large pastures represents a cost-efficient method of cropping native vegetation, maintaining a functional ecosystem, providing local employment in an industry that is indefinitely sustainable, and providing a healthier meat."
—Craig J. Knowles, wildlife consultant

It is the working theory of The Nature Conservancy's preserves in Nebraska and its just-opened preserve in Oklahoma that bison grazing, together with the effects of occasional fires, will tend to bring back native grasses and lead to a stable ecosystem. The process has also been the subject of research at Custer State Park in South Dakota, at the Konza Preserve of Kansas State University, and elsewhere. In recent years, small, museum-like preserves of native grasses, harbingers of more extensive future restoration, have been established through the persistent efforts of volunteers. The most remarkable of these preserve "islands" is within the giant circle formed by the nuclear accelerator at the Argonne National Laboratory outside Chicago. Another lush example is found on the grounds of the Kauffman Museum in Newton, Kansas. These precious areas nurture an incredible richness of species compared with the desolation to which most Plains and prairie grassland has been reduced. One writer noted their "scintillating interdependence that constitutes a single living whole."

Devoted souls who care about bringing back the native grasses can be found everywhere. In Chicago, they have banded together in a loose organization called the Wild Onion Alliance. ("Chicago" comes from the Indian name for a wild onion, and the city and its surroundings have a surprising number of vacant spaces suitable for restoration.) Such people set a powerful example and issue effective appeals for physical labor and vigilance from a large force of concerned citizens. Each community, they say, must

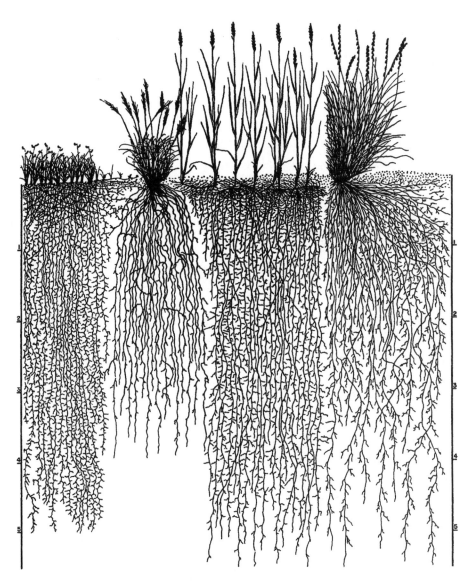

When researchers excavate the root systems of grasses, they find that they penetrate to extraordinary depths. This drawing shows the tops and roots of dominant grasses common to mixed prairie: from left to right, buffalo grass (which is similar to blue grama), purple three-awn, western wheatgrass, and sideoats grama. Depths are in feet. Reprinted from *Prairie Plants and Their Environment: A Fifty-Year Study in the Midwest*, by J. E. Weaver, by permission of the University of Nebraska Press. Copyright © 1968 by the University of Nebraska Press.

develop its own "prairie consciousness" in order to push back the concrete, the alien bluegrass lawns, and the cornfields. After ten years of hard work, they have brought back a forest preserve north of Chicago to its ancient state of viability through persistent seeding amid existing vegetation, a method they have found to work better than plowing and planting anew.

There are now such fragments of restored prairie in many states—too small to support bison, but inspiring examples of what can be done. Unfortunately, the extraordinarily labor- and money-intensive work that has gone into these experimental and educational plots is too expensive and demanding to be applied on a regional scale. But The Nature Conservancy hopes that the cropping of grasses by bison, who tend to bite off the top parts of grass rather than tear away the near-ground growing shoots as do cattle and sheep, may aid the recovery of native grass species that cannot survive under livestock.

Native grasses are adapted to occasional heavy grazing, and many grasses actually grow more vigorously when grazed. A free, nomadic bison herd might graze a given grass area one year but not return to it for several years. The constant pressure of fenced and maximum-stock grazing, however, has tended to favor grasses of European origin.

The effects of fire were also undoubtedly crucial to maintenance of the original grasslands. Some fires were induced by lightning and others were set by Indians. Periodic fires, though many researchers like to classify them as disturbances, clean out dead grass materials that do not decay rapidly in dry climates and return them as ash to the soil nutrient cycle. They also create ecological mosaics—spotty patterns where different plant species offer different habitats to different animal inhabitants. Fire stimulates the germination of certain seeds. It is well documented that after a fire, a new round of more productive growth begins, offering new, protein- and energy-rich shoots that please grazers. Fire may even help to prevent outbreaks of pests and plant diseases.

Scientists like Al Steuter, who is in charge of the bison at The Nature Conservancy's Niobrara Valley Preserve in Nebraska, have worked out the sequence of what they call patch dynamics. An area that bison have been lightly grazing accumulates more dead grass and is thus prone to fire. After a fire, helped by increased penetration of sunlight and warmer soil temperatures, a new round of growth begins; bison may be particularly attracted to burned areas for two or three years. Gradually, however, they turn their attention elsewhere, and dead grass begins to build up again, setting the stage for the next fire.

Indians certainly employed fire, and it seems likely to Al Steuter that their influence altered the grasslands to favor species that could support a wider range of grazing intensities. Without fire, he says, woody plants tend to take over grasslands. Steuter points out that since most lightning-induced fires occur in the growing season, when grass is greener, they are naturally less fierce than dormant-season fires and produce a characteristically small burn patch. Ninety percent of lightning-caused storms in the West burn out or are rained out before reaching an acre in size. The human-set fire regime at the Niobrara Preserve tries to replicate the impacts of Indian- and lightning-set burns.

Bison's observant nature and great speed meant that they were seldom endangered by the relatively erratic and mostly small-scale fires of presettlement days. Fires are less perilous to fast, alert animals in open country than viewers of *Bambi* might expect. The fires at The Nature Conservancy preserves should thus be compatible with bison, especially when their free-range area is expanded and there is little possibility of their being trapped by fences.

In short, there is a remarkable match between bison and their ancestral grassland home. The hardiness that enabled bison to survive the severe climate of the Plains is especially impressive compared with cattle's vulnerability. Bison can even reduce their metabolic rate when exposed to intense cold and are much better than cattle at finding sheltered places to wait out storms. One bison ranger and researcher, even though he favors using cattle along with bison on small areas of public lands for ecological maintenance, says flatly, "Clearly, bison are relatively better suited to a continuous year-round presence on a northern mixed prairie natural area than are cattle."

Particularly in the tallgrass prairies east of 94 degrees west longitude (a north-south line passing just east of Kansas City), the abundance of vegetation is astounding, particularly the number and seasonal variety of brightly colored wildflowers. The Buffalo Gap National Grassland in South Dakota distributes guides to forty-six species of grasses that can be seen on its nearly 600,000 acres—from crested wheatgrass to buffalo grass to little bluestem to something known as stinkgrass—and displays dried samples of the major grasses in its visitor center. A similar list contains eighty-nine wildflowers: western yarrow, white prairie aster, cutleaf goldenweed, nipplewort, prairie coneflower, miner's candle, lambsquarter, and dozens more. Some of these plants are extraordinarily well adapted to a dry climate: Barr's milkvetch develops a root deep and strong enough to anchor and sustain it for forty to fifty years.

Bird and small mammal populations are extremely diverse on the Plains. Hawks and owls, turkeys, pheasants, flycatchers, flickers, and dozens of other birds are common in grassy areas, while a surprising variety of waterbirds (especially herons, geese, and cranes) frequent rivers and lakes. Grouse, once unbelievably common, are now rare.

The diversity of grasslands is particularly significant for bison. Polycultures, such as the mixed grasses and forbs that bison eat, turn out to be more productive than monocultures. In other words, an acre of mixed prairie grasses produces more biomass—food for humans or animals—than does an acre planted solely in corn or wheat. In a sense, this should hardly be surprising, since peoples in the Western Hemisphere have been planting beans and melons among their corn for thousands of years. But it is only recently that a trend in the social sciences, called rational peasant analysis, has dared to assume that indigenous people who have survived for millennia just may know what they're doing. Unfortunately, our style of development is almost always at their cost. We could surely have learned much about bison from the Plains tribes, but we killed off long ago the hunters who were the keepers of bison lore.

Bison's famous roaming, like that of other wild grazers on the Plains and on the great grasslands of Africa and Asia, was not merely an inborn predisposition. Bison and other grazing animals become visibly stimulated, in ways we do not yet understand, on entering a new, rich pasture area, and, of course, roaming gave access to continually new forage. Roaming also helped minimize encounters with predators, who more easily concentrate on a sedentary herd, and moving in herds promoted ready self-defense against predators when they appeared. Roaming presumably was also a response to the eventual fouling of a grazed area by urine and dung.

Grazing by millions of bison and other species not only did not degrade the Plains and prairies but promoted coexistence and coevolution of animals and grasses in a remarkably rich and productive symbiotic relationship. The crucial role of the frequency of grazing, as opposed to overall intensity of grazing, went unrecognized during most of the history of the Plains. Received ideas about how many grazing animals can be supported by a plant community have nothing to do with wild species such as bison. This previous thinking derives from rainy European areas, where domestic animals were kept on the abundant grass of small, fenced pastures and a simple rule of thumb sufficed: do not overstock (that is, have too many animals for the total grass available). But an observant and thoughtful former Rhodesian game official named Allan Savory has recently extended our understanding of how wild and domestic animals interact with grasses in dry environments. The inventor of the term "short-rotation grazing," Sa-

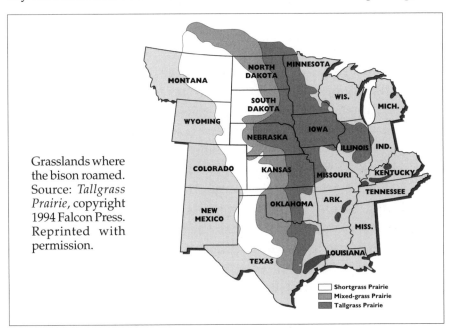

Grasslands where the bison roamed. Source: *Tallgrass Prairie*, copyright 1994 Falcon Press. Reprinted with permission.

27

vory has applied a systematic ecological analysis to the problems of ranching, and we will see later how his ideas are being put into practice by bison ranchers. But his thinking also bears on the history and future of wild species such as bison.

Savory's fundamental strategy was to study closely what occurs at the soil's surface over time. Grass that looks relatively healthy, he found, can still be in trouble if the plants are widely spaced and the soil in between is bare and hardened, offering no foothold to new young plants. Conversely, grass that looks severely nibbled down may actually be capable of good recovery if it is composed of numerous young, vigorous plants spread uniformly over the whole pasture. (Unlike leafy plants, grasses grow from the bottom; that is why mowing a lawn does not destroy it.)

Bison grazing in historical times was often intensive in local areas and its impacts were considerable, especially when combined with the bison's wallowing and trampling. However, herds would soon move on to other areas while an affected area recovered. Savory contends that such temporary, intense impacts are in fact essential, whether the grazers are bison or livestock, for they stir up soil and push seeds into the ground so they can germinate successfully.

Jack Norland, a researcher in range science at Montana State University, has concluded from his own work that "bison naturally exhibit short duration grazing behavior when grazing large pastures." Thus, if large enough pastures are available, building a lot of internal fencing and moving animals around among different pastures is unnecessary. Left to themselves, bison move constantly, not staying in any one place for more than a day. Both herds and individuals distribute themselves over all of an area, and bison come back to regraze areas at varying time intervals. Norland argues, "Just leaving the bison alone in an adequately large area (with suitable habitat) is the grazing system that would be easiest, most efficient, and would offer the least chance of damaging the pasture. This would also probably be the most productive. Of course proper stocking rates [numbers of animals per acre] are needed for this to work."

We may see for ourselves that an unmanaged herd will prosper on ample acreage by observing the healthy bison in Yellowstone National

Park—now about 4,000 animals and likely to grow to some 20,000 before the 2.2 million acre park becomes overpopulated. As we shall see, management of public lands for true multiple use, combined with expansion of bison herds on Indian reservations, could add many more millions of acres for bison. However, on the relatively small areas where bison ranchers have been operating, Savory's novel management strategies can substitute for natural grazing patterns. Yet even on public lands, some managers continue to follow traditional agricultural practices rather than learning to rely on simulating major ecological processes of fire, bison grazing, and natural plant succession.

Although Savory's general analysis of the grazing process and its relation to the health of grasslands is an important advance, his management recommendations are restricted to limited-acreage situations. For the future of bison, we must give priority to Norland's conclusion that bison grazing in large, unfenced areas provides ecologically satisfactory natural rotation. The ultimate bottom line is this: large herds of bison can be sustainably (and profitably) kept on suitably large unfenced ranges on the Plains. As long as land remains divided into small parcels, the always precarious micromanagement of grazing impacts becomes necessary; yet cattle raising, burdened by the costs of internal fencing and intensive management, will continue to degrade the land and, if left without subsidies, to cause ranchers to go broke. Nature is giving us a signal that in our current land-division practices we have been thinking like real estate agents and that we must instead learn to "think like bison."

It appears that the only way to replicate the ecological symbiosis that free-roaming herds once had with grasslands is to put bison, elk, pronghorn, and deer back on large territories, along with their appropriate predators (including humans, hunting on a year-round basis), and let them reestablish coexistence with the grasses and the myriad other forms of life there. With bison and their companion grazers, it seems almost certain that the best management is no management. A few large ranches, following the Ted Turner operation's lead, will be able to implement this policy, but for the most part the task will fall to our public lands. Full implementation will probably require a century and will test to the utmost our temptation to imagine that, with our limited understanding, we can do things as well as nature.

Bison affect other features of grasslands besides grass, particularly streamside vegetation. A large herd of bison visiting a water hole or riverbank tramples it severely. In times past, however, when bison had access to unbounded expanses of land, their visits were intermittent, a fact that mitigated their impacts. Certainly bison do not display the predilection for sticking close to water that cattle have, perhaps because of their origins in wet southern Asia. Sharman Apt Russell says it well:

> The effect of cattle on riparian areas is well documented. Unlike wild ungulates, cows tend to stay near water, to wallow in it, to lounge on the stream banks, and to trample the same ground over and over. As they lounge, they eat—grasses, tree shoots, whatever they find. On the John Day River, they eat, steadily, the willow and red-osier dogwood that act to slow the force of floods and protect the banks. They eat the grass that shields the soil from sun and wind, keeping soil temperatures low and reducing evaporation. They eat the sedges that are filtering out sediment, cleaning the water, and building up banks at the same time. When this kind of vegetation is overgrazed, the look of a stream changes drastically. Trees such as willow, aspen, alder, and cottonwood disappear as mature trees die out and the young shoots are consumed. In areas with deep alluvial soil, the stream begins to downcut, creating deep channels that result in a lowered water table.

Bison, on the other hand, tend to drink and then move on—far and fast. Bison do wallow, both in dry depressions to dust their coats and in wet depressions to cover themselves with a layer of mud for protection from insects. Nevertheless, they wallow mostly on high, level areas, and their wallowing produces bare, depressed areas that promote species diversity because they become tiny wetlands after rains.

Bison Digestion

Bison consume a greater range of plants than do the cattle that have replaced them. They respond flexibly to forage quality and abundance. Moreover, bison seem to digest what they eat more efficiently than cattle, perhaps because of different digestive-tract bacteria and protozoa; they can certainly achieve protein and energy intake equal or superior to those of cattle.

Bison ferment their cud more than cattle do, and perhaps for this reason, along with their superior nitrogen recycling, they have a higher digestive coefficient—that is, they get more out of the dry matter and fiber they eat. Actually, the nutritional needs of bison may be slightly different from those of cattle, although herd managers tend to treat them alike and rely on cattle rules of thumb in critical matters such as how many acres to allow for each bison. (On the high, dry Plains, a bison may need fifty acres.)

Bison diets tend toward grasses and sedges [grasslike plants with solid stems], though they will eat forbs and shrubs (like willow) if they have to. It intrigues scientists that bison can subsist on low-quality, high-fiber diets, whereas cattle require finer fare. In fact, bison digestions are rated between 3.7 percent and 6.1 percent more efficient than those of cattle. Nature has equipped them well for survival on the Plains.

Like other ruminants, bison emit large quantities of methane, a gas that is a major contributor to the greenhouse effect. In this meat-eating epoch, there are more than a billion cows aboard the planet, producing some 15 percent of the methane in the atmosphere. Methane is also produced in voluminous quantities by the flatulence of a human population explosion nearing 6 billion, by decay processes in rice paddies and swampland, and by the digestive processes of the planet's staggering population of termites. Thus, it seems likely that the bison population's methane output, whether that of the past or that of bison brought back to the Plains in the future, is not a significant factor in the global methane level.

Indians and Bison

Even before they had horses, Indians hunted bison successfully. On hands and knees, their human identity concealed with wolf skins, they stalked and killed individual bison with bows and arrows. They surrounded small groups of bison, confused them by shouting and waving, and finished some of them off with bows and arrows. Most dramatic of all, they drove whole herds off cliffs that the Sioux call *pishkun* and whites call buffalo jumps; people waiting at the bottom clubbed and butchered the fallen animals, leaving deep deposits of bones over the centuries.

Some Plains tribes who lived in settled villages along rivers and practiced extensive gardening to produce much of their food—the Pawnee, Arikara, Mandan, and others—also hunted bison in semiannual hunting expeditions. However, in traditional tribal life, whether settled or nomadic, the bison provided for an impressive proportion of the people's needs. In fact, Plains Indian life would have been unthinkable without bison. Both Indian traditional stories and later white writings conjure up the thrill of the bison hunts: riders galloping bareback after the dangerous racing animals, shooting arrows faster than a gun could be reloaded. As whites later remarked, the bison was the Indians' general store. Shirts, leggings, dresses, belts, and moccasins came from the hides, as did tipi covers. Bison bladders made good water containers, and rope could be braided from rawhide strips. Spoons, ladles, and cups could be fashioned from horns, which were also important in headdresses.

Bison robes were a basic household resource, used for keeping warm, sleeping on, and sleeping under. Tanned hides were used for storytelling artwork. Knives, arrowheads, shields, and personal ornaments came from bone and hides; bones also made scrapers and hoes. Bowstrings and arrow wrappings came from sinews. Harnesses for horses and dogs, pouches for carrying things on horseback, lariats, snowshoes, sled runners, even covers for balls used in ball games—all came from the bison. So did ceremonial objects like masks, rattles, and winding sheets for the dead. (Even the tails found use—as fly whisks!)

Hump meat was considered a particular delicacy, along with tongue, brains, heart, and liver; dried and crumbled jerky pounded into a cake with berries and fat produced pemmican, a portable, preserved high-energy food. Bison were by no means, however, the sole item in tribal diets. Reading explorers' accounts gives the impression that Plains tribes ate nothing but bison meat, perhaps because the early mountain trappers and explorers themselves, lacking Indian knowledge of the region's plant resources, had to depend entirely on game. It is now recognized that so-called primi-

Bison, unlike cattle, just love to run, and they are astonishingly fast. At distances greater than a mile, they can outrun racehorses—in fact, they are credited with speeds of up to fifty miles per hour. Photo: South Dakota Department of Tourism.

tive peoples ordinarily enjoyed a much wider, richer, and healthier diet than humans now consume—dependent as we are on just three seed-bearing cultivated grasses (wheat, rice, and corn) for most of our caloric intake. Thus, it should not be surprising that Indians ate not only large amounts of bison but also quite a number of plants. During the winter, particularly, people without sources of carbohydrates could not have survived on bison meat alone because it is so low in fat. Indeed, the limits on Indian populations on the Plains may have been set by the amount of nonmeat foods available, not by the supply of bison. It appears that tribal groups may have nomadically followed the development of prairie turnips (or Indian breadfruit), succulent roots that they tracked more intently than they tracked the bison herds and dug up with sticks made of sharpened elk antlers. And buffalo-bellow plant flowered at rutting time, signaling people when it was time to head for the hunting grounds. Indians also ate the scarlet buffalo berry. Prairie chickens (pinnated grouse) were a tasty staple, as they were for the whites, who later exterminated them in many areas; they survive now only in rare places where traditional rotation of crops is still practiced. The grouse depended on seasonal grazing by bison to "open the grass," so they declined with the herds—a correlation that inspired a sad Indian lament, "O come back too, prairie chickens!" Surveying the fate of the species, William Least Heat-Moon reflected, "As goes the prairie chicken, so goes the prairie and its people."

Antelope were another staple food over much of the Plains, as were elk in some places. Ian Frazier gives a much more exotic list of Indian foodstuffs, which included geese, ants, dogs, grasshoppers, beaver tails, wild peas, chokecherries, rose pods, wild plums, turtle eggs, wild artichokes, morning glory roots, wild onions, juneberries, and cottonwood bark. All in all, then, the diet of the original Plains inhabitants was rich, varied, and without question more healthful than the current American diet heavy in beef, salt, sugar, and fat.

The Balance Upset

The size of the herds that existed when whites first landed on the continent began to diminish early in the nineteenth century. A great drought struck the Plains in 1840, and another drought in 1867 supposedly starved millions of bison on the southern Plains. Diseases from introduced Euro-American livestock probably also contributed to some decline. Nonetheless, the bison-centered ecological balance that had prevailed on the Plains since the last ice age was not fatally disrupted until the arrival of whites. The first few trappers, explorers, and fur traders seemed to pose little threat. But after them came buffalo hunters, preying on the bison. Then came traders, making their living off the hunters and trappers and Indians. Then settlers took possession of the land to extract the accumulated richness of its soil, and gold miners invaded the Black Hills. Bandits, gunfighters, lawyers, and storekeepers arrived to live off the townsfolk and settlers. Finally, the military and its civilian helpers killed or rounded up the remaining Indians.

The water and land were at first exploited by open-range cattle barons and their hired guns, but then came "the plow that broke the Plains." Wave after wave of farmers built sod houses, plowed, planted, watched their crops shrivel or blow away, and went bust. So in time a new variety of predator appeared on the Plains: not carnivore, not even human, but nonetheless voracious. Banks gobbled up the farms. Giant grain-trading corporations learned to manipulate commodity prices, producing waves of bankruptcies. Seed companies, fertilizer companies, and equipment companies racked up sales to failing farmers. These new predators were mostly legal fictions called corporations: self-replicating organisms driven by an ineluctable need to maximize profits, protected by law from personal liability claims. They steadily sucked money from the farmers, driving them to try ever harder to squeeze money from the land. For a time, the farmers fought back through populist political organizations. They even formed a new party and sent a few representatives to statehouses and to Washington, but their uprisings were soon beaten down.

As Ian Frazier sums up the situation in his book *Great Plains*:

This, finally, is the punch line of our two hundred years on the Great Plains: we trap out the beaver, subtract the Mandan, infect the Black-feet and the Hidatsa and the Assiniboin, overdose the Arikara; call the land a desert and hurry across it to get to California and Oregon; suck up the buffalo, bones and all; kill off nations of elk and wolves and cranes and prairie chickens and prairie dogs; dig up the gold and rebury it in vaults someplace else; ruin the Sioux and Cheyenne and Arapaho and Crow and Kiowa and Comanche; kill Crazy Horse, kill Sitting Bull; harvest wave after wave of immigrants' dreams and send the wised-up dreamers on their way; plow the topsoil until it blows to the ocean; ship out the wheat, ship out the cattle; dig up the earth itself and burn it in power plants and send the power down the line; dismiss the small farm-ers, empty the little towns; dry up the rivers and springs, deep-drill for irrigation water as the aquifer retreats....

The Bison Heritage

When historian Frederick Jackson Turner declared in 1893 that settlement from sea to shining sea had closed the American frontier, only a few hundred bison remained, almost all in vestigial herds maintained by a handful of preservationists. There were some in Texas, a few in Montana, some that poachers missed in Yellowstone, a few dozen in (remarkably) the Bronx Zoo. By the 1920s, most Americans believed that the bison had vanished entirely, along with the Indians—both remembered only by their presence on the nickel coin. Nonetheless, during the latter decades of the twentieth century a sustained recovery program, with both private and public support, has had great success. In 1995, there were some 200,000 of these impressive animals in the United States and Canada, and their number is growing rapidly. The species is no longer endangered. Bison are steadily gaining new friends among the public at large, among wildlife biologists, among conservation organizations, among Indian tribes (including some with no historical connection to bison), even among politicians. The greatest of American animals is coming back.

But bison restoration on a significant scale will not be easy. Bison are wild, freedom-loving beasts. These weighty symbolic virtues also pose difficult problems—conceptual and practical, economic and political, cultural and ecological. Indeed, if we are to let bison be bison, we will have to modify some of our current ways of being human. These changes will benefit us as well as bison, but they will be profound.

Chapter Two
The Managed Land

Originally, whites' hunting of bison for robes and meat was seasonal, focusing on the fall and winter, when bison were fat and their fur luxurious. But bison had a brush with extinction after it was discovered that bison leather served well as industrial belting and in carriages, furniture, and even leather wall paneling. Traditional sources of leather could not meet the growing demand of post–Civil War industry. Thus, when the railroads pushed into the West, hides were transported east by train, year round, in unimaginable quantities. A sizable trade also developed in tasty bison tongues, which could be shipped when salted. During the late nineteenth century, white hunters kept their gun barrels hot, some of them hunting bison for the army, and "Buffalo Bill" Cody alone was said to have killed 4,280 bison in eight months to feed railroad workers. Historical records of this industrial hunting era are still painful to read:

> *Each of us was carrying a rimfire, .44 caliber Henry repeating carbine, short, light, easy to aim and fire with one hand, best of all weapons for running buffalo.*
>
> *We rode up the coulee, keeping out of sight of the herd until, at the head of the coulee, we charged out and right in among them. They instantly ran, gathering compactly together. . . . And our horses were as eager for the chase, for the killings, as were we. With ears set fiercely back, they did their best to get us close up to the left of the cows, so that we could put a single, killing shot into their lungs or hearts. The pace at*

which we were going seemed to us like the swiftness of lightning. Well we knew that, at any moment, our horses might step into a badger hole and we go down to be trampled to death; that a hard-pressed bull might turn and gore us. It was that danger, that constant risk, that made the chase so exciting, so fascinating. Oh, how we loved it all: the thunderous pounding and rattling of thousands of hooves together; the sharp odor of the sage that they crushed; the accuracy of our shooting; the quick response of our trained horses to our directing hands. Always the run was over all too soon. Never was a horse that could keep up with a frightened buffalo herd for much more than a mile. When I had shot my sixth cow, my horse was all in, winded, and wet with white foaming sweat. I brought him to a stand and sat watching Eli. . . . Then he, too, stopped, turned, came slowly back, and equally slow, I rode to meet him. "How many?" I asked.

Grinning, he answered: "Eighteen. Eighteen cows with eighteen shots." Hard to believe, but there were the proofs of it, blackly strewn upon the yellow-grassed plain. To select, chase, and kill eighteen cows in the run of a buffalo herd was something to talk about, to be remembered. I have never heard of anyone's equalling the feat.

Another hunter wrote:

[Johnny Cook] made up for this lost day late in June. The air was hot and still, the buffalos thirsty. . . . Around a thousand came in a straggling dusty run to the creek, black tongues out, pushing and tromping each other at the water. Afterward they spread out over the second bottoms. All had shed their old hair and were smooth, fine animals. Half were down and chewing their cuds when the hunter got close, one large bull up and looking. At about eighty steps Johnny started to shoot into the mixed herd with the Fifty, taking first bead on the watching bull. He cringed a little when he was hit, but not half of the resting ones rose at the report, and Johnny got three dead shots before the closest began to move a little towards the creek. He dropped the leader. When the rest just stopped, excitement ran through the young

hunter. He knew he had a real stand going, his first. He recalled Charlie Hart's advice: never push the shooting fast enough to heat the barrel, and always get the outside ones, those starting to walk away. . . . After about twenty-five buffaloes lay dead, the smoke was so thick and so slow in spreading in the quiet air that Johnny had to wipe his stinging eyes and find a new location where he could see. . . . Finally Johnny quit, even before the last were out of range. He already had eighty-eight scattered over the narrow creek bottom and felt ashamed somehow, the glassy eyes staring as he passed, the arcs some made by their kicking a saddening thing to see.

Most hunters were not so sensitive, and while the skins and tongues were shipped east, huge numbers of carcasses were left to rot. People even shot grazing bison from passenger trains, considering it sport. So gross were the excesses of the trade that fitful efforts to control or end buffalo hunting were made in Washington and in some state capitals. Protection laws were indeed on the books in Idaho, Wyoming, and Montana by the 1870s, but they were not enforced. Finally, inspired partly by military minds such as that of General Philip Sheridan, bison hunters wiped out the remaining herds utterly, depriving the Indians of their "commissary" and forcing them into dependent reservation life. "For the sake of a lasting peace," said Sheridan, "let [the buffalo hunters] kill, skin and sell until the buffaloes are exterminated." Sheridan's kind of peace was achieved, but luckily extermination was not. One person, incidentally, who resisted the final slaughter was a military man, Captain Moses Harris. Horrified by poaching of the dwindling herd of bison in Yellowstone, he bent official hands-off orders and forcibly discouraged poachers, thereby saving the remnants of the herd until meaningful protection was enacted in 1894.

As Richard White writes, "By 1882 there were an estimated 5,000 white hunters and skinners at work on the northern plains; by the end of 1883 the herd had vanished. The slaughter was so thorough and so quick that not even the hunters could believe what they had done. In the fall of 1883, many outfitted themselves as usual. But there was nothing to hunt except piles of bones bleaching in the sun and wind."

Settlement of the Plains

PRAYER OF THE HOMESTEADER

Lord, can it be that this is not your land?
Your ways are peaceful ways through country lanes,
But you have never walked upon these plains,
We never see your face beneath these skies.
Come to us, Lord.
Man should not live alone within the world;
He is not strong nor wise.
Bless our thin crops.
Teach the small trees to grow.
Stretch us your kindly hand.
We must have comfort in this alien land.

But this land fights
Its hard brown sod protests against the plow,
Its stubborn grasses cling.
Our young crops are beat flat by roaring hail,
And when the rains should visit us in spring
There comes a hot strange gale,
Like desert wind blown over glittering sand
That dries the little wheat.
Lord, did you mean that men should farm this land?

There is no doubt that the process of settling the Plains was almost inconceivably arduous. Mari Sandoz has ably dramatized the hardships and defeats of the early sodbusters, among them her own Swiss father, in *Old Jules*. And in *The Buffalo Hunters* she reminds us that the would-be settlers were fleeing from an almost equally difficult life in the cities of the East: tenement fires, Civil War draft riots that killed a thousand in one day, hunger, privation. Even though both the settled, farming tribes and the nomadic, bison-following tribes knew the Plains intimately and had survived there for eons, the newcomers were mostly unprepared.

As Richard White puts it:

> *German Russians, fresh from the steppes of the Ukraine, found the grasslands a familiar and comfortable place. Migrants used to the forests of eastern North America or of northern Europe, however, found it terrifying. Beret, a character in O. E. Rølvaag's novel* Giants in the Earth, *called it "the great stillness where there was nothing to hide behind." Finding the Plains forbidding, the ambition of many settlers was to transform it.*

The peak of the settler rush came between 1905 and 1915, when large areas of land that were ultimately to prove unfarmable were put to the plow. Homesteaders from the Midwest tried to use their midwestern farming practices to wrest a living from 160 acres with half the rainfall they had expected. Later, homestead grants were increased to 320 acres, but that still proved too small for survival. After World War I, demand for farm products dropped and a drought began. Both people and soil, driven by the harsh prairie winds, began to leave the land—a process still going on today.

The "black blizzards" that created the Dust Bowl were to make rural life impossible, but from the beginning, living on the Plains meant facing extremes of fierce summer heat and deadly winter cold. Weather could change from balminess to blizzard in a matter of hours, and stock and people caught away from home often froze to death. Rains came capriciously, sometimes in torrential thunderstorms, which could be followed by years of unforgiving drought. Hail could wipe out crops instantly. Many settlers lost their land claims, their crops, their livestock, their children, their spouses. A large number of wives fled back to the East. The endless open spaces and the loneliness of farm life bore heavily on people whose origins were in thickly settled regions, whether in America or Europe; women especially, who were frequently kept in virtual confinement by their husbands, suffered the worst of frontier life. The families that remained were phenomenally hardy, but even with good luck and endless resourcefulness they suffered, lived on tenuous hopes, and, understandably, often went crazy. In a particularly hot period, writes Mari Sandoz,

Many of the settlers [in western Nebraska] lost their cattle, even milk cows, and some their horses and pigs. Two men and a woman were sent to the insane asylum on the first passenger [train] east. Down at the edge of the [sand] hills a mother of three hung herself. North of Hays Springs a man killed his brother with an axe, sneaking up behind him and splitting his skull almost to the neck. There was much lawing [using legal chicanery to seize farmers' lands].

Rural populations on the Plains peaked in the 1920s and have been declining since. A major exodus took place during the Dust Bowl years in the 1930s, when a series of dry years led to dust storms so severe that dust in the air reached ships off the Atlantic coast. The windblown soil literally buried many farmsteads. Some of the abandoned land was bought up by the federal government, reverted to grassland, and is now managed as Forest Service or Bureau of Land Management (BLM) grazing land.

The rivers of the Plains flow eastward over a landscape so evenly and gradually tilted that they often run virtually parallel. In the bottomlands, the meandering of these rivers over the millennia has deposited rich soil—in Kansas, a stream cut at the Land Institute near Salina reveals topsoil still ten or twelve feet deep. Cottonwoods and other trees thrive near water and provide habitat for many birds and small mammals. Along rivers, irrigation can make farming feasible even where underground water cannot be pumped. Viewed from space, these farmable areas form long, narrow fingers of green reaching westward along the Missouri, the Niobrara, the Platte, the Smoky Hill, the Arkansas, and intervening smaller rivers. Even though farming of these bottomlands is not a highly profitable undertaking, they seem likely to remain in field-crop use indefinitely.

The uplands between the rivers are grass covered, and in many counties as far east as the middle of Kansas only a fraction of these uplands have ever been plowed, though in other places a lot of acreage has been successfully sown with that special human-bred grass we call wheat. But the upland soil is mostly thin, and water is available only from the scarce and unreliable rains or from the aquifer. Pumping water from the aquifer has enabled farmers to grow corn or other crops in some places for a few decades. But in the great sweep of a century or so, even if farmers learn to husband the aquifer and use water more sparingly, the chronic erosion brought by monoculture farming will return most of the land to grass. Even now, great areas of it are cattle ranches, with here and there a bison-ranching operation. For a time in the 1880s, when the open range was first being fenced, giant (often British-owned) cattle ranches dominated the Plains. But in the bitter winter of 1886 about 60 percent of the cattle died, and today only smaller-scale operations survive, though these are still impressive by eastern standards—spreads of 30,000 acres with 5,000 cattle on them are not unusual.

Just under Plains soil, especially in eastern Wyoming, lies 50 percent of U.S. coal reserves: immense amounts of low-sulfur coal. A lot of this coal is under public land where, as we shall see later, bison could also roam. As oil grows scarcer worldwide, strip mining of coal will probably increase; it may continue for decades, until a combination of the coal becoming less accessible and alternative sources of energy growing cheaper finally drives

During the Dust Bowl, hundreds of thousands of homesteaders were forced to leave the Plains when their farms met this fate. Photo: U.S. Department of Agriculture.

the mines out of business, and the landscape can be restored to grassland.

There is also oil under the Plains in Oklahoma, Kansas, and Wyoming, and even in North Dakota. A visitor driving through the area sees many oil wells working and also many no longer in use—their output cannot compete with cheap oil from the high-production Persian Gulf, African, and Latin American states, from which most U.S. oil supplies now come. The oil economy, too, operates by boom and bust, and right now bust prevails. Even at present depressed world oil costs, it is barely cheaper to generate electricity from oil or gas than to do so from wind power, so it seems unlikely that higher-cost American oil production will ever revive significantly. In any case, even our remaining nationwide reserves are small compared with our enormous oil consumption.

Concentration of Landownership

American agriculture is no longer based on family farms—the kinds of place town kids spent their summers on, helping out with the animals, lazing about the old swimming hole, and eating Grandma's cherry pie. We do still have some family farms, particularly in specialty-crop areas, where small enterprises can be, in market terms, both efficient and competitive. But today in the nation as a whole, 5 percent of the landowners hold 50 percent of the farmland acreage. Farms handed down through families are in sharp decline; only about 40 percent of transfers, whether by sale, inheritance, or gift, still take place within families. Each year 3.5 percent of farms change ownership; thus, in about thirty years there is a virtually complete turnover.

The biggest change in landownership—and one that is continuing—is the fact that absentee landowners now far outnumber resident farmer-owners. Nine out of 10 landowners are nonfarmers; 98 out of 100 of them are white; 2 out of 3 are more than sixty years old. Some of them are former farmers who live on their land (36 percent) or on other farmland (19 percent), but at least half live elsewhere, so much of the rental income they derive from tenants goes (and stays) outside the tenants' communities.

During the heady optimism of the New Deal, America was still a predominantly rural nation, and the federal government put into effect ambitious programs, from crop price supports to rural electrification, designed to bolster family farming—and to bring about, many believed, a kind of decentralized Jeffersonian democracy: free-spirited people living on their own land. Today this ideal is moribund. As a U.S. Department of Agriculture (U.S.D.A.) researcher now puts it, "Widespread farm ownership along with land-to-the-tiller was a primary objective of land policy at one point, but is now infeasible given the current structure of agriculture, nor is ownership necessary for access to profitable farming." In the contemporary agricultural world, profit is the measure of all things—and rural communities are in precipitous decline everywhere, not only on the Plains.

Despite the concentration of ownership, however, landowner-tenant relations have tipped in the tenants' favor; it is not easy to find people willing and able to take the risks and do the work of operating farms, and in sharecropping areas the landowner now often gets only 40 percent of the crop. Many think that sharecropping died out after the Civil War, but it is alive and well: 41 percent of all farmers now rent all or part of their farms from somebody else. Generally, landowners share in decisions about what to plant, how to cultivate, and when to harvest; tenant farmers are not the independent operators of yesteryear. And by the same token, landowners will be major players in any private-land transitions from cattle raising to bison raising.

Agricultural land represents, as the U.S.D.A. puts it, "a small and declining proportion of the national wealth." Moreover, since many landowners own relatively small properties (two-thirds of them own fewer than 180 acres) and are not people of great wealth, they have limited political influence. The power of the farm lobby now comes primarily from organizations like the Farm Bureau, whose base is large farmers and farm corporations. As in so many areas of American life, money talks but votes now only whisper.

The biggest landholders in the United States today are corporations: timber and paper corporations, oil and coal and agribusiness corporations, utilities, railroads. Landownership is highly concentrated, and in agriculture the concentration is growing. (Kansas and eight other states have laws limiting total landownership, but they are not enforced. More than a million acres in Kansas are held, illegally, in greater than 5,000-acre totals.) We often recommend land reform to impoverished Third World countries. But perhaps, as suggested by demographer Frank Popper—of whom we will hear more later—we could use some land reform here too. As he notes, "Land is primarily a social weapon. It is a means by which its possessors protect their economic, political, and other interests."

Depopulation of Rural Lands—a Global Problem

Farming populations remain dense in most of the nonindustrialized world (nowadays often referred to as "the South," though not quite accurately). However, it is seldom realized how far the process of depopulation has gone in the rural areas of much of Europe and America. When it was revealed in 1987 that more than a hundred Great Plains counties had reverted to populations lower than "frontier" levels (two persons per square mile), it seemed a shocking revelation.

However, the Plains experience is part of a worldwide pattern. There has been a parallel sharp decline in the numbers of people living on the land in Spain, Italy, and France. Even in relatively undeveloped places like rural India, the process of concentration in landownership has been relentless, and the resulting unequal distribution of wealth accounts for much of the poverty (and consequent mass migration to the cities) of such areas. But in "Northern" countries it is, above all, corporate land ownership that has grown—and surviving family farmers often are forced to become corporate too. ("Get big or get out" was and is the advice given to American farmers by our government.) As agribusiness triumphs, few independent family farms remain, and the work of the large-acreage industrial farms is done with the aid of legions of petroleum-driven machines, so the work force has decreased to only a few percent of what it once was. For example, harvesting today is carried out by crews of migratory contractors, who, with their own machinery, work their way gradually north during the harvest season. What is happening here is the familiar process of raising productivity while rendering human labor superfluous, often taken as an achievement of capitalism; financial writers glow at higher "productivity" statistics. Such productivity increases may or may not fulfill the promise of cheaper goods—often the gains are siphoned off by investors and management. However, the social costs paid by society as a whole—in unemployment, underemployment, dislocation, and declining real wages—are indubitable, and large, and lasting.

The emptying of the countryside is particularly poignant in France. France is the most blessed in soils and climate of all European countries. Peasant farming has sustained itself there for more than a thousand years, and the French people are, it hardly needs saying, deeply attached to the high quality of their traditional foodstuffs. The French government has also believed that the maintenance of French traditional culture depends on preserving the vitality of rural France's small farms and has thus provided substantial government farm subsidies. But the evolution of a global and highly competitive agribusiness market has already forced many small French farmers off the land. "Cardboard" tomatoes and cosmetically perfect but tasteless cheap fruit are proliferating in France too—along with the heaviest pesticide ap-

Sideoats Grama

plications per acre in the entire world. The new international trade treaty known as GATT (General Agreement on Tariffs and Trade, to which the French government showed some resistance) will further drive farming everywhere toward the agribusiness model and hence further depopulate the French countryside—where well-to-do Britons and even Americans are now buying up vacated peasant houses, adding modern conveniences, and using them as summer or retirement homes. The only bright side to this story is that extensive, largely depopulated areas of the south of France have sunshine almost year-round, which should make it easy for France to switch rapidly to solar-thermal electricity generation if its aging nuclear plants begin to falter.

Similar forces, exacerbated through the Western Hemisphere trade pact known as NAFTA (North American Free Trade Agreement), will drive peasants off the land in Mexico, sending them to the cities and to the United States. In fact, there is hardly a developing country in the world, including China, with its billion-plus population, where rural agriculture is not in a deepening process of social dislocation, with profound global effects.

In America, only 2 percent of the population now farms or engages in related agricultural occupations, and a large percentage of farmers are part-timers whose basic income is provided by off-farm jobs. We have experienced a migration from rural to urban living so profound that it is hard to visualize in the abstract. But it is plainly visible in the towns that small-farm counties once supported; Larry McMurtry dramatized the process well in *The Last Picture Show*, and you have only to drive across the Plains to see it continuing.

The phenomenon, however, manifests itself everywhere. Even in California's stunningly rich Central Valley, areas dominated by large-scale agribusiness support only a fraction of the town activities (stores, cafés, doctors, dentists, lawyers, and so on) that family farming areas of the valley support. Where most people can make a living only as hired hands or as sharecroppers, communities wither.

The Universal Dole

We live in a system called capitalism, but it might better be called subsidism. There is hardly a significant economic interest in the country that does not benefit from public funds. The money flows are so voluminous, varied, and complex that nobody has yet been able to track them comprehensively, even on a state level. Perhaps a wall-size electronic display could cope with the complexities involved so that citizens could literally see at last where their money was going.

Critics of the subsidy system have begun to appear, working from different ideological perspectives—some are conservatives who regard it as a travesty of free enterprise, and some are liberals who regard it as a looting of public funds. The process whereby regulatees "capture" supposed regulatory or administrative agencies and turn them to the purposes of private profit has long fascinated academics, but nobody has yet figured out how to do anything about it. Meanwhile, the debate is becoming more ardent, the vocabulary more heated: "welfare aerospace," "welfare cotton." There was even, as we learned in a recent budget debate, welfare mohair production, though a warier Congress eliminated this, along with honey and wool subsidies, in 1994. But hundreds, probably thousands, of other enterprises remain on the public dole. (In economic arithmetic, whenever the government provides something to somebody below market cost, it is a subsidy, exactly equivalent to sending out a check.) So it should be no surprise that critics have mounted a concerted attack on "welfare ranching" and farming. As *Time* magazine noted, farm support programs now pay almost half their benefits to farmers making more than $100,000 per year; reforms being discussed in Congress would save some $4.3 billion.

When some congressional whim cuts off the subsidies, as happened to the merchant marine, the industry in question generally closes down. More recently, aerospace executives have professed themselves uninterested in conversion to peacetime production, with its messy competitiveness. Ranchers who stoutly defend the favors they receive from government are thus hardly more greedy than the national norm; they could justly claim to be asking for no more than the next person is getting.

Confining ourselves to land questions, the government sells national-forest timber to lumber companies at a loss—in most national forests, it spends more on roads and other aids to the companies than it gets from them in timber fees. It subsidizes corporate producers of sugar and small producers of grain. It spends enormous sums on levees, channels, and locks for navigation, subsidizing the inland barge trade for the benefit of agribusiness. It subsidizes land- and energy-intensive highways and airports at the expense of the no-longer-subsidized railroads. It operates a nationwide research and advisory system devoted to furthering the interests of agricultural producers, especially large firms. And it simply sends out a lot of checks: in both Canada and the United States, according to Andrew Nikoforuk, "more than half of farm income in former bison haunts now comes out of taxpayers' pockets. The great frontier is really a welfare state." In North Dakota, farm subsidies provide more than half a billion dollars annually to the state's economy—four-fifths of net farm income. Subsidies, of course, have the general effect of preserving the status quo when it could no longer survive unassisted. Ranchers enabled by subsidies to keep going with cattle have little incentive to switch to more profitable bison.

"Getting the government off our backs" is an oft-heard phrase among people who are actually seeking to keep their own subsidies intact while abolishing any regulations they might have to comply with. So it is not surprising that the ranching industry, operating as it does in thinly populated states, where politicians are easily accessible—indeed, are often ranchers themselves—has been able to perfect and defend the subsidy machinery in a way that must make other industries envious.

In the ten westernmost states, about 30,000 grazing permittees receive government subsidization as the beneficiaries of below-cost grazing leases, costly (and usually ecologically damaging) programs to "improve" pasturelands by providing water for cattle, road access, fencing, efforts to remove species that compete with or prey on stock, and so on. About a third of these leased lands are in former bison country.

It is difficult for city people to understand the power that a handful of ranchers have over the political process, both local and national. This power is founded on long-term presence of dominant families, important connections with rising and established politicians, and long-term public tolerance. Challenges to it are not taken lightly: admitted environmentalists in ranching areas sometimes receive death threats, and on occasion their wives and children are terrorized. Forest Service employees who attempt to carry out mandates from headquarters to "preserve the resource" often find themselves transferred when political pressures are brought to bear on their superiors.

In an attempt to increase the visibility of ranching issues, conservation groups have been recommending "adopt-an-allotment" programs whereby people interested in the ecological health of nearby rangeland get to know intimately a given allotment (which may be some thousands of acres) and its permittee and, if possible, encourage the rancher to adopt less-destructive livestock policies. (It is sometimes thought that ranchers treat their own land better than leased public land, but range degradation seems to be the same on both.) In rural communities where the dominant ranchers have brooked no opposition for generations, this takes a lot of courage; it is most likely to occur in areas where "outsiders" have achieved a certain political weight. On the whole, such groups are likely to be aware of the ecological and economic advantages of bison.

In recent years the powers of the ranching lobby have been cut back a bit, especially in Montana, where a tide of "modem cowboy" immigrants running small, modern businesses have brought environmental ideas with them. Montana's urban areas are small, but today they overbalance the state's thinly populated areas, and their elected representatives have begun to reflect this. In fact, in 1992 Montanans' sole congressional representative, Democrat Pat Williams, sponsored a bill to add 1.6 million more acres to the wilderness system. (Williams throws an occasional bison barbecue for the Montanans in Washington.) Standing timber remaining in Montana is dwindling, and mining is expected to remain minimal, supporting only about 6,400 jobs. State officials are realizing that if they want to preserve something worthwhile for tourists to look at, they cannot allow the landscape to be destroyed.

However, from a nitty-gritty political standpoint, ranchers and farmers are still firmly in control of the statehouses and congressional delegations of a half dozen states. We will address in Part III the hardball political question: given the public will for and ecological desirability of getting cows and sheep off a good many public lands and getting bison (plus antelope, elk, etc.) onto them again, can we conceive a strategy that could find support from ranchers and other Plains dwellers, as well as from taxpaying members of the national public and environmentalists interested in the welfare of the grasslands ecosystem?

Tracking the Money

Lynn Jacobs, one of the most learned among critics of public-lands grazing, estimates the total expenditures to support ranching in the ten westernmost states at a billion dollars per year. This sounds like a lot, but not in light of the details that follow. Analysis of the ten westernmost states will not suffice, of course, for an overall program for the Plains, which extend into the next tier of states to the east, but it gives some idea of the workability of the basic idea. If we add the Dakotas, Nebraska, Kansas, Oklahoma, and Texas and omit the coastal states plus Nevada and Utah, which are outside bison range, the total should be nearly as great. Where does all this money go?

Low grazing fees are a tradition on public lands, and they account for a major part of the subsidization. Plans to raise fees toward levels approaching parity with rentals of comparable private lands have always been bitterly opposed—though ranchers forced to rent private lands at market prices regard the favored status of their permittee competitors as unfair. Grazing fees are not, as most people imagine, fixed numbers, like prices in a mail-order catalog. They are set through a complex formula that supposedly takes into account a rancher's expenses; the process works rather like the budgeting that welfare workers negotiate with their clients in order to avoid bankruptcy and homelessness. The result, studies have generally shown, is that lessees get land for something like a fifth of its fair market value. (Ranchers pay market rates, which run about five times higher than federal fees, when, as commonly happens, they sublease permit land from another rancher.) In 1986, grazing-fee subsidies totaled $75 million for the ten westernmost states, or $3,500 per rancher. (During the Clinton administration, they actually increased.) Under these circumstances, grazing permits are extremely valuable, often used as bank collateral; possession of an established grazing permit sharply raises the price of base ranch properties.

Heretofore, the government has shown no inclination to try to break even on its leasing program. Much fee income goes right back into range "improvements" as a further subsidy to ranchers rather than into the federal treasury. Thus, both the BLM and the Forest Service run regular losses on their range operations, just as the Forest Service does on timber; it gave $8.1 million to the Treasury in 1987, for instance, but spent $31.4 million, and the BLM spent even more. It is almost impossible to track the precise extent of subsidies in such situations, but when the two agencies themselves attempted to calculate their total deficits in 1987, they came out with $50.8 million.

Some public-land agency expenditures are not listed as range related but nonetheless constitute ranching subsidies, such as clearing of brush and thinning of trees to promote pasture, piping in of water for stock, fencing to minimize livestock impacts on streams, much fire suppression and road building, installation of cattle guards on roadways, and so on. Lynn Jacobs,

Native to areas where winters are severe, bison are much hardier than cattle and overwinter without being fed or brought inside to shelter. (Cattle have frozen to death in large numbers on the northern Plains.) Photo: Michael H. Francis.

who has spent a great deal of time with officials discussing their budgets, concludes that such activities would add another $140–190 million.

To these figures must be added the costs of Soil Conservation Service work; the administering of a large number of loans (in 1987, grazing associations had borrowed $56.7 billion from the government); incentive payments to wool producers; disaster relief (in 1988, $140 million was spent on feed for "drought-stricken livestock," and in 1989, $900 million was appropriated for disaster relief to farmers and ranchers); agricultural marketing programs; research services; and so on. In arid regions, ranchers also benefit from irrigation water, the provision of which is extremely expensive to the taxpayers.

State agencies in ranching states are likewise busy providing costly services to ranchers. In addition, there are tax loopholes that are equivalent to subsidies. For example, a corporate owner of land worth millions can put a few cows on it and pretend it is agricultural land, thus lowering taxes; one Arizona company did so, winning a tax decrease from $92,000 to $150. For similar tax reasons, H. Ross Perot claimed to be a goat rancher on 200 acres he was actually clearing for condominiums and hotels near Austin, Texas.

Any analysis of government outlays for ranching must include the budget of the Animal Damage Control program. ADC is often accused of being a rogue agency that, though placed under the purview of the U.S. Department of Agriculture in 1986, is not really responsible to anybody except its rancher clients. (Its advisory committee has two scientists, eight livestock people, and eight other members representing commodity interests.) ADC is thus a kind of counterkingdom to the agencies charged with protecting wildlife.

Ranching is a risky endeavor, and ranchers are beset by reduced demand for meat, competition from cheap meat from abroad, and corporate takeovers; it is understandable that they should be angry, and predators are conveniently available as scapegoats. So ADC poisons, traps, snares, and shoots predators from air and land in seventeen western states—on public and private land—including bears, bobcats, and mountain lions. Targets even include the endangered swift fox, which eats prairie dogs, whose holes and consumption of cattle forage so outrage ranchers. ADC particularly poisons coyotes, an intelligent and resourceful species that has filled the predator niche from which we removed wolves, and that will prey on unprotected sheep. Adult coyotes are sometimes poisoned with illegal compounds given out by ADC offices; federal investigators once confiscated enough poisons "to kill every man, woman, child, and mammal in the western U.S.," which ranchers had been using on bald and golden eagles. Coyote pups are often killed in their dens with flamethrowers, smoke, or hooks or simply by having their heads smashed in with shovels.

Pictures of animals painfully killed by ADC have begun appearing in the media with enough regularity to horrify a lot of taxpayers. Less emotionally, the program has lost support because it has begun to be understood that predator losses are only 2 percent of the losses that ranchers suffer—respiratory and digestive malfunctions of livestock account for 51 percent. Moreover, poisons kill at least twice as many cattle and calves as predators do.

ADC spends about $36 million of public money annually, 53 percent of that on its various extermination programs, which continue to dominate its activities despite announcements from headquarters that it is moving away from lethal methods and encouraging ranchers to use human shepherds or guard dogs (or burros or llamas, which are even more effective) and to confine their sheep at night. Although ADC claims that it is now strongly promoting the use of nonlethal methods, so much outrage has built up among animal-rights and biodiversity advocates that several organizations now exist for the sole purpose of exterminating ADC itself.

Meanwhile, attentions from ADC do not actually seem to reduce predator populations, and coyotes are killed at a cost of $100 to $2,000 per animal. (A lamb is worth around $80.) Kansas, which has no ADC program, has significantly lower lifestock predation losses than do neighboring Nebraska and Oklahoma, both of which spend hundreds of thousands of dollars each year on predator killing. Public protests have been having some effect; in 1992, they led to a brief hiatus in ADC activities on BLM lands, which were found to violate the National Environmental Policy Act (NEPA); however, business as usual soon resumed under "emergency" authorizations. The Forest Service, even more obligingly, has been having ADC prepare environmental assessments on its own operations.

Lynn Jacobs, totaling all these figures, guesses that they amount to around a billion dollars a year and reports that a suppressed Forest Service analysis came out with roughly the same estimate. Later we will consider some potential future uses for this money.

A Different Future

"Grass no good upside down."
> *—Pawnee chief observing plowing by Plains settlers*

It is time to think of the Plains in new ways. As Native Americans are demonstrating by their reintroduction of bison on many reservations, bison can again become part of the natural Plains landscape—and, for Indian people, not only a source of self-sufficiency in food production but also a powerful spiritual and religious presence. For whites, bringing back the bison and their companion grazers on a large scale in Plains parks and

Bison challenge us to think anew about the future of the Plains.

on other public lands will provide us the opportunity to see what a sustainable ecosystem in the Plains is like. And growing numbers of bison on private ranch lands will help us learn what a permanently viable agricultural system could be. Moreover, because the Plains are also very windy, they could become producers of a significant amount of wind-generated electrical energy, making the region self-reliant in energy.

Thus, in the next few decades, a period when most of American society is virtually certain to be wracked by increasingly severe social problems, many of them with ecological roots, the Plains could become a serene beacon showing the way to a sustainable future. There is no easy technofix for the thinning of the ozone layer; we are going to have to live with whatever its consequences turn out to be. We will not be able to reverse global warming. It is doubtful that we can avoid famines, resource-conflict wars, and ensuing disruptive human mass migrations. At home, we must somehow learn to live with a further decline in American real per capita income and the disintegrative effects of our consumerist economy on families and communities. But on the Plains, the potential exists to demonstrate that humans can inhabit our planet in a newly responsible, permanent, comfortable, and civilized way.

Statistically, modern oil-propelled agriculture looks impressively productive. For several decades, in fact, despite extensive paving over and erosion and desertification of farmable land, the world's farmers defeated the predictions of pessimists that increasing population would outrun food production. (This trend has recently turned downward, however; there is now less grain on the planet per capita than in earlier years, and formerly sanguine agrotechnologists admit that the prospects for increased yields are not bright.) But at present, as we shall see in detail later, we put far more petroleum calories into agriculture than we get out in food calories.

In time, what William Catton has called our species "overshoot" in population will require correction. Barring some catastrophic plague, population reduction will probably not happen quickly. But cheap oil and gas will no longer be available for producing cheap food and all the other things we use them for. And in time, more costly food will drive down population, as will growing social disorder.

American agriculture presently accounts for only 3–4 percent of our total energy consumption. We may assume that the government will guarantee full fuel supplies to the agricultural sector for as long as possible; no government contemplates with equanimity the possibility of food riots. At the moment, nations addicted to oil income are pumping oil as fast as they can, and in fact an international oil glut exists, greatly to the temporary advantage of the industrialized countries. But in the long run—probably a matter of four or five decades—oil will become scarcer and considerably more expensive, to the point at which oil substitutes made from our considerable coal reserves will seem reasonable. And when the coal also dwindles, Wes Jackson predicts, "our last available fossil fuels will be spent on agriculture, perhaps to make nitrogen fertilizer to offset the consequences of soil loss." Well before that time, agriculture that produces a net surplus of energy will become essential. This is possible on the Plains, if nowhere else in America.

Part II Bison Present

A new fondness for bison has been growing in the land, like a variant of what Freudian psychology calls "the return of the repressed." The familiar bison profile is becoming a standard icon, having proliferated first in tourist goods sold in the bison heartland, but then almost everywhere in the country. Artists are painting bison. There are bison jewelry designs, bison note cards, bison emblems on clothing and hats. A movie company uses a moving herd of bison as its logo on film credits. Television retells American history in lavish programs full of bison images. The great, shaggy beasts are rising into national consciousness again, and they have a lot of helpers—some, as we shall see, motivated by fun, some by profit, and some by a sense of spiritual or ecological propriety. The presence of bison in our national life is becoming reestablished, both in imagery and in fact.

Indian tribes, nonprofit organizations like The Nature Conservancy, and government parks and refuges are bringing back wild bison in the context of open western landscapes. The Conservancy has been operating a 54,000-acre preserve in the Niobrara Valley of Nebraska since 1980, and it recently opened a 50,000-acre bison preserve near Pawhuska in Oklahoma. Yellowstone National Park, with the largest free-ranging public herd in the United States, extends over some 2.2 million acres, and a half dozen other parks have sizable herds. Indian tribal lands suitable and available for bison total some 12 million acres. Ted Turner, who believes that bison ought to return as a natural part of the American landscape, has used some of his media wealth to put bison on a 128,000-acre spread in Montana, and also bought two huge ranches in New Mexico, of 300,000 and 338,000 acres, for bison. (Turner's reported goal is to own a million acres for bison.)

Bison have become a business for many people. These include a steadily growing band of former cattle ranchers who are raising bison to sell as stock or meat and to provide a wide range of buffalo artifacts. A young bison calf is now worth three or four times what a cattle calf brings. The marketing of bison products is becoming vigorous. If you happen to want a genuine gigantic buffalo head looking down at you from the wall of your house, you are now in luck: a mail-order company called Thundering Herd Buffalo Products will give you one for between $1,750 and $2,000. If that makes you squeamish, you could have a soft, cuddly stuffed toy buffalo, with imitation-leather horns, for $35. Or you could go for 10 eight-ounce buffalo top sirloin steaks, for $99.00 plus $21.00 shipping; this works out to $24 per pound. The Denver Buffalo Company will sell you top sirloins, rib eyes, roasts, "buff dogs," and smoked buffalo sausage at similar prices. The M&S Company in Rollins, Montana, makes buffalo jerky in three flavors, which it will ship to you for $15.95 per pound. If you are concerned about the effects of fat and cholesterol on your arteries, you might be motivated to spend that sum upon reading that buffalo has almost 85 percent less fat than beef.

Bison are finding a place in our hearts and minds and, for that matter, in our stomachs. Their place on the American land is growing too. In the following three chapters, we will explore the status of bison on Indian land, on public land (and quasi-public nonprofit land, including zoos and preserves), and on private land.

There is a spectrum of ideas about how much management by humans is appropriate for bison, but correlation of management style with landownership categories is by no means exact. Only one public herd (at Yellowstone National Park) is truly unmanaged—the animals are allowed to roam wherever and whenever they wish and are never rounded up, culled, or vaccinated; the only human limitation on them is that if they wander outside park boundaries, they are liable to be shot, by ranchers or by Montana or Wyoming wildlife officials. Indian ideas call for bison to be allowed to be bison in the same manner as at Yellowstone, but tribal herds are generally still relatively small and so far exist on limited and fenced areas. On the lands of federal wildlife refuges, state parks, and The Nature Conservancy, bison are often intensively managed, even when their keepers are devoted to their value as wildlife. Zoos and small preserves, maintaining very small bison herds on restricted acreage, usually feed and otherwise manage them. And on many private ranches, though their owners often respect the independence of the species, bison are confined in rotational grazing pastures and rounded up yearly for injections and culling; troublesome mature bulls are routinely eliminated, horns are removed, and so on; in short, bison are treated almost indistinguishably from cattle—as a species subject to the infinite ingenuities of human will.

To a significant degree, the struggle for the future of the bison is a struggle for land. As we shall see, bison can be kept, in good health, on relatively small pieces of land. But to let them be bison requires an expansive terrain and a willingness to let nature take its course. Neither of these essential components of the future of bison is secure or certain.

In white law, bison occupy an anomalous position. On public lands such as parks and preserves, they are "wildlife"—in the same category as elk or bears—subject to federal or state authorities (which sometimes issue hunting licenses) and watched over by game-management officials. On public lands leased for grazing, bison have the same character as bison on private lands: they are private property and can be bought, sold, and managed subject to only minimal and seldom-applied U.S.D.A. regulations aimed at protecting their basic health. On land belonging to nonprofit organizations like The Nature Conservancy, they are private property devoted to the public benefit; we have no accepted name for this land or the bison on it, which might be termed "social property." These human distinctions, of course, mean nothing to bison and will probably tend to break down over the decades if the total number of bison rises into the tens of millions.

Original bison range extended into the Southwest, where the Taos Pueblo has owned a herd for many decades. Recently bison motifs have been growing in popularity in Southwest Indian jewelry and other artwork. Some Southwest Indian spiritual imagery involves bison, like this kachina. Marigay Graña collection, photo by Marigay Graña.

We live in an era when every square meter of the earth, outside of the few remote territories still in the hands of indigenous peoples, belongs to somebody. Our fences, perhaps the most omnipresent physical signs of this possessory pattern, run over even the most seemingly vacant rangelands of the Plains. A piece of short-grass rangeland may be literally worth less than the cost of fencing it, yet it will remain fenced as long as a few cows can be supported on it. The fences will come down only when the value of the land for cattle sinks below what it is worth for bison—and even then, as long as traditional private ownership patterns prevail, only internal fences will go down, not boundary fences. As we will see later, new forms of co-operation among ranchers could assemble quite large areas for jointly managed bison herds, perhaps several hundred thousand acres together. But that is still only a fraction of natural bison scale. Thus, we will ultimately need greatly expanded government ownership of Plains land—in several multimillion-acre blocks, on the scale of Yellowstone—because without it,

Bison calves seldom stray more than a few yards from their mothers in their early weeks. The pair communicate through frequent and varied grunts. The calf's original orange-rust color darkens with time. Photo: Rich Kirchner.

bison will not be able to roam the indefinite ranges natural to the species. The Yellowstone herd, precious though its freedom is, must not remain the token wild bison herd that it is today.

We may develop in this country a substantial bison-ranching industry that produces meat and deals with bison largely as if they were domestic stock—creatures who, though alive, are treated as if they were mere machines for meat or hide or egg production, controllable by humans in the interest of profit. But if this pattern is allowed to become predominant it will be a disgrace to our species, and a tragedy for the bison.

Chapter Three
Bison on Indian Reservations

To Native Americans, the bison is not merely an animal, in any sense familiar to Euro-Americans, but is a spiritual presence connected to the ultimate realities of the world. Bringing the bison home, then, is for Indians above all a cultural goal, and educating young people about bison is a way of educating them about spiritual issues. Bison were, of course, a source of food, robes, tipi covers, and many other Indian necessities. (In using the terms "Native American" and "Indian" interchangeably, I am following practice common among the tribes themselves. Similarly, I use both "Euro-American" and "white.") But bison and people had been created together, and there had been a time, in the worldview of the Lakota Sioux, for example, when bison and people were interchangeable—they could turn into each other, they could interbreed and have children, and it was a matter of self-determination whether you wanted to have a bison form or a human form. Moreover, bison had a herd structure, a community structure, and even a language, which were taken as models for people to follow. There were the young cows and the older cows and calves, the young bulls and the older bulls, and the tribal social system was built on that; the bison, as your brothers, would show you how life should go and how you should conduct yourself. Even today, Indians speak of bison as "our four-legged relatives" or "our people" and "buffalo people." Buffalo were intimately connected with the origins of human life. Mari Sandoz, in her foreword to *The Buffalo Hunters*, mentions hearing "an old Pawnee of the buffalo days" tell this version of the beginning of the world:

Once, long ago, all things were waiting in a deep place far underground. There were the great herds of buffaloes and all the people, and the antelope too, and wolves, deer and rabbits—everything, even the little bird that sings the tear-tear song. Everything waited as in sleep.

Then the one called Buffalo Woman awoke, stretched her arms, rose and began to walk. She walked among all the creatures, past the little tear-tear bird, the rabbits and all the rest and through the people too, and the buffaloes. Everywhere as she passed there was an awakening, and a slow moving, as when the eyes were making ready for some fine new thing to be seen. Buffalo Woman walked on in the good way, past even the farthest buffaloes, the young cows with their sleeping yellow calves. She went on to a dark round place that seemed like a hole and she stood there a while, looking. Then she bowed her head a little, as one does to pass under the lodge flap, and stepped out. Suddenly the people could see there was a great shining light all about her, a shining and brightness that seemed blinding as she was gone.

And now a young cow arose and followed the woman, and then another buffalo and another, until a great string of them was following, each one for a moment in the shining light of the hole before he was gone, and the light fell upon the one behind. When the last of the buffaloes was up and moving, the people began to rise, one after another, and fell into a row too, each one close upon the heels of the moccasins ahead. All the people, young and old and weak and strong, went so, out through the hole that was on Pahuk, out upon the shining, warm, and grassy place that was the earth, with a wide river, the Platte, flowing below, and over everything a blueness, with the tear-tear bird flying toward the sun, the warming sun. The buffaloes were already scattering over the prairie, feeding, spreading in every direction toward the circle that is the horizon. The people looked all around and knew this was their place, the place upon which they would live forever, they and the buffalo together.

Such stories were common among Plains tribes. Their earth-centeredness embodies the ecological truth that humans are indissolubly connected to the rest of the natural order.

Another story about Buffalo Woman has been retold and illustrated by Paul Goble. In it a buffalo cow turns into a beautiful woman, marries an Indian man, and has a son, but she is scorned by her human relatives and finally returns to bison form—taking her son, also transformed, back to her original herd. There the distraught husband joins them and, with his son's help, passes a test in which he correctly identifies his wife and son among the herd members and thus becomes a member of the herd himself. The relationship between people and bison made that day, it was said, would last until the end of time. In the Lakota phrase, *Mitakuye oyasin:* We are all related.

As the Indian medicine man Lame Deer put it, "There is power in a buffalo—spiritual, magic power—but there is no power in an Angus, a Hereford.... When we killed a buffalo, we knew what we were doing. We apologized to his spirit, tried to make him understand why we did it, honoring with a prayer the bones of those who gave their flesh to keep us alive, praying for their return, praying for the life of our brothers, the buffalo nation, as well as for our own people.... To us life, all life, is sacred." And he went on: "You can't understand about nature, about the feeling [Sioux] have toward it, unless you understand how close we were to the buffalo. That animal was almost like a part of ourselves, part of our souls."

A sled for young children made from bison ribs. Courtesy of Museum Collections, Minneapolis Historical Society.

This profound connection to bison is at the core of the Indian restoration effort because people sense that bringing back the bison will teach Indian people how to live their lives. Indeed, some of the restoration impulse has to do with being able again to communicate with bison on a daily basis. Moreover, because almost everything the Plains tribes did involved bison, bringing them back will be a powerful aid to preservation of native languages. Indians not only relied on bison for food, they also made practically all household objects from one part or another of the bison.

Some of these uses will surely revive—there is a brisk market among whites for buffalo robes, and Indians themselves will use them as they become more common and affordable. Presently horns and skulls, which to

Indians are religious or quasi-religious artifacts, decorate houses of whites. In Indian eyes, this does not serve the dignity of the bison—symbol of the unity and strength of Indian culture, a sacred gift from the creator.

Bison at Pine Ridge

Alex White Plume directs the natural resources program of the Oglala Sioux (or Pine Ridge) Indian Reservation in southwestern South Dakota. He is a tall, handsome, rather gangly man, with a narrow face and deep brown eyes. Although he is a tribal official with heavy responsibilities, he has a meditative, thoughtful way of speaking. I met him in the dusty reservation village of Kyle, in a double-wide mobile home (painted barn red with white vertical stripes) converted to office use by the Parks and Recreation Authority of the tribe. It is a bustling office, with three Indian women working at computers, sending faxes and answering telephones, and various people coming in and out on business.

The literal meaning of "buffalo" in Lakota, Alex White Plume says, is "His Great Owners"—so "in actuality, he owns us; we don't own him. As a

Left: Spirit of Three Buffalos, by Art Manchego. Contemporary Indian painters often use bison imagery in their work. Reproduced by permission of Art Manchego and Saga Cards of Enchantment, Albuquerque. *Right:* This buffalo horn bonnet was probably used in the Buffalo Dance of the Gros Ventre tribe. Courtesy Buffalo Bill Historical Center, Cody, Wyoming. Gift of Mr. and Mrs. Larry Larom.

result of that the stewardship idea came into being. It's very different from ranching. The cattle industry has been on our land for approximately 130 years, and what they did has totally ruined our grass—exotic grasses have taken over, though in those pastures where we have buffalo it's now recovered to almost 95 percent native grasses, the same that used to be there." (By far the biggest proportion of the reservation's 2.8 million acres is still being used for cattle.)

There were bison on the reservation starting in 1933, on about 4,000 acres; after a lapse between 1947 and 1972, they have been reestablished. The tribe now has about 32,000 acres devoted to bison and some 500 head. "We don't overstress the grass, overstress the animals. Each animal has about seventy acres of land, so year-round there's never a short supply of food." No rotational grazing—moving the animals from pasture to pasture—is employed; as Alex says proudly, "Once you start handling the buffalo, they become gentle and then they're not buffalo any more. But ours are kept in a totally wild state. They're pure buffalo. If you go up in our pastures, they still make their defensive formation—the bulls will make a line and the cows and calves will get into the center. It's a beautiful sight to see!"

The tribe's objective is to have about 10,000 head in ten years, along with an increasing number of elk, concentrated in the sparsely populated western and northern areas of the reservation. Meat from the bison is at present used exclusively by reservation people in ceremonies: sun dances, the naming ceremony (through which a baby becomes a member of the community), and the making-of-relatives ceremony, a kind of adoption ritual. Alex White Plume says, "We don't sell the meat, but we give it out for the ceremonies, and in this way we're helping our future. That's the whole purpose, to make sure we're doing things that are culturally relevant." It is still being debated whether meat should eventually be sold to non-Indians as more becomes available.

Alex said that when the tribe gave 168,000 acres of its northern badlands region to the federal government to expand Badlands National Park, it was supposed to receive in return surplus bison from national parks, but this turned out to be "another broken promise. Now we have a bill in Congress to get that land back." (The tribe does get some income from operations of a lodge in the park, and several other tribes have received excess park bison.)

Hunting permits are a substantial source of income for the tribe; the current price is around $4,000, but Alex thinks it can gradually be raised to $10,000. Hunters with that kind of money are primarily interested in the head (for mounting) and the hide, but the tribe makes available a tow truck with winch that can haul an entire carcass to a slaughtering and freezing plant if the hunter desires.

I have been told by Indians that the re-creation of the fierce joy of the buffalo hunt in *Dances with Wolves* affected them powerfully. But tribal buffalo hunting today is not so dramatic. A couple of guys in a pickup can go out and bring in a bison without having to be much in the way of stalkers or marksmen. This does not mean, however, that the act lacks spiritual significance, any more than driving to church in a car necessarily negates white religious devotion. The felled animal is spoken to in a ritual of gratitude; sacred eagle feathers wave sage smoke over it. Children watching the process learn about the ways of their ancestors, how death leads to life, and how bison are coming back into daily tribal ways.

InterTribal Bison Restoration

Originally, tribal lands and their animal inhabitants were not "owned" at all but were used according to traditional patterns of sharing. White notions about possession of land still sit uneasily with Indians who prefer to live in traditional ways, and Indian bison-restoration efforts are aimed at building up tribal herds, not herds owned by individual tribespeople—though at Pine Ridge there are presently three individual Indian ranchers who have small "seed" herds, leasing land from the tribe for them, and two more are about ready to start up. (It is a common practice for would-be bison raisers, white or Indian, to "borrow" animals for a few years, keeping most of the calves when they return the original, or equivalent, animals.)

The InterTribal Bison Cooperative (ITBC), which was founded in 1990, exists to help along the bison-restoration efforts of thirty-one participating tribes in thirteen states, and more are becoming interested. The group has been very active in consulting with tribes and helping train young people to work with bison in the framework of tribal culture and tribal needs. It has also helped secure federal money for a number of tribes (its own operations are funded by foundation grants) to aid in building up their herds, which Congress has been persuaded will help improve the diet and welfare of the reservation people. The ITBC's executive director is a wildlife biologist named Mark Heckert.

It was a hot summer day in Rapid City, South Dakota, when I met Heckert for breakfast. Like other young folks in the area on such a day, he sported a tank top. He is a big, solid, hearty man with a relaxed, centered manner. Although he has worked as a wildlife biologist for the Native American Fish and Wildlife Society and on various other tribal projects before serving as executive director of the ITBC, he is a white man, from Washington State. He has straight black hair and a tattoo on his shoulder, and, though he is forceful and articulate, he sometimes slips into a lightly teasing way of interacting that I was to find was a common social denominator throughout the Plains. All in all, it was easy to see why Indians would feel comfortable hiring and working with him.

He was captivated, he said, by the bison project "because it was a forum and springboard for doing all kinds of ecological restoration. Using the buffalo, which has such a strong cultural attachment for Indian people, you could change grazing on the reservations, and you wouldn't have to do things like prairie dog poisoning. Prairie dogs and bison are ecologically inseparable, and bison act to keep the prairie dogs in check—they infest only under overgrazed conditions. And you don't have to kill coyotes. You don't have to bring in exotic plants. So it all just seemed a very natural thing. Since white people have been out here, the whole aim has been to break the natural system, to make it conform to the needs of these unnatural animals, cattle. You've got to change the grasses. Cattle deal poorly with wolves and bears, so you've got to get rid of them, and if the cattle are not economically profitable you have to squeeze more and more out of the land all the time, so you end up with this never-ending cycle of poison, fertilize, shoot, overgraze, fence—it just becomes a domino effect. And if you get caught in that you have to continue doing more and more every year."

Working on tribal bison restoration has given Heckert a way to go be-

Tribal bison-restoration efforts are moving rapidly. Fred DuBray, president of the ITBC and director of the Cheyenne River Sioux bison program, now has 750 animals on 50,000 acres, but since the reservation, which is in central South Dakota, encompasses 2.5 million acres, the potential herd size is enormously larger. DuBray has remarked that in principle he would like to see the whole reservation devoted to bison; he is looking forward to having 5,000 animals before ten years are up. Like the Oglala Sioux's, the Cheyenne's lands are adjacent to parks, so they have to be fenced along the boundaries.

Recently, said Mark Heckert, the ITBC facilitated a government grant to help the Northern Ute begin utilizing some 3 million acres on their reservation in Utah for bison. A congressional appropriation of $400,000 is expected to be followed by further funding, allocated according to the acreage suitable to bison and the tribal members' level of interest.

The Southern Ute, in southwestern Colorado, have 304,000 tribally owned acres and a small herd (13 bison) maintained on an "aesthetic and cultural level," being used in dances and other ceremonies. The Lower Brule Sioux, in South Dakota, have 140 bison on 4,500 acres. In addition to using the bison for ceremonial purposes, the tribe issues hunting permits for about ten bulls each year at $1,250–$1,750 each—and for about fifteen cows at $900 each. The Crow tribe recently rounded up its bison and counted a total of 1,065 in the Bighorn Mountains on the western end of their reservation and are now ready to sell some animals. The Crow have some 3 million acres altogether, but their bison are presently in a 70,000-acre area naturally enclosed by buttes, so they need only a half mile of fence. In Wyoming, the Northern Arapaho hope to set up a research program with the U.S.D.A., the Wyoming Livestock Board, and the state's Game and Fish Commission.

Bison have also been important to some of the Rio Grande Valley pueblo tribes in the Southwest. The Taos Pueblo has seventy-five bison on some 2,200 acres, and a buffalo dance, though not publicized, is still being performed at the Cochiti Pueblo. This region was at the western edge of original bison habitat.

yond the political limitations he encountered earlier in his career while working for state agencies. The tribes, he feels, are more "pure conservationist—because they're not trying to save things just to make money off them; it's part of their culture." Maybe this is where deep ecology started, he muses—the philosophical position that human-centered management, however well intentioned, can never replace the wisdom of nature and that our only reliable strategy is to massively reduce our own impacts. Heckert had gone about as far as you can go with the environmental movement's approach, which accepts the gulf between humans on one side and animals and the natural world on the other, affording no real ethic or connection. You reach a point, he says, "where probably the best thing you could do would be to kill yourself. But for Native Americans, there's never been that gap to be bridged. They intuitively realize the reason for preserving the land. So I found it easy to go along with tribal philosophy."

A buffalo-horn spoon made by the Ute. Courtesy of the Denver Art Museum.

But Heckert's training in biological science has not made it altogether easy for him to understand Indian views on bison. Sometimes when Indians are talking about the spiritual side of their attitudes toward buffalo, he says, "It's really scary! I used to think they were talking metaphorically, but now I don't know what the hell is going on. But I'm just a technician. The guys who are really doing the work are the Indian guys out at the grass roots.

"Indians just like having bison around—whether it does anything for them or not, that's a moot point. They're powerful animals—they're perfectly tailored to the ecology of the Plains. They don't need supplemental feeding, they don't need exotic grasses, they don't need the care and husbandry that cows need. We've line-bred cattle for a thousand years, which are essentially a wetland, lowland species, and we've tried to move them out here into an upland arid area. So they spend endless time in riparian areas, and you've got to keep unfrozen water open for them in the wintertime. You've got to pull the calves because they can't reproduce naturally. And sheep are even worse—they're just off the scale."

The ultimate goal of the Indian bison-restoration movement involves a massive bison presence on the continent. The ITBC tribes together have some 12 million available acres, which should be able to accommodate at least 120,000 bison, scattered through many states.

Mark Heckert cautioned that different tribes have different ideas about bison—and about everything else. "A Mohawk from upstate New York, a Cree from northwestern Canada, and a Hopi are as different from each other as we are from the Chinese and the Yugoslavs." It is thus hard to guess which tribes may decide that bison are within their cultural framework, but once they do, the ITBC helps them out with the mechanics. The Onondaga in upstate New York, for instance, have decided to keep some bison on their reservation, though most people are unaware that this was formerly bison range.

Although Indians are not mainly interested in bison for economic reasons, subsistence food production for the tribes would certainly be welcome. Many Indians have no respect for cattle and believe that eating them makes you weak. By contrast, bison meat represents, as Heckert put it, "a power food," powerful both spiritually and nutritionally. You cannot talk for long to anybody from the Pine Ridge Reservation without being reminded that it is the poorest in the nation, but poverty levels on almost all the reservations are appalling, and many elderly Indians, especially, suffer from diseases caused by deficient diets. Easy availability of local bison meat, high in protein and low in fat, should lead to a drop in heart disease and probably in other medical problems as well.

Craig Knowles, an independent wildlife biologist who has consulted with members of the Fort Belknap Reservation, the Northern Cheyenne River tribe, the Assiniboines, and the Gros Ventre tribe about their bison programs, says that because self-sufficiency in meat is an important objective, tribes could offer bison to their members in reservation stores. And ultimately tribes may establish their own slaughtering and freezing operations so they can market bison meat off-reservation; it appears that the potential market is limited basically by supply. Recently a rancher-owned cooperative slaughterhouse opened in North Dakota, but Mark Heckert is seeking to develop a mobile slaughtering rig for the reservation herds, probably occupying a semitrailer or two, that could go where the bison are

These "exotic animals" have been around for almost a hundred times longer than the Department of Agriculture. Photo: Mark Kayser, South Dakota Department of Tourism.

and could deal on the scale of five animals at a time rather than employing the massive assembly-line, high-investment, high-overhead operation characteristic of modern slaughterhouses. "Also," he points out, a mobile operation "would enable Indians to make traditional use of the internal organs and so on, which slaughterhouses just dump in the grinder. But government just doesn't understand these projects. A lot of people in Washington think that Indians are extinct and buffalo are too. It's an educational thing. We have to show the benefits in dollars. Well, we can do that comfortably: job creation, money pumped back into the economy. And we can also show that it's good for the environment. So we keep trying to break through with the U.S. Department of Agriculture—they're beginning to be interested in sustainable agriculture."

But the distance the U.S.D.A. has to go may be seen from the fact that it focuses solely on cattle, swine, sheep, and chickens. A rancher who wants to roll the dice by trying to raise these species may qualify for a loan, but bison are excluded as "exotic animals," in the same class as the emu.

Knowles thinks that the Northern Cheyenne River tribe should aim for 100,000–500,000 acres of unfenced pasture, stocked more heavily than is usual with cattle because bison move around and utilize forage more efficiently. The tribe ran a successful longhorn-ranching operation on the then unfenced reservation in the 1930s. But the government, seeking to turn the program in the direction of more intensive management, sent in the Civilian Conservation Corps to cross-fence the reservation and establish water sources within each of the resulting pastures. Today the reservoirs are silted up and the wells are nonfunctional; pasturage near remaining water sources is overgrazed, as is almost universally the case with cattle. Knowles contends that the currently fashionable holistic resource management system of rotating animals from pasture to pasture is not in wide use because ranchers are too busy during the grazing season with making hay and fixing fences.

Blue Grama

Heckert also expresses doubts about the system. "It has its virtues, but we'll never be able to imitate a natural rotation system because we just don't know what was going on prior to the white invasion. Presumably the bison just rotated themselves—they probably grazed an area intensively for a short period of time and then moved on, in a migrational pattern, though this wasn't very large. Overall, it was a constant medium-grazing regime." And Indian lands are large enough that, in time, something like this can be allowed to happen again. Perhaps 10 percent of the reservations can become bison lands, Heckert guesses. "We want to open up the maximum area that we can, to allow the animals to go through their own regimes, and not try to hamstring them by making them conform to small areas. You put a lot of them in a small area and you're going to get overgrazing. We have to stop thinking within the constraints of the last hundred years of agriculture, when small, intensive management was the norm."

Whites interested in bison are often committed to narrow ideas about "scientific" management that lead them to disparage Native American criteria of stewardship, which are based on millennia of intimate contact with

the natural order rather than on controlled experiments and scholarly publications. Some white biologists, however, have come to believe that a traditional stewardship model is more rational, in the long run, for native peoples. The Lakota, biologist Richard Sherman has said, "always planned for
the worst-case scenarios when stewarding their resources, as allowances
were made for such things as severe droughts, wildfire, and other phe-
nomena. . . . One needs only to compare basic program practices. For example, a typical modern management (non-Indian) technique when as-
signing stocking rates for a parcel of land is to allow for the average year.
Operating by indigenous beliefs, the Lakota would stock the area more
lightly by perhaps 10–20 percent, thus ensuring their own survival and that
of the resource during lean times."

Several Indian tribes in the Midwest have established fine records of
sustainable operation of their forest resources—the Menominee in Wisconsin still have the same amount of timber on their land as was there in 1865,
and the Anishinabe (Ojibwe) at the tip of Lake Superior have fought off
government pressures to intensify their lumber operations beyond a sustainable cut. The basic Indian goal is the reestablishment on the reservations of the natural ecological balance or reciprocity among humans,
plants, and animals that existed before Euro-American occupation. On the
Plains, a restored population of bison would be a sign that things had been
put back together again on a sustainable basis. As Fred DuBray puts it, "We
recognize that the bison is a symbol of our strength and unity and that as
we bring our herds back to health, we will also bring our people back to
health." In Mark Heckert's view, this could be called sustainable agriculture "because you can get what you need to survive without inordinately
disrupting the system," and the result would be self-governing tribes in
which the bison are thriving again, the ceremonies have been revived, and
the bond between Indian people and the bison has been reestablished. At
Pine Ridge there is an ongoing program of teaching stewardship: grand-
parents go into the schools and explain to the children that all the parts of
the natural order are necessary and interrelated; they pass on the store of
traditional knowledge that has been kept in the memories of the elders of
the community. The comeback of the sacred bison—and, more specifically,

the appearance of a one-in-a-million white bison—would "mean a spiritual recharge for our people," as Alex White Plume puts it. "There's talk locally that the time is approaching, so people are beginning to get ready, learning the old songs and revitalizing the ritual that they need to go through. It might be within the next ten years. I hope it's during my lifetime." (As we shall see, this hope was soon answered, in a fashion.)

Indian women have their own perspective on bison. Traditionally, women followed the hunters on the chase and dealt with the skinning, butchering, distribution of meat to families in the community, hide tanning, and later utilization of all the parts of the animals; this was manifestly a central function in tribal life. Restoring bison on the reservations could thus bring women's roles back into their proper communal place. In what a *Today* show narrator described as a "sacred odyssey into the past," a Sioux woman named Edna Little Elk was recorded on video demonstrating to a group of about a hundred young people exactly what her grandmother had taught her seventy years ago, when there were no more bison and Indian ways were ridiculed. But she remembered everything about

Bison cows tend to have narrower faces and are thought to be more intelligent than bulls. They are also more cooperative.

how women dealt with bison—how the animal was cut up, what the different pieces were used for, how it was all done ceremoniously, "using everything for a good reason." Her grandmother had had a vision that someday the buffalo would be back. "We have to remember this," her grandmother said. "Someday people will need these techniques again."

A replica hoe made from a bison shoulder blade.
Courtesy Buffalo Museum of America,
Scottsdale, Arizona.

Indians and Ecology

In Indian tradition, decisions must be made with the interests of "the seventh generation" in mind. This fits in perfectly with the sustainability criterion that white ecologists have recently developed: "meeting our needs without jeopardizing the chances of future generations," as one formulation puts it. The relation between bison and humans seemed indissoluble in 1903, when Chief Red Cloud said, "We told [the whites] that the supernatural powers, *Taku Wakan*, had given to the Lakota the buffalo for food and clothing. We told them that where the buffalo ranged, that was our country. We told them that the country of the buffalo was the country of the Lakota. We told them that the buffalo must have their country and the Lakota must have the buffalo."

Reestablishing the relation between humans and bison that prevailed for the many millennia before Euro-Americans arrived is a goal that, at least in the plannable future, Indians do not see as conflicting with the interests of white ranchers, including those now holding leases on Indian grazing land. "We're not trying to run them off," Mark Heckert says. He points out that large areas of unused reservation land, much of which are marginal for cattle raising, could support bison.

Indian ways of dealing with bison diverge from the management practices that many white ranchers currently have in mind. The official mission of the National Bison Association is to preserve the "integrity of the bison," but, as we shall see later, actual ranch practices do not always fulfill this ideal. If tribes can get excess bison from Yellowstone, as far as possible they want to put them out to pasture and let them alone. They are willing to vaccinate them in order to set ranchers' minds at rest about brucellosis, a disease bison carry that ranchers fear can be transmitted to their cattle. But Heckert is not greatly concerned about the brucellosis issue. "Brucellosis," he says, "is a political disease. We go out of our way to reassure our neighbors who have cattle herds, including Indian ranchers, but brucellosis doesn't hurt bison." And since most tribes are chronically short of investment funds, the practice of leaving bison as wild as possible seems not only spiritually desirable but also economically inevitable. "Let bison be bison!" says Heckert. And DuBray has been quoted as saying, "When you farm buffalo, you can't help changing them. They are big, dangerous animals, and you find yourself eliminating the more aggressive ones for your self-preservation. . . . They should never be domesticated; that will destroy them."

At a conference of experts on public-lands bison in 1993, DuBray made an impassioned plea for leaving bison alone on large acreages, a goal that, he argued, can be achieved by cooperation among ranchers. Indian and non-Indian ranchers alike can band together and amass three or four thousand acres, enough to support a herd of bison in a good way. DuBray told how moved he was by seeing a recalcitrant bull finally squeezed into a hydraulic chute (to the cheers of white onlookers) where it let out a mighty bellow that he will never forget. It taught him, he said, that bringing back the bison in numbers is not enough: if they are treated like cattle, with "this intense kind of management stuff," they will not really be bison.

Indians identify with bison in ways that are difficult for whites to understand. The "vindictive earnestness" that General Sheridan urged on the exterminators of bison was also mercilessly applied to Indians; he advocated "total extermination of the Sioux—men, women, and children." At the conference, DuBray described how tribal bison at a Denver auction show in 1991 had shown their sense of pride in the ring. "If somebody got too close, they would run them out of the ring." Then some ranched bison were brought in, with their horns cut off; they huddled in the center of the ring. Another tribal member, watching, said, "Boy, that really makes me feel bad, that makes me think of myself in boarding school—those buffalo are ashamed to come out here because they have no horns. Just like they did to our people when they sent us to boarding school, they cut off our hair, it made us ashamed to be Indian people. I can see that in their eyes."

Indian thinking closely parallels modern ecological science. DuBray went on:

> In the Indian way of life, we are not superior, we are just another participant here, equal to the buffalos, eagles, all these other animals, plants, trees . . . are relatives, are all necessary for our existence, we're necessary for theirs, we all fit together, without each other we can't exist. So . . . do we want to make the same mistakes we made in the past or do we want to do something different? . . . When [buffalo] are intensely managed their social structure is broken up. They react to the land just like cattle do, stand around, because you've taken all that away from them, you take the young calves away, wean them, keep them separated from the older bunch, they never get to learn what it is to be a buffalo, how to interact. There's a lot of it that's inside of them, instinct, but some of that is learned behavior from their peers, just like us.

DuBray called on the assembled wildlife experts and park managers and range scientists and geneticists to meet the real challenge that bison offer us:

> It's every one of ours duty to make change, because this earth is the only one we have and it can only do so much. . . . If [buffalo] are standing around in a feed lot, is it even worth bringing them back if that's their future? One of our elders told me, one time, that if you're going to bring these buffalo back, first you have to ask the buffalo if they even want to come back. I don't think they would want to come back if they have to stand around in a feed lot for the rest of their life. On the other hand if they get to be buffalo and do what buffalo do, then I'm sure they would want to come back.

Indians are well aware of the complex ecological connections that link bison to grasslands. Like some scientists and the staff of The Nature Conservancy, DuBray believes that bison can help "enhance the land in a holistic way." Indians have always believed what whites have felt they need to prove—that the way in which bison graze helps to maintain the dense, deep-rooted grasses that grew on the Plains before the whites brought their cattle and sheep and the European grasses and weeds that spread through overgrazed lands.

Preserving and Extending the Tribal Land Base

From the Indian perspective, one conceivable fate for the enormous Great Plains rural areas that Euro-Americans can no longer inhabit profitably—subsidies or no—is simply to give the land back to the Indians from whom it was originally taken, so that bison can return to it. On most of the Plains, the original land seizures go back only a few generations, something like 130 years; it is a relatively short history to be undone, and ample records remain to work with.

Reservations that have been whittled down to their present extent could at least be restored to their original dimensions, and broken treaties could be honored. When the reservations were established, Mark Heckert says, it was promised that they could be expanded to meet the needs of the people—some thought then that the Indian tribes would grow and flourish and need to recapture their old homelands. There was, of course, another line of white thinking—not entirely dead yet—that anticipated the dying out of Indian cultures and, in the bureaucratic term favored during the Eisenhower era, the "termination" of reservations. Aiming at this goal, the federal Bureau of Indian Affairs forced tribes to divide their land into individually owned parcels, and the natural course of dog-eat-dog capitalism forced many Indians to sell out to whites.

Heckert offers as one Plains example the Cheyenne River Sioux reservation which now has four times the number of people it had when it was established—and only a third of the land base because so much of the reservation has been sold off to whites. Like many other tribes, the Cheyenne River Sioux are slowly buying back land—partly with funds generated by sales of bison. But they always meet resistance because land going back into "tribal trust" is taken off the tax rolls—though it was, of course, a windfall in the first place for the counties (and states) to get tax revenues from the reservations, which are legally autonomous entities. In the final analysis, the counties cannot stop the process of Indians' recovering their own lands. Still, as Heckert puts it, "They can sure slow it up. And if you do it on a large enough piece of land, the state and county governments will both actively oppose it," just as they oppose putting land into national forests or national parks.

On the Plains as in the rest of the country, it will take many decades for the tribes to repurchase the reservation lands that were first stolen from them physically in the settlement process and then wrenched from them fi-

Buffalo jump, or pishkun, in Montana. Bison were lured to the vicinity and then stampeded over the rise from the right. Indians sometimes guided the bison toward the edge by piling up rocks to form a wide funnel. By the time the rushing mass of animals reached the cliff, they could not stop and landed below, dead or crippled. Hundreds were sometimes slaughtered in this way. Some sites were apparently used for thousands of years. Archaeologists, such as those whose marking stakes are visible here, are finding layers of bones more than twenty feet deep and evidence of long-established camps nearby.

nancially. But reacquisition of their land base has gained broad support among Indian people; without the land, a growing consensus has it, Indians cannot continue to be Indians. With it, as Heckert says, "there is absolutely the potential for self-sufficiency of large groups of people based on the buffalo economy"—although this, he thinks, will be over the resistance of the government, which aims "to break down all cultures and homogenize them so they're not independent—because if they're independent, they won't do what the government says."

As Fred DuBray has said, "This isn't farmable country. Without federal subsidies, farmers would just dry up." The question of whether lands no longer worked by white farmers should go back into Indian hands has not yet arisen as a real political issue, though it probably will in time. The major obstacle is a peculiarity of capitalism: the insistence that everything, however useless, must have an "owner." Counties that take over properties whose taxes have not been paid for years hustle to find private owners for them, at derisory prices if need be, and sooner or later they find them. Minute corners of land are, it always turns out, owned by somebody—usually an absentee owner, willing to speculate on the future. And in the arid West, so far there has always been somebody willing to buy or rent even the most derelict land and put a few cows on it. In practical terms, fenced rangeland will only be considered truly abandoned, and thus potentially capable of return to the Indians, if it can no longer pay its rent from the meager profits of cattle. Considering the recent past and the shrinking prospects of Plains ranching, this point may not be far away.

Whereupon, at least in theory, land could begin going back to the Indians and becoming bison habitat again. Thus, with a stunning irony, lands that white ranchers and settlers claimed because they were "vacant"—except for their Indian inhabitants—could go back to their original occupants. This would be a historically novel and noteworthy form of justice: Native Americans are one of the few ethnic groups anywhere on the planet whose homeland had not previously belonged to somebody else—though the tribes now resident on the Plains were mostly forced there from farther east by white pressure, and thus they displaced earlier inhabitants. Indeed, the past odysseys of what we now think of as Plains or western tribes covered thousands of miles. To give only a few examples, the Sioux originated in the lake region of what we call Minnesota; the Crows moved west from the Missouri in the 1700s; the Cheyenne, who had been based in Minnesota, hunted in the Black Hills, but some of them moved south to present-day Oklahoma and Kansas. After whites forced the tribes onto reservations, they were often simply loaded onto trains and transported thousands of miles to territory totally unsuited to their culture and ways of finding food and shelter.

Little by little, tribes are recovering from the cultural desolation that whites inflicted on them. The present Plains tribes still possess the communitarian ethic needed to handle bison as common tribal property on unfenced range. And it is not inconceivable that some of the federal land presently rented out for cattle could become part of a Native American Bison Refuge, perhaps along the lines of the existing Fort Niobrara National Wildlife Refuge but much bigger. This is, in fact, a project of the InterTribal Bison Cooperative, as Mark Heckert explained. The proposal is to use the land for experiments to learn more about the ecological effects of traditional tribal practices. A strong case can be made that present management practices, which are based on cattle-management notions, do not work very well. And, as the National Biological Service recently reported, ecosystem-level protection is imperative; too many natural communities, including the tallgrass prairies, are endangered or threatened. "We need a place, or a group of places, where we can do research on what's best for the animals and the people at the same time," said Heckert. "On private ranches they don't have the latitude to do experimentation because they always have to make a profit. So we'd like to develop a place that is large enough for a functioning ecosystem—a watershed or a series of watersheds." Such a refuge could conceivably be put together on federally owned national grassland territory if scattered grassland holdings could be pieced together into big enough chunks. We will learn more of such possibilities in the next chapter.

In Lakota, *Wopila tatanka* means "Give thanks to the buffalo." As the years pass, more and more tribes will be in a position to render this traditional thanksgiving. Meanwhile, along with the national parks, the tribal lands offer bison a natural habitat and an opportunity to multiply without human manipulation and control.

Increasingly, visitors to reservations will encounter bison, with their wild spirits free to roam, as a familiar part of the landscape and a promise of a better tomorrow.

Chapter Four
Bison on Public Lands

The sight of a bison herd stirs most people deeply. The animals have a fascinating power and self-possession; their unique shape and surprising grace make them compelling to watch, even from a distance. And a closer encounter with bison, whether from the safety of a car or (very cautiously) on foot, makes the adrenalin flow: one is manifestly in the presence of the wild, the unpredictable, the tantalizingly unknowable. Bison demand attention from humans who confront them, just as they require it from one another. They challenge us to look, to understand, and to respond with a bodily intelligence most modern people get little chance to exercise. It is no wonder, then, that bison are becoming major tourist attractions all over the country, particularly on public lands, where large herds live in natural or near-natural conditions.

There are bison on public lands of many types: national parks, state parks, national and state wildlife refuges, recreation areas, even military bases. These herds are thriving, and some new herds are being established. But this bright picture is shadowed by the fact that the tens of millions of acres of original bison habitat that fall into the national forests, national grasslands, and Bureau of Land Management holdings are still dedicated solely to cattle and sheep. The long-term prospects are that bison and other wild grazing species can be allowed to come back on significant western portions of such lands, but a vigorous political struggle will be necessary to accomplish this.

Journalists sometimes make fun of bird-watchers as if they were a negligible minority, but the fact is that more Americans take trips to watch wildlife than go to all professional sporting events combined. Young and old, we go out into nature in our cars and boats, on our bikes, in our four-wheel-drives and even our wheelchairs, bringing our binoculars, our cameras, our species identification books. We spend a lot of time watching wild species, hearing rangers talk about them, and hiking through their habitats. We also spend a lot of money in the process; a recent study of national forests showed that areas immediately around the forests provide nine jobs, presumably mostly tourist-service jobs, for every timber job provided by the forests. And bison watching has become an increasingly popular recreational activity as the great beasts reenter public consciousness.

Bison in Yellowstone National Park

About a million people each year get their first real look at wild bison through visiting Yellowstone National Park, where many of the park's four thousand or so bison easily tolerate the presence of humans and graze unperturbed on road shoulders and hotel lawns as well as on remote grasslands.

Bison receive varying treatment in the different public herds. Yellowstone's herd is genuinely wild. Bison are not fed, vaccinated, or interfered with in any way inside the park. They are never rounded up; all ranchlike corrals and other facilities left from an earlier era have been dismantled. Park rangers in Yellowstone formerly shot "excess" bison to keep their herd's numbers down; in 1967, however, a policy of "let nature take its course" was adopted, combined with boundary control in cooperation with the wildlife departments of Wyoming and Montana. Yellowstone bison today have the run of the park's 2.2 million acres (3,458 square miles), totally unmanaged and left to roam. The herd grew to a summer count in 1994 of 4,200 animals. This still leaves a lot of room for more, but bison seeking ampler winter forage venture increasingly out of the park down the Yellowstone River valley. Rather than seeing these animals shot, the InterTribal Bison Cooperative has offered to save as many as 2,000 of them, quarantine them until they are certified as disease-free, and distribute them among tribes seeking to build up their reservation herds. However, because the U.S. Department of Agriculture and various agencies of the recipient states must be involved, this is not likely to happen rapidly.

A few other managers of public herds follow similar policies and generally leave their bison alone, but extensive handling is common. Park pastures are divided into fenced paddocks, and bison are rotated from one to another when rangers consider it desirable to delay grazing impacts. Yearly fall roundups are held; some have become popular public events. Female calves are vaccinated against brucellosis, animals are weighed, calves are branded (or ear-tagged) for identification and record keeping. The drug dosing prevalent with cattle is sometimes extended to bison: at the Antelope Island State Park in Utah, for example, injections include, besides brucellosis vaccination, "Eight-way Ivomex, Primer, vitamins A, D, and E, Penicillin, and Vibro Lepto 5." In some places with limited acreage, like the Fort Niobrara National Wildlife Refuge, paddock areas are small and frequent rotation is necessary.

On many public lands, bison are only one among a number of species being preserved. Grazing is not only appropriate but also necessary for the long-term health of park grasslands. Native grazers that share range with bison include elk, antelope, deer, and bighorn sheep. All have their own fans, who visit public lands in increasingly large numbers.

Since bison are an outstandingly successful species biologically, with the potential for rapid population growth throughout an immense range, serious predation on them is essential to their long-term health and that of the grasslands ecosystem as a whole. Historically, wolves, bears, and Indians filled the predator role; in modern American conditions, however, most types of ecosystems have been distorted by extermination of the original cast of predators. Attempts are being made to reestablish wolves in Yellowstone and in central Idaho; despite opposition by ranching interests, federal courts finally approved a small experimental reintroduction in 1995.

Wolves can bring down weakened or solitary bison and bison calves that get separated from their mothers; they prey quite successfully on deer and elk, and sometimes on pronghorn young or ailing enough to be slowed down. In wildlife areas where domestic livestock is not present, current objections to the reestablishment of wolves should greatly diminish. Contrary to popular folklore, wolves do not appear to pose significant hazards to humans, and there is widespread new public familiarity with the actual lives of wolves, as described in Farley Mowat's *Never Cry Wolf* and as seen in the movie based on that book. Kevin Costner's lovable wolf friend in *Dances with Wolves* has also given viewers a more matter-of-fact look at the species. Indeed, a constituency has been growing for these close cousins of our domestic dogs, and considerable wolf reintroduction in the Rockies seems likely in the next few years, as well as some natural spread southward from Canada.

Historical accounts tell of grizzly bears killing bison, and this may still happen occasionally in Alaska, where the bears remain numerous. However, Yellowstone's grizzlies have been observed preying on bison only during the spring melt, consuming the thawing carcasses of bison that had died during the winter.

Even if natural predation regimes can be reestablished in some areas, in

This bison evidently drowned in a bog. Drowning after breaking through river ice may also have taken a significant toll on the great bison herds of the past. Photo: Michael H. Francis.

the long run humans are likely to be the chief predators of bison, and in time it will behoove us to fill this role responsibly. For many years to come, however, animals whose numbers surpass the carrying capacity of a given area will be so valuable to other parks and to tribes or ranchers seeking to build up herds that export of live animals should be the rule, along the lines planned by the InterTribal Bison Cooperative. Only after many decades will all available land be filled and park bison need to be culled.

When the time comes, this prospect is likely to spark fierce opposition from those who cannot countenance human killing of any animals. Not all such people are unrealistic about carrying capacity; some recognize and accept that starvation will occur, as it already does among deer stressed by overpopulation. Moreover, some who might favor humane killing of excess animals oppose sport hunting—though some such people see nothing wrong with having other people slaughter steers for their steaks and hamburgers. Perhaps fittingly, the more successful we are in reestablishing natural predators of bison, the longer we can put off the day when we ourselves must become their responsible predators. In these issues, as in many others, Yellowstone National Park is an arena in which new possibilities must be explored.

One place where elk have center stage over the roughly 175 free-roaming resident bison is Jackson Hole, within the 430 square miles (some 275,000 acres) of Wyoming's Grand Teton National Park. This is a famously scenic lowland area bordered by dramatically steep peaks. The elk are fed in the winter by the National Park Service and have multiplied greatly. (They also carry brucellosis, as do about a fifth of the bison.) But the bison there are so popular with tourists that "bison jams" sometimes occur along the main highway and a tourist resort maintains a bison-sightings billboard to assist visitors in finding bison to observe. As is the case in Yellowstone just to the north, debates over management plans are based on the assumption that the herd will remain free-roaming, with as little human intervention as possible. Both Yellowstone and Grand Teton are fine places to observe bison being bison; any drive through these parks will almost certainly take you past bison, sometimes at close range. (Visitors should keep in mind that it is foolhardy to approach bison on foot.)

Bison in Other Parks

Within a day's drive of Yellowstone are most of the country's present sub-stantial public-lands bison herds, as well as a number of major bison ranches. The National Bison Range, operated by the U.S. Fish and Wildlife Service at Moiese, Montana (forty-five miles north of Missoula), has about 18,500 acres and 370–475 bison, along with hundreds of mule and white-tailed deer, elk, pronghorn, bighorn sheep, and mountain goats. It is also an easy place to get a look at bison because it has a 19-mile self-guided auto-mobile tour route; hiking off the road, however, is discouraged. The bison herd here originated with animals from the nearby Flathead Indian Reser-vation who had been saved by a Pend d'Oreille Indian named Samuel Walking Coyote. The refuge is fenced into eight grazing units, and no sup-plemental feeding is done. Every fall the bison are rounded up, a time of considerable public excitement—there is even a small grandstand at the corrals. The herd is maintained at about 40 percent males and 60 percent fe-males; excess animals are sold through sealed bids. These sales bring in siz-able sums to support the refuge.

Custer State Park, in the southwestern corner of South Dakota, is lo-cated on the shoulder of the extraordinarily scenic Black Hills, where they meet the Plains. (The Hills were named by Plains tribes for their dark-col-ored tree cover, but the bison-oriented tribes used them only as places for religious ceremonies.) Custer, which still enjoys some impressive stonework buildings put up by the Civilian Conservation Corps during the Great Depression, has the second largest public herd in the country, after Yellowstone: currently some 1,500 animals on 113 square miles, or about 72,000 acres. This park has made a determined effort to promote tourism in general and bison tourism in particular. A wildlife loop road takes automo-biles through bison range, and a guided bison safari is also offered.

On a beautiful, cloudless morning I talked with Ron Walker, who is in charge of Custer's bison, in his office in a converted ranger residence. As organizer of a 1993 bison symposium, Walker is a kind of nerve center for the public-bison field. He is a quiet, trim man, perhaps forty-five, who has been at Custer for twenty years. A gleam appears in his eye when he talks about the possible resurgence of vast herds: "Maybe not 60 million, but

Bison in Badlands National Park. Photo: Mark Kayser, South Dakota Dept. of Tourism.

great herds, and it'll be a wonderful day—and a very profitable day." Walker feels that Indian reservations will see a great expansion of herds. But his perspective is partly that of a seller of surplus bison from Custer to avid ranchers; the prices, he says, have become unbelievably high. On the whole, he thinks the major factor in the scaling up of bison herds will be that ranchers will learn to combine their acreages into big, low-overhead operations. When I asked him how big these should be, he replied with a grin, "As big as you can get!"

There are no prospects of expanding Custer's area, but there have been talks about combining its herd with that of Wind Cave National Park, which abuts it on the south. There are logistic problems and some bureaucratic ones, but Walker thinks they can be surmounted. He seems good at getting people to work together and laments that university research on bison is still so scattered. People in many colleges and universities are doing good work on scientific problems involving bison, but they are separated into the usual academic compartments. Hence, their contacts with one another are infrequent and the influence of their work on public understanding and support of bison, or on practical operations of parks or ranches or reservations, is limited.

Custer's bison are intensively managed, partly with the goal of financial self-sufficiency through sale of animals. A yearly roundup is popular with volunteer buffalo-hands and the public, and it is followed by the sale of animals either directly or through video auction. All calves, whether to be sold or not, are weaned from their mothers by the end of January; the managers argue that this improves the health of the cows. Custer's bison have an excellent reputation, and they are bought by ranchers from as far away as the state of New York. Ten bull-hunting permits are sold each year as well; rangers accompany the hunters and point out takable bulls—some of which are solo bulls, way back in the woods, so the hunting demands some skill. Walker revealed that the park uses a wrecking truck to pick up dead bulls, and will chill and quarter them or take them to a Rapid City butcher for the hunters.

Supplemental feed is given to the cows just prior to calving, and since 1991 the range has been divided into several sections in order to prevent overgrazing of big bluestem grass, a favorite of bison, in one area. Attempts to move the herds into undergrazed areas by other means have been imaginative—using mountain lion urine and rattlesnake scent—but unsuccessful. A program of disease control and genetic studies is also in place; the latter has revealed that the park's methods of bull selection have narrowed the herd's genetic base. New selection criteria based on blood tests will, it is hoped, improve this situation.

Wind Cave National Park has 28,500 acres and around 300 bison, plus hundreds of elk and antelope and innumerable prairie dogs. Wind Cave's herd goes back to the very beginnings of bison restoration: in 1913, thirteen bison arrived from the New York Zoological Society and the American Bison Society to inhabit this first federally financed game preserve. The park's stated goal is to let the herd live as it would have before the arrival of whites. However, roundups are held for vaccination of heifer calves and culling of animals, and they are carried out with helicopters, which can push animals through the park's mixture of ponderosa pine, savannah, and prairie. As far as possible, culling is done in a way to emulate natural predation (on yearlings only, however). Management may soon become more intensive; park officials are awaiting the arrival of a computerized grazing model.

Badlands National Park, also in southwestern South Dakota, occupies 382 square miles, or about 244,000 acres overall. It contains the only mixed-grass prairie in the entire National Parks system, and has 300–600 bison, a "semi-free-roaming herd." Despite the addition of 133,000 acres from the Pine Ridge Reservation, the park is considered too small to accommodate a naturally roaming herd like Yellowstone's. It is very dry country, with water limited to a few springs and impoundments. Working with researchers from Colorado State University, park officials hope to develop models of multispecies carrying capacity for prairie parks. These would provide guidance in stocking the park with other grazers and smaller animals. Meanwhile, bison are rounded up periodically for vaccination and selection of excess animals, which are given away to state Indian tribes wishing to augment their herds. Visitor-bison interactions are supervised by park patrols, which also keep a lookout for poachers. (Bison rustling does occur; though ranchers do not see it as a problem, it may happen fairly frequently on larger and chronically understaffed public lands.)

Theodore Roosevelt National Memorial Park, in nearby western North Dakota, occupies 108 square miles (70,446 acres), including some badlands and wilderness, and has 300–750 bison in two units, along with some elk, feral horses, and other species, readily visible on a wildlife route designed for car tourists. Attempts are in progress to use satellite reconnaissance and computer models to improve range—here, in hopes of reducing invading exotic plants—probably a doomed enterprise without a full range of native grazers, though a good portion of the park is wooded or shrubby. Interestingly, though the park no longer can afford yearly roundups, its management does not see much need to reduce the herd, since new fencing mostly prevents bison from escaping onto neighboring ranches. But there are occasional culling operations, using a helicopter and riders to corral the animals. National parks are not permitted to sell bison, so surplus animals are given to the Fort Berthold Reservation tribes or to other National Park Service units, state parks, or zoos. The herd is free of disease, but brucellosis regulations still forbid shipping park animals out of state.

The Fort Niobrara National Wildlife Refuge, near the prospering town of Valentine in north-central Nebraska, is an old cavalry fort that has served bison preservation since 1912. Today about 500 bison, 40 elk, and 275 multicolored longhorns occupy the refuge's 19,000 acres and can be viewed on a self-guided auto tour route, which features ponds favored by elk.

The refuge's goal is a fifty-fifty gender ratio, which is thought to be the natural norm and is usually approximated by public-lands bison, though ranchers prefer to get rid of most of their bulls for reasons examined in the next chapter. Animals are rounded up each fall, new calves are branded, vaccination shots are given, and some bison are selected for sale. Since

Left: In the spring, bison like to rub on vertical objects to help remove their excess winter hair. They seek out trees, big rocks, power poles, and fence posts. In Fort Niobrara National Wildlife Refuge, bison have rubbed this fence post in a characteristic shoulder-high pattern. *Right:* Pronghorn are the speediest North American animal. They normally share grasslands with bison and often graze along highways, where it is illegal to fire guns. (The roadsides stay green because of runoff from the pavement and because the highway department plants clover and alfalfa for erosion control.) The lowest strands of barbed-wire fences on national grasslands are kept higher than normal to accommodate the pronghorn's habit of going under them on their knees—sometimes on the run. Pronghorn are now considered a unique species, not members of the antelope family. Ranchers receive state compensation from the state for wildlife damage, as well as fees from hunters going after pronghorns and deer, so they do not always view the animals as competitors who might take grass away from cattle. Photo: Michael H. Francis.

1988, the summer range has been subdivided by fencing, and rotational grazing, which is believed to permit greater herd size, has been employed.

The Niobrara River valley, where the refuge and The Nature Conservancy's preserve discussed later in this chapter are located, is an extraordinarily beautiful place, and because a considerable stretch of the river is raftable, it has been attracting large numbers of visitors interested in outdoor recreation. The river flows through a partly wooded valley that it has carved several hundred feet below the surrounding Plains. Grasslands spotted with trees run southward, giving way to the Nebraska Sand Hills, an amazing area of the most extensive sand dunes in North America. The Sand Hills have recognizable dune shapes but are covered with enough thin soil and grass to support modest numbers of grazing animals; the fact that ample aquifer water lies only a few feet below the surface inspired unsuccessful efforts by early settlers to plow and plant there. Part of the area is also a candidate for inclusion in a national park.

A Future Grasslands National Park

We have safely preserved mountains, seashores, canyons, and forests, but our heritage of grassland is virtually unrepresented in the National Park system. Yet grassland is the richest ecosystem there is, in terms of numbers of species supported. It is also a critical factor in our nation's history. Over the years, attempts have been made in Kansas and Oklahoma to establish a national grasslands park, but so far they have been defeated—through a combination of feared loss of local tax revenues and antifederal sentiment. But the Niobrara valley, which has a very sparse human population and includes much intact and untouched land, is a prime, though very modest, prospect. The Sierra Club has proposed that 171,000 acres be designated a Niobrara–Buffalo Prairie National Park. This would include the existing Fort Niobrara National Wildlife Refuge, The Nature Conservancy's preserve, and newly acquired small strips of additional land set back from the river. So far, Nebraska has virtually no public lands of any kind (one small national grassland in the northwest corner of the state and three small national forests, plus a handful of minuscule state lands), so its growing outdoor-minded public should prove supportive of the national park idea. A

Nebraska representative in Congress, Doug Bereuter, backs the park idea, though on an even smaller scale. A seventy-six-mile stretch of the Niobrara River has been given official wild and scenic river status by Congress, and the legions of rafters now gaining familiarity with the area should provide some national political push for the park idea, which is being mulled over by the National Park Service. The state has always been almost obsessively devoted to agriculture, but there are some signs of a growing appreciation for nature among Nebraskans in general, such as the fact that native wild-flowers and grasses are now being planted along all state highways.

People can become very attached to grasslands, which burst into bloom during the summer months with modest but pretty flowers and provide abundant habitat for badgers, rabbits, prairie chickens, bobcats, and many other creatures. Surely, in time, we owe our descendants a de-cent-sized grasslands park in which, as could the pioneers, "you can see forever." This would mean at least a million acres where we could recreate a past we nearly destroyed, and where bison and elk could live in age-old balance with their natural predators. Something on this scale might yet be accomplished, probably on the borders of Oklahoma and Kansas.

Smaller Public Herds

When we depart from the region dealt with above, public bison herds and the areas they occupy are usually much smaller. Visitors can, however, still get a good idea of how bison look, move over the landscape, and interact. The biggest herds are at Antelope Island State Park in Utah, with 750 animals on an island in Great Salt Lake, and at the Wichita Mountains National Wildlife Refuge in southwestern Oklahoma, with 575 bison on 59,000 beautiful, mountainous acres, along with wild turkeys, longhorns, elk, white-tailed deer, and endangered bird species.

National wildlife refuges, run by the U.S. Fish and Wildlife Service, total more than 90 million acres, of which perhaps a quarter are on the Plains. At present the federal refuges are primarily "bird farms," heavily oriented toward game species of waterfowl, but cattle are often present, despite their trampling of nests and other negative effects on waterbird life. Many Plains refuges are large enough to support bison along with a full range of other wildlife species, including the predators that are essential components of a functioning ecosystem. (The states maintain wildlife refuges as well, total-ing almost a million acres, although only part of this area is on the Plains; these refuges present similar problems and opportunities.)

As we will see in the next chapter, bison ranches have become so numer-ous that except in parts of the Northeast nobody in the country is impossi-bly far from a bison herd. Indeed, whereas large and public herds are mostly on the Plains, no state, east or west, lacks bison these days, mostly in the hands of small ranchers who fancy them—and know that they can sell excess animals for high prices. Except in areas outside their original range, where they suffer from parasites and disease, bison thrive. They are popular with neighbors, nearby townsfolk, and tourists who happen to see them. In a shadowy way, these little herds are making their presence felt throughout the territory that their ancestors once dominated. But they are not yet easy to locate, and sometimes viewing them is not allowed, or at least not invited. Luckily, public herds are also well distributed through-out the country.

In Arizona, for example, the state's Game and Fish Department pre-sides over about 100 bison in House Rock Valley, using land on a coopera-tive basis with the Forest Service, the Bureau of Land Management, and local ranchers. In southwestern Minnesota, Blue Mounds State Park has 45 bison on 146 acres of fenced pasture; through the auction of surplus ani-mals, the herd more than supports itself financially. Unfortunately, because their range is so small, the bison must be fed hay and grain during the win-ter. Kansas, although it is as lacking in parklands as Nebraska, has several small game refuges and a wildlife area run by the state's Department of Wildlife and Parks, which provide a home to some 360 bison in all. The Sullys Hill National Wildlife Refuge in North Dakota has 30–35 bison on 1,380 acres under "reasonably natural" conditions (with winter feeding, however). To these, as quasi-public lands, we must add The Nature Con-servancy's preserves, presently totaling around a thousand bison in three states but with plans for significant growth in the Conservancy's new Ok-lahoma preserve.

There are even bison on military land. It is particularly intriguing that the military, which has traditionally been the country's greatest single source of environmental pollution, now has a standing interest in wildlife conservation on its properties—a rather startling turnabout. This explains why at Fort Wingate, an ancient frontier fort near Gallup, New Mexico, there is a flourishing small herd of U.S. Army bison. Nobody knows quite how they got there, but they have been there a long time; they are considered wild and thus the "property" of the state's Game and Fish Department. The fort is now on caretaker status, without an active mission, but the army does not plan to give it up; a few staff people remain to oversee the bison and the many archaeological sites on the base. There are four bison at the Tooele, Utah, Army Depot—overflows from Fort Wingate. The army also has a small herd at the Anniston Army Depot in Alabama, which was within bison range in the 1500s, and there may be more. The U.S. Army possesses 11 million acres in the country as a whole, and in the region where bison naturally roamed there are a great many military installations, some with large vacant portions where bison could qualify as original wildlife. It is conceivable, therefore, that someday we might see many more bison on military land. A wildlife preservation mission would make for excellent public relations in an era of declining military budgets.

Other public agencies have bison as well. For example, the Tennessee Valley Authority maintains eighty-seven bison in its Land Between the Lakes recreation and environmental education area. They occupy a mere 200 acres, but forage is abundant and they are left "unworked." Unfortunately, the damp southeastern climate fosters parasites; biological methods of fly control are being tried.

Canadian Bison

In Canada, about 8,000 bison occupy extensive federal lands in four provinces or territories. For western Canadians, bison are readily accessible. Wood Buffalo National Park, located in Alberta and the Northwest Territories, contains 17,300 square miles with some 3,000 bison. (The "wood buffalo" were long thought to be a subspecies distinct from the Plains buffalo. After long and ardent taxonomic debate, most experts now consider them merely a variant population, with minor differences in conformation and hair.) There are several other large herds in Canada and some small ones, such as the Nisling River herd in the Yukon, totaling about 200 animals; some of these bison proved troublingly fond of the herbage along the fertilized road shoulders of the Alaska Highway, and at least nine were lost in motor vehicle accidents. It is not known how many vehicles were "lost," but the remaining bison became a hot political issue. They were finally captured and are now kept in a sort of bison jail—a fenced game farm and ranch. But their progeny, possibly less fond of roadsides, will be released. The manager of the herd laments that these "problem bison" have had a negative influence on public support, resulting in a temporary setback for the project.

Public Grazing Lands for Bison

How much acreage could conceivably be opened to bison if they were given access to public grazing lands in the same way cattle now are? Keeping only to those areas that qualify as prime bison habitat (in the states of Montana, North Dakota, South Dakota, Wyoming, Nebraska, Kansas, Oklahoma, and Texas), we can try to assess the possibilities by adding up the land now managed for livestock grazing.

Of the Bureau of Land Management's 470 million acres, 167 million are leased out for stock. Virtually all of this land is in the West, so at least a third of it would be prospective bison territory. The 155 national forests total 188 million acres; between them and the national grasslands, 87 million acres are leased for grazing. Most of this is also in the West, since there are only a few small national forests anywhere else. In a rough way, we can therefore estimate that some 100 million acres of leased public lands are, in principle, prime potential bison habitat. Even half of it would be enough for at least a million bison. Between them, the Forest Service and the BLM also manage another 97 million acres of "public range," and some of this, too, could support bison.

The twenty-odd national grasslands, totaling nearly 2.1 million acres, were bought by the federal government from bankrupt individual farmers during the Dust Bowl days. Some of this land, which under the Bankhead-Jones Farm Act of 1936 was supposed to provide demonstrations of how to farm these fragile areas, went under the jurisdiction of the U.S.D.A. (and hence its Forest Service), and some went under the Department of the Interior (and hence its Bureau of Land Management). Both Forest Service grasslands and BLM lands tend to be scattered or checkerboarded with private land rather than existing as large, solid holdings, so some new land acquisition or trading will be essential in order to provide sufficient areas of open range for bison and other wild grazers.

Mere government ownership of land does not, of course, imply that bison restoration will be possible there, much less easy to accomplish. A joint Forest Service–BLM pamphlet, *Livestock Grazing Successes on Public Range*, describes as one of its success stories the Oglala National Grassland, which is in the Nebraska National Forest and thus near the former heartland of the bison range—but nowhere in its text is heard an encouraging word for bison. Moreover, bison do not yet enjoy protected winter range outside Yellowstone (or other federal lands), though this is a common practice for elk and antelope.

Indeed, the livestock mentality that still dominates the federal lands bureaucracy still considers bison to be exotic animals. The perversity of this position can scarcely be overstated. Cattle, after all, are originally Southeast Asian creatures, domesticated over the centuries in the damp climates of the Old World and only recently imported here. They require elaborate human assistance to survive, while bison have been doing just fine on their own in these parts since the last ice age. It is cattle and sheep that are exotic and have little or no defensible natural role in the North American landscape.

State policies, too, are in need of a turnaround. The federal Pittman-Robertson Act of 1937 enforced the setting aside of hunter-derived revenue for wildlife management, and the states were thus encouraged to acquire some 900,000 acres of refuges. These have on the whole been successful; the beneficiaries, however, have been deer, pronghorn, elk, mountain goats and sheep, moose, bear, beaver, and game birds such as pheasants and wild turkey—not bison. Similarly, although federal agricultural policy since the 1985 Food Security Act has been to set aside highly erodible lands and pay farmers for not plowing them, no bison have benefited. As we will see later, these lands are almost entirely in small parcels, often of fewer than 100 acres, but in some areas they constitute potentially continuous bison habitat.

The priorities of the Forest Service are crystal clear from its budget: 70 percent goes to timber operations and only 5 percent goes to fish, wildlife, soil, and water. Forest Service personnel have sometimes pointed out, as an excuse for not fostering bison, that the basic Grazing Act does not mention bison. However, the 1960 Multiple Use Sustained Yield Act mandates "multiple use management for outdoor recreation, range, timber, watershed, and wildlife and fish purposes for *all* national forest lands" [italics added]. Robert Williamson, director of range management for the Forest Service, thinks it possible that a few bison are being run by ranchers on land that is part of the national grasslands. After talking with Williamson, I made some calls to officials of individual grasslands and found that although private ranchers were raising bison adjacent to several grasslands, apparently no federal land was officially being used for bison yet, though a few bison do wander from a nearby game ranch into the Carson National Forest in northern New Mexico. More recently, I heard of two ranchers using Forest Service land in South Dakota; also, Ted Turner's operation in Montana and the Durham Ranch in Wyoming have both negotiated inconclusively with the Forest Service about extending their bison operations onto federal land. Indians, says Mark Heckert of the InterTribal Bison Cooperative, are eager to work with the Forest Service to manage a model grassland featuring bison.

Little Bluestem

Williamson—and the same is probably true of most other Forest Service people—is not antibison. Nor is the Forest Service against bison, and the BLM story seems to be the same. It is just that they are not for bison either. Despite bison's undeniable status as native fauna, the desirability of restoring them on public lands has never become a visible policy issue. As wild animals, bison do not exist for the Forest Service. They might, however, exist as ranch animals: Williamson assured me that a rancher could apply for a permit to run bison on a grassland and would probably get it. The application would have to go through the usual NEPA environmental-assessment process, but since bison are widely regarded as easier on land and water than are cattle, this should not raise obstacles. "Demonstrating control would be the main problem," according to Williamson. He knows of ranchers who have trained bison to be very manageable, but in general, he says, "you can't just cowboy them," and fencing has to be sturdier than for cows. In other words, the Forest Service would probably tolerate bison as long as they were managed like cattle and did not stir up too much opposition from neighboring cattle ranchers. Mark Heckert reports, however, that the North Dakota ranchers running bison on Forest Service land have not had escape problems and get along fine with their cattle-raising neighbors. As we will see in the following chapter, bison ranchers find that effective fencing actually does not present insurmountable problems.

Thus, in general, although the Forest Service is not hostile to bison, its present role is passive: to provide low-cost pasture for cattle ranchers, as it provides low-cost (often below-cost) trees for the timber industry. This compliant posture comes out of a long history in which the agency's orientation, ultimately dictated by Congress, was to work with ranchers and lumber companies to get out the meat or timber, and ecology be damned. Service on the grasslands was considered to be a kind of Siberia, and promotions were unlikely. The staff on the grasslands were mostly local range people or former ranchers, and they saw their mission as the demonstration of better grazing practices rather than ecological preservation. (Later, in some areas, oil and gas leasing became their primary concerns.) But public pressure for more environmental sensitivity in the management of public lands and greater demand for recreational use of these lands have already caused some changes in the Forest Service, and in the BLM as well. Wildlife biologists are now part of every national forest's staff, and they are sometimes listened to. Reacting to public concern about the chronic degradation of land under its care, the BLM even has a program called "Bring Back the Natives," officially aiming to improve wildlife management generally, restore 75 percent of the agency's riparian and wetland habitats by 1997, enhance fisheries, and conserve and recover endangered species. BLM officials now realize that past mining, lumbering, livestock management, and road building have created an overwhelming need for habitat restoration—which has the virtue of bringing with it appropriations and jobs. The handful of showcase projects undertaken so far, however, focus on fish and waterbirds; descriptions of the program do not mention bison or other grazing wildlife. Public pressure for natural restoration still must be translated into practical measures for restoring bison, other wild grazers, and their natural predators in a large part of Plains federal landholdings. Meanwhile, for those in charge of the people's grass, the bison that used to inhabit it are still considered just too much trouble.

Wildlife Biology on the National Grasslands

The area known as Thunder Basin in eastern Wyoming is high, dry, and windy. Containing the biggest open-pit coal mine in the world, oil wells scattered across its landscape, and closed-down uranium mines, it has sometimes been referred to as an "energy sacrifice zone." But the area is also the site of the Thunder Basin National Grassland and is potential bison habitat, so I went there to take a look.

Some of the open-pit coal mines are a mile long, but they seem almost insignificant in the sweep of the landscape. Although hard-rock mineral mines, along with people hoping to cash in by claiming and developing federal land, still remain beneficiaries of the 1872 Mining Law, coal operations (along with oil and gas) are regulated by the federal Surface Mining Control and Reclamation Act, which has since 1977 required the mines to refill and restore closed pits to "equal or better" than the original condition of the surface. Thus, the Thunder Basin Coal Company has spent hundreds of thousands of dollars on grass seed and other replanting efforts, and of some 5,600 acres affected by its mines, about 3,500 have been permanently or "semipermanently" reclaimed. At the company's biggest mine, extraction of coal is expected to continue until the year 2017, after which time most of the land should be undisturbed grassland, available for livestock or wildlife. A layer of topsoil is returned after the pits are refilled, and the affected land, on which the companies attempt to tailor surface contours in line with surrounding terrain, is apparently more productive of forage than it was before mining. Pronghorn are especially numerous in the mine areas, along with elk, mule deer, various birds of prey, and small mammals.

Coal, gas, and oil companies pay royalties of 12.5 percent for their extracted commodities and are also subject to various state taxes. Under the federal Mining Law of 1872, however, no royalties or reclamation fees are required of other mining companies, though some state reclamation laws exist. Hard-rock mining extracts about $4 billion worth of free minerals from public lands annually. Growing public resentment of this policy led to the passage of reform bills by both House and Senate in late 1994, but they lapsed in conference. It is conceivable that this leak in the federal budget may someday be stopped up.

A recent oil and gas boom has receded, but the region is still prospering on the strength of coal. Long coal trains snake over the landscape at fifteen-minute intervals, bound for distant and some not-so-distant power plants, and the towns of Douglas and Wright (a modern company town) are thriving.

These elk are on reclaimed land that was formerly a coal-mine pit. Like bison, elk usually tolerate fairly well the presence of human beings and their buildings, roads, vehicles, and fences. Thus, they do not require the totally protected areas without which grizzlies, wolves, and some other species cannot survive. Photo: Bob Moore, Thunder Basin Coal Company.

I called on Tim Byer, wildlife biologist at the Thunder Basin National Grassland. Byer is a helpful, well-organized person. He is primarily a bird expert, studying golden and bald eagles, prairie hawks, and other raptors that prey on small grassland mammals, and his office is full of maps and charts he develops for this work. He is also studying the potential for reintroduction of the black-footed ferret into some of the extensive prairie dog towns on the grassland (one is four or five miles long). On the wall of his office hangs a poster, produced by a local coal company, of elk grazing just outside the Black Thunder Mine's crushing and loading structure.

Byer told me that the grassland's half million acres are scattered over eighty-nine townships and are badly checkerboarded. Still, if ranchers manifested a desire to run bison on grassland allotments, staff would duly process their applications. On the other hand, if a movement developed to bring back bison as wildlife, in the same way that pronghorn now inhabit the grassland, major studies of impacts would be necessary. So far, no political heat has been felt under that particular pot.

Byer said that the Forest Service still poisons prairie dogs. This is partly to keep their population density low enough to prevent their nibbling from baring too much ground and leading to erosion. And partly it is out of concern for ranchers who fear that the prairie dogs will eat up forage before cattle get to it and that cattle will step in prairie dog holes. Ironically, poisons are probably one of the main reasons why the ferrets, who originally kept the prairie dog populations under control, are on the verge of extinction. (Bison are evidently alert enough to avoid prairie dog holes; bison ranchers do not worry about them.)

Relations between government agents and local ranchers are not always cordial, but as Byer says, "They own land; we have to work with these folks." One paradoxical result of such tensions can be seen in fire-suppression policy. People in the Forest Service are, of course, well aware of recent research about the ecological virtues of fire, its natural role in ecosystem maintenance, and its tendency to improve forage. Staff of some forests even do brush-control burning, but on the whole they are still intent on suppressing grass fires, presumably because ranchers never wish to lose a grazing season by seeing "their" grass go up in flames.

Tim Byer can see no reason why ranchers who decided to move into bison raising could not build on existing grazing associations to amass acreage sufficient for bison. At present, usually five or six cattle ranchers get together and propose a management plan for the allotments they wish to lease from the grassland, giving a total number of "animal units" to be allowed. They can then share this total as they wish, either by dividing up the total number of animals or by sharing months of use of individual areas. Yet few seem likely to abandon their cattle-raising traditions to try bison, since building stronger fencing is expensive and many ranchers are right on the edge of bankruptcy as it is.

Byer also works with the staff of Wyoming's Fish and Wildlife Department. As he says, "I went to school with all these guys, so we can usually work things out." As we have seen, bison have a dual legal character, considered private property on ranches and wildlife on public lands, and Byer thinks this is a basic reason why public policy is vague or nonexistent; he confirms my impression that there are no rules or regulations whatsoever about bison within the Forest Service.

One curious aspect of the Thunder Basin Grassland is that ranchers are allowed to drill wells to make water holes for their cattle where the aquifer is not too far down, though this tends to be costly. Oil companies are also allowed to drill, but if a hole hits only water they are obliged to notify the Forest Service, which may decide to develop the hole into a water well suitable for stock or wildlife. (By now there are a lot of these wells, some of them artesian, or self-flowing.)

Although the Classification and Multiple Use Act of 1964 envisaged application of the multiple-use principle to BLM lands and the 1976 Federal Land Policy and Management Act directed the BLM to plan and manage on the basis of multiple use, there are practically no bison on BLM lands either. Glenn Secrist at BLM headquarters in Washington told me that there is a herd of several hundred bison in the Henry Mountains of Utah, grazing mostly on BLM land; there is a herd in Wyoming ranging on BLM as well as Forest Service lands; and there may be some in Montana. Would-be users of BLM lands would have to apply for permits and go through the usual environmental analysis; the agency would also be concerned about fencing—Secrist has heard of problems in this area. The BLM's operations are quite decentralized, and each state office would process permittee applications; it is quite possible that local officials are not exactly enthusiastic about bison, but Secrist says that no significant policy issues about bison have arisen on the national level. He anticipates a growing number of applications to run bison, but the agency regards its existing grazing regulations as applicable to bison as well as cattle. As on Forest Service lands, ranchers could amalgamate leased BLM acreage into cooperatives big enough to make good sense for bison, though some persistence and ingenuity would be required. This would not be necessary in western Wyoming and eastern Montana, however, where BLM lands are in large chunks. Secrist himself recognizes that bison need to roam, and he spoke longingly of "getting rid of all those fences"; indeed, he confessed that he sometimes thinks of getting into bison ranching himself.

The future of presently leased public lands is thus not entirely bleak. There is the potential for ranched bison on federal lands, which could add up to hundreds of thousands, and ultimately millions, of acres, though this will not happen quickly. But at present, with a few exceptions, federal lands remain cow country from coast to coast.

Potential for Government Stewardship

As we will see in the next chapter, there are sound economic reasons to expect a great proliferation of bison raising on both private and leased public land. From the standpoint of wild bison, however, it is reasonable to ask whether, given a congressional mandate to do so, government land agencies would actually be capable of fostering them. It is encouraging that the federal agencies and their state counterparts have had considerable success in restoring and augmenting other species—almost always with hunting in mind—in some 4,400 areas encompassing almost 40 million acres, public and private. In national forests, parks, and wildlife refuges, white-tailed deer rose from half a million in 1920 to more than 14 million in 1989 (4 million were shot in 1980). Elk numbered only about 100,000 in 1920 but had come back to 500,000 in 1989, mostly in national forests. (We think of elk today as predominantly a forest species, but, like pronghorn, they lived on grasslands in large numbers before settlement drove them into higher, rougher country.) Antelope and mammals such as squirrels, beaver, and black bear—all prey animals for hunters—have also increased. Some game birds, such as ducks, geese, pheasant, prairie chicken, and grouse, have done well too.

These increases have occurred despite intensive use of wildlife refuges for activities including cattle grazing, oil and gas drilling, off-road vehicle travel, and military operations, both aerial and on the ground. More than 60 percent of the refuges in the federal system have been affected in some of these ways. Air force bombing practice is actually permitted in the Copalis National Wildlife Refuge in Washington state.

There are a growing number of strong voices for bison in public agencies. Glenn E. Plumb, a wildlife biologist at Badlands National Park in South Dakota, puts it this way: "Bison should be the preferred alternative when the natural area is medium to large, economics are acceptable, facilities exist to permit proper handling, and management plans are sufficiently simple so as to preclude very difficult herd manipulations." (The degree of handling that Plumb envisions would not please some bison partisans.) Plumb adds, "Stewardship with bison may continue relatively uninterrupted throughout the year at a lower stewardship cost per acre." However, he believes that cattle may have a role in stewardship plans for smaller (or less well funded) areas, where using cattle part of the year may help to optimize economic stability and ecological integrity of management. Keeping some cattle around intermittently, he feels, could thus help bison and other wild species.

Nonprofit Bison Herds

The Nature Conservancy, a national organization devoted to the preservation of intact natural areas (which it often buys to save them from commercial development, then later hands over to public agencies) has a long-standing interest in bison and their role in maintaining healthy grassland ecosystems. It now has four Great Plains preserves on which bison have been or soon will be introduced. As we saw in an earlier chapter, the Conservancy's overall strategy is to preserve "disturbance" patterns caused by

Nature Conservancy Preserves

Cross Ranch Preserve in North Dakota amounts to 6,000 acres and has seventy-five bison. Thirty animals are rotated among three pastures in a northern unit of 900 acres of northern mixed-grass prairie and bottomland forest, while forty-five animals inhabit 1,440 acres in a southern unit of northern mixed-grass prairie and woody draws.

Samuel H. Ordway Memorial Prairie in South Dakota has eighty-five bison on 1,540 acres now but will soon have about double that on a single unfenced pasture of 3,500 acres; spring burns will be carried out to create a shifting landscape patch mosaic, and bison will distribute their grazing accordingly.

Niobrara Valley Preserve in northern Nebraska has 250 bison on 7,500 acres of Sand Hills prairie and riparian wetland–woodland–grassland area along the Niobrara River. A random program of burning areas of high fuel accumulation creates a landscape patch mosaic.

The newest Nature Conservancy bison are on the Tallgrass Prairie Preserve near Pawhuska, Oklahoma, which received 300 bison in late 1993. These bison are in a 5,000-acre area, which will be gradually enlarged as the herd grows over the next eight to ten years to around 1,100 on some 30,000 acres; the fences that presently divide the property will be removed. A randomized burn regime will be adopted, whereby areas will experience fire about every three to five years; studies will focus on how the bison move around in the resulting patch mosaic. Manager Bob Hamilton first got into bison work through interning at the Conservancy's Ordway preserve, during the period when the Conservancy removed cattle and introduced bison. He told me that it is anticipated that about 600 head will be sold each fall by sealed bid. These sales, like those at other preserves, will help substantially to keep the preserve operating. This means, of course, yearly roundups, at which brucellosis vaccinations will be continued. In time, the Oklahoma herd may reach 1,850 bison on the total land area of 51,000 acres, generating a yearly surplus of some 900 animals. Hamilton and his family, he says, have been eating bison for a long time and now, in fact, eat no other meat.

periodic intensive bison grazing and occasional fire. (As Ron Walker of Custer State Park emphasized, bison cannot do the job alone.)

A minimal management approach is used, allowing the bison to behave as naturally as possible, though mature bulls are often removed "to reduce containment problems"; fencing at the preserves is five- to six-foot barbed-wire fences rather than the woven-wire fences common for bison. Culling is done to simulate predation; calves and older adults are chosen. No supplemental feeding is done, and population levels are kept moderate to light compared with typical cattle stocking. Vaccinations for brucellosis and tuberculosis are carried out.

Other conservation and wildlife-oriented organizations also have bison. Most of the herds are easily observable by the public, and the organizations generally provide educational materials to help inform people about the past, present, and future of bison. One spectacular example is the Catalina Conservancy, which maintains approximately 200 bison on Catalina Island, twenty miles off Los Angeles on the California coast—once a playground for Hollywood celebrities, whose presence was reported to mainland newspapers by carrier pigeon, and now a delightfully isolated beach vacation spot. The island is a comfortable, safe place—kids steal each other's bicycles, but serious crime is rare because escape would be possible only by ferry or other boat. Thanks to its former owners, the Chicago Wrigley family of chewing-gum fame, most of the rugged, chaparral-covered, twenty-mile-long island is now owned by the Conservancy (not to be confused with The Nature Conservancy), a sophisticated environmental organization engaged in an ambitious program to restore the island's native vegetation. But along with 86 percent of the island, the Conservancy also inherited a herd of bison, originally brought over in 1924 to be filmed in *The Vanishing American*, directed by George B. Seitz on the basis of a Zane Grey story.

After the filming, the bison were left on the island because it was cheaper than shipping them back to the mainland, and they thrived; the original fourteen, together with nine more brought from Colorado to broaden the herd's gene pool in 1934 and fifteen bull calves imported from Montana in 1969, multiplied to around 500. They have now been reduced to some 200 to decrease browsing and grazing pressure on the island's vegetation. Catalina was originally about 85 percent forest and chaparral, but when whites brought goats and sheep to the island, their incessant nibbling soon cut this to 15 percent, giving much of the island a semidesert look reminiscent of Greek islands—products of similar ecological devastation. Now the sheep are entirely gone and the goats are almost eliminated as well. Only the bison and a sizable population of feral pigs remain; the pigs are hunted in deer season.

The Catalina bison owe their arrival on their paradisiacal island to Americans' love for imagery of the old West and their survival to the Wrigleys' profitable exploitation of human nervous chewing habits. Ironically, they owe their continued presence, a fairly blatant contradiction of the Conservancy's overall restoration aims, to the fact that they are popular with tourists; they also, of course, do a lot less damage to vegetation than do livestock. And although they occasionally rub hard enough against a road sign post to knock it askew, they have not been known to damage the power poles that cross the island—a fact that will turn out to be significant for the future of bison on the Plains. Enthusiastic tourists take a tram tour that bumps them up to the island's surprising heights, where they almost always encounter small groups of bison. Sometimes Catalina bison can even be seen wading in the salt water in a picturesque cove.

Bison in Zoos

The Bronx Zoo still keeps about a dozen bison in a pasture surrounded by trees that is reminiscent of ancient Eastern bison habitat. A bronze plaque reminds visitors of the crucial role the zoo played in maintaining the species when it was all but extinct. The San Francisco Zoo has a similar herd on about five acres. Like many zoos, it is plagued with budget and management problems, and critics in the local Watchbison Committee feel that it has not been maintaining a sufficiently high level of care for the animals. Over the years, the bison's area has been whittled down to the equivalent of two or three football fields. With thirteen bison—one vasectomized bull and twelve cows—this is the equivalent of a padded cell for a free-roaming beast like the bison. The irrigated grass in the enclosure, however, looks surprisingly good, though not all of it consists of types palatable to bison. The animals are also fed pellets and hay and appear healthy. Unfortunately, it is hard to keep visitors from feeding them pizza and other human food, which is hard on their digestion and may carry disease organisms.

A local bison enthusiast named Phil Carleton worries that the surrounding largely residential neighborhood has not been prepared for a bison breakout, which might result in frightened neighbors asking the police to kill bison. (Recently police fired forty-three shots to bring down a dairy cow who had wandered onto a southern California freeway.) Carleton points out that escaped bison, unless they are panicked by people, quickly settle down to quiet grazing on lawns and can then be driven back inside their paddock.

A concern at zoos is that people sometimes enjoy teasing bison. In San Francisco, the paddock's arrangement formerly facilitated this because it had a fenced corridor protruding into the paddock for feeding the animals and people used this vantage to harass them. Daring teenagers sometimes climb the fence and sprint across the pasture; so far none has been hurt. Tourist buses make regular stops for viewing and photography.

The Denver Zoo also has a bison herd, and bison are an attraction at many other zoos as well. Unfortunately, because of the limited space available in all but a few zoos, seeing bison there is not at all like observing their natural ways of living and tends to be depressing. Like marine mammals trained to do appealing tricks in exhibition parks, zoo bison are martyrs—living in confined and straitened circumstances but serving to give watchers some faint idea of the strength, grace, and natural majesty of their wild relatives.

Chapter Five
Bison on Ranches

The ranching of a wild animal is a paradoxical undertaking that offers infinite challenges but also enough gratification to attract legions of enterprising folks. Ranchers often seem to be torn between their realization that bison are naturally wild, free-ranging animals and their desire to manage them efficiently, conveniently, and profitably. Since most ranch owners and hands—and also people working with herds in parks and preserves—come out of the cattle industry, their traditions push them strongly in the latter direction. But bison are not docile like cattle. They tend to evade human control and maintain their own autonomous agendas. It is small wonder, then, that some ranchers have attempted interbreeding programs to mix three-eighths bison with five-eighths cattle (for one example) and come out with a manageable but still hardy "beefalo." But the progeny are generally not fertile, and the hoped-for advantages have proved minimal.

In recent years, a good many ranchers of both cattle and bison have turned for guidance in managing their herds to the ideas of Allan Savory, which were discussed earlier. Savory's approach, which he dubs holistic resource management to emphasize that it includes much more than ideas about stocking practices, has been criticized by some range researchers, who have their own, simpler versions of rotational grazing and who claim to have disproved some of his contentions experimentally. Savory is a passionate expositor who does not gladly suffer those he considers fools, and he has a considerable number of allies among ranchers. He believes that cattle and any other grazing animals, if properly managed, can be good for grasslands. A number of bison ranchers, like a few cattle ranchers, have recognized that conventional rotation schemes, even with modest numbers of animals, still lead to damaged pastures, and they have found Savory's ideas practical and useful. His workshops, newsletter, and training programs have brought his ideas widespread recognition, if not universal acceptance.

The Savory approach basically attempts to do what predation and animal instincts did before humans usurped control of the land: spread grazing impacts evenly, over time as well as area, with a frequency such that grasses can recover before they are grazed again. In his consulting work, Savory usually recommends accomplishing this through a complex system of fencing—though, with cattle, herding by mounted riders can accomplish most of the job. Ranchland is subdivided into "paddocks," often arranged radially like pie slices and sharing a common watering tank at the center. A herd in its entirety is then rotated from paddock to paddock on an intricate schedule planned with relative paddock productivity, rainfall, and seasonal nutrition demands in mind. There may be as few as eight or as many as a hundred paddocks. Often, where paddocks are small and numerous, yet animals may total several hundred, the herd is moved every few days. (Cattle and bison can both be trained to change paddocks at the sound of a small whistle.)

The crucial factor, Savory argues, is to ensure that the animals have enough time to graze the whole paddock but not enough time to nibble given grass plants twice. Then the animals are moved to another paddock, where the process is repeated. "Time grazings according to the needs of perennial grasses," he advises; overgrazing can occur if animals stay in one area long enough to rebite a regrowing plant or if they come back to a spot before a severely grazed plant has recovered. The brief but heavy grazing and trampling each paddock receives, Savory contends, mimics as closely as can human control the original impacts of grazing wild herds. Occasional trampling is good because it breaks the soil surface, making possible seeding and development of new plants, and it is especially effective when it is done by excited animals. The buffalo stampede was a classic example, but even cattle (whose behavior these days, as Savory puts it, is characterized by "unbroken calm") can be stirred into lively activity by throwing granular salt or protein cubes over an area to be trampled.

Savory has a scientist's persistent curiosity about the grazing process and has spent twenty years revising and perfecting his ideas. He believes that his analysis provides the key not only to stopping the degradation and desertification that has cursed the American West and, indeed, most grasslands of the world but also to raising the productivity of the animals grazing them. He regards conventional stocking practices as oversimple and arbitrary because they are based on ignorance of ecological succession principles. They usually result in too light and too continual grazing, which is inevitably spotty and actually causes the takeover of grassland by woody plants (brush) that ranchers and government agencies have been spending millions to eradicate. Moreover, Savory considers the prescription of rest or total absence of grazing, advocated by some environmental groups and by some land-agency officials, as strongly counterproductive. Such observations, predictably enough, have not been welcomed by the range establishment, and it seems unlikely that Savory's ideas will ever predominate in government-agency or university thinking. Meanwhile, as he sees it, millions of acres of land will continue to degrade.

Ranchers sometimes try the Savory system and experience solid success, then turn it into the same kind of rigid routine as conventional stock rotation and soon find their pastures looking terrible again. In the end, it may be doubtful that even Savory himself, much less ordinary ranchers, however observant and thoughtful, can in fact be so subtly responsive as to replicate the intricate, subtly balanced flow of free-ranging bison across the land closely enough to bring back the ancient richness of the Plains. Indeed, Savory recognizes that his system, a simulacrum of the natural grassland ecosystem, works best with large herds—2,000 to 5,000 head—on very large acreages. Yet because land is so subdivided today, he argues, we must do the best we can with small herds on small ranches.

Savory's approach turns on the assumption that since we have removed natural predators from the grasslands—including, in the North American case, Indian hunters—we are forced into trying to micromanage grazing impacts on grasslands. However, not every ecologist agrees with all of Savory's assumptions. He contends that herds once moved in large part to avoid predators, yet wolf and bear predation on bison appears to have been limited, and even human predation was moderate until repeating rifles appeared on the Plains. Also, omnipresent fencing simply goes against the grain of many wildlife biologists. Savory's critics argue that people accept his system as management gospel even in situations in which no management of any kind might be preferable. Advocates of letting overgrazed public land rest claim that the Savory system offers false hopes of regeneration. Savory has little patience with such critics, saying that they lack a realistic understanding of how grass reacts to grazing patterns.

Bison "Management"

Bison are curious about human beings, as they are about everything else. They pay close attention to changes in their environment and have even been seen, for mysterious reasons, attempting to refill newly dug fence-post holes by pushing the dirt back in with their noses. They shove around farm machinery left in their pastures. They are not afraid of human beings and will sometimes approach people very closely, but they usually dislike being touched and sometimes butt or even gore people who infringe on their dignity in some way. Ranchers say, "Never turn your back on a bison," especially if you are located between the bison and an open area.

Bison certainly require less labor than cattle, but they do need better, hence more expensive, fences and corrals. They also require ranchers to adapt to their intelligence, curiosity, resourcefulness, impetuousness, and strength. Still, of the roughly 140,000 bison in the United States as of 1994, a large majority are on private ranches. The national total is rising sharply, with conservative predictions of 175,000 by the year 2000. (The Canadians expect to have another 120,000.) Two trade groups, the National Bison Association and the American Bison Association, have been trying to strengthen demand for bison, improve distribution, help people get started with bison, and facilitate the sale of live animals. In November 1994, the two groups merged under the name National Bison Association, with headquarters in Denver. Judging by the combined memberships, there are around 2,000 bison ranches in the country, and they are everywhere, even on Kodiak Island off the Alaska coast—where the resident grizzly bears wisely leave the bison alone.

Moreover, there are now Plains bison in Europe. Exporting animals has become quite a sideline for several American ranches, and there are now small bison ranches abroad: in Quebec, on the Camargue grasslands in southern France, in Switzerland, and a few in Belgium and other corners of Europe. On the remote and still ecologically intact border between Poland and Belarus, by the way, lives a small herd of wisent, the only native bison outside North America—forest-dwelling descendants of the great bison depicted in prehistoric cave art. They survived World War II but are now endangered by logging.

Predictably enough, most people concerned with bison exude optimism about the prospects of bison ranching. Sales of bison meat, after remaining relatively flat for many years, began surging upward about ten years ago, and at present, demand far outdistances supply. But the scale of bison raising in the United States is still minute compared with that of the cattle industry: we support some 116 million cattle, and such is the American desire for beef that about 125,000 of them are slaughtered each day. Predictions are that around 20,000 bison should be available annually by the year 2000, compared with about 11,000 today. It is hard to imagine that this could satisfy the demand, especially if even marginally better distribution becomes available. At present, many ranchers sell meat, and sometimes bleached skulls, heads, and hides, directly to customers through mail-order lists and local deliveries. There is something to be said for continuing and expanding this pattern of highly personal local production and consumption, as opposed to the giant national mechanism of contemporary American food merchandising, in which nobody knows where food comes from, how long it has been in transit, or what has happened to it en route. And John Flocchini of the Durham Ranch in eastern Wyoming says that his operation has already developed a worthwhile market for bison meat in western Europe.

Given the small present size of the bison industry, it is easy to see why there has been a sharp rise in the value of live bison for breeding stock. At the moment, John Flocchini says, it is primarily a breeder's market. Flocchini is around thirty and, despite the fact that he operates out of a ranch house and nearby office set in an otherwise uninhabited valley, he is a sophisticated and articulate man who might have recently stepped off a university campus with an M.B.A. His ranch grew out of the Flocchini family's meat-distribution business in California and is a thriving operation. John says that he has been negotiating to start grazing bison on another large property to the south, which would make possible a significant rise in production. He emphasizes, "Meat is still the mainstay of this operation. The breeding stock market is gravy for us, though an eight-month-old weaned heifer calf goes for $1,000–$1,500 these days." There may be a speculative element in such prices, and John would not be surprised to see a crash. "Some of the people who are diving into it are not doing their homework real well."

"Hobby ranchers" are the surprisingly numerous people who simply like to keep a few bison around, raising them for fun rather than profit. Bison can stir strong affections in humans. Dana Jones, forty-three, a hospital emergency-room clerk who grew up in bison country in western Montana, lives on ten acres north of Seattle where she keeps nine bison behind a sign reading "Danger: Buffalo—Private Game Refuge." Jones says the human bond with bison is undeniable but also unexplainable, though it may have something to do with early human history, when the presence of a big animal meant dinner. She has, according to a story in the *Seattle Post Intelligencer*, "buffalo chimes on the porch, buffalo robes on the couch, buffalo paintings on the walls, the head of one of her butchered bulls on the living-room wall and, near the door, the skull of a buffalo cow that died giving birth." Jones takes pride in being the only single female bison rancher she has ever heard of. After some local publicity she began to get a lot of calls, and whether her bison are a business or a hobby, she says, "They've engulfed my whole life." About ten times a week, she takes Kiwanians, Rotarians, schoolchildren, and church groups on hayrides through her pasture, giving them a basic lecture on bison. Understandably, Jones is known locally as "the buffalo lady," and she extends her passion for the great beasts by visiting schools, showing classes a video and telling children about the history and comeback of bison.

A German sausage maker lives nearby, and he butchers about one animal a year for Jones, turning it into both meat cuts and jerky. In her house there is now a bison-items gift shop, where Jones sells skulls, robes, and heads, but she sells the meat to regular customers whom she has educated about proper cooking methods. Because she gets to know individual animals well, she arranges to be away when the butcher comes. But the income from sales just about finances her operation.

Like other noncommercial or semicommercial bison keepers, Jones does not manage her herd, except for culling older males. In time, to avoid inbreeding, she will need to bring in a new bull from outside. She pays no veterinarian bills, so the animals have to fend for themselves. "The buffalo are either healthy or they're dead," she says. "They thrive on neglect. They've survived for hundreds of thousands of years by being wild animals, relying on their instincts. I let them be buffalo." She does feed them treats occasionally (they are fond of apples), but aside from maintaining

Bison are sometimes used as a means of attracting tourists to roadside cafés, "museums," or "ranches" featuring exotic birds and animals. At such places they are kept in tightly crowded conditions, which make them a depressing sight. This bison and her calf are confined in a small "ranch" operation in Nevada. Normally bison are accustomed to grazing across immeasurable expanses of grassland. These bison not only live in a pen measuring about thirty by forty feet, they also must walk about in deeply trodden filth.

her fence—by which the bison let themselves be confined most of the time, as long as they have grass and company—Jones leaves them alone. If she has to attend to something inside the fence, she goes in by tractor, and she knows the warning signs of bison body language. Once, when she failed to keep track of where one of her bison was, she got butted and her pants leg was ripped. But Jones still literally holds out a hand to the bison: a cow recently let her scratch away (through the fence) at her shedding winter coat. One of Jones's favorite pleasures is to sit in her hot tub, twenty feet from the buffalo fence, "listening to the buffalo snort and watching their hot breath turn to clouds of mist." She has no plans to enlarge her operation, though she could rent more land next door; she likes it the way it is. Her only move to improve the business side of her herd has been to build a corral so she can more easily sell young heifers.

Then there are people who raise modest numbers of bison on small ranches—a hundred animals or even fewer—and derive only part of their livelihood from the herd. Quite a number of producers (the industry term for bison ranchers) have intermediate-sized herds of 100–250 animals but are often eager to expand. A few bison are not usually troublesome to manage, especially if they have been raised in a fenced area since birth.

Major Bison Ranches

"What it comes down to is this:
bison are half the work— and twice the money."

—*Former cattle rancher*

Bison ranching as a substantial commercial venture was pioneered by Roy Houck in South Dakota. Mostly because Houck just liked them, he kept around seventy bison on his cattle ranch. Then came the terrible winter of 1966, when Houck noticed that the bison came through the blizzard quite well while he suffered heavy losses of cattle. Houck, who died recently, was a canny man and a daring one. He decided to get into bison in a big way and began by buying bison from Custer State Park and anywhere else he could find them. Learning to manage the animals was trying, for they were much faster and smarter than cattle. When he was loading them into a truck from a chute, for instance, they would move into the truck, turn around, and shoot back out in the time a cow would have needed to take a step or two. For ten years, Houck and his family bought and bred bison, refenced, and set up corrals to build the herd into the largest private herd in the world—some 3,500 animals. Realizing the critical need to gain publicity for bison ranching and to sell bison meat, Houck formed the National Buffalo (later Bison) Association and served as its president for many years. It is remembered that he would come to board meetings with enough proxies in his pocket to ram through whatever measures he wished. (He evidently had plenty of political savvy, since he rose to be state senator and lieutenant governor.) In 1974, finding that cattle slaughterhouse operations were not satisfactory for bison, Houck built his own processing plant and began marketing not only bison meat but also hides, heads, and skulls.

Houck attracted wide public notice because it was his ranch on which director-star Kevin Costner and producer Jim Wilson filmed much of *Dances with Wolves*. After a handshake contract, from which Houck said he never made much money, Fort Sedgewick was built on the ranch, including a fiberglass replica of its sod house, with walls removable for the convenience of cameras, and the famous hunt and other bison scenes were shot nearby. No real bison were killed, of course; the magic of special effects ensured that.

Like the Houck ranch, the handful of other leading bison ranches are large operations in acreage—it is not reasonable to take on bison as a sole occupation unless you are willing to think in terms of tens of thousands of acres. All the same, most of these ranches have adopted a fencing-and-rotation scheme, and most writers in industry publications seem to take it for granted that ranchers will use it.

The major exception is the Ted Turner operation. The broadcast magnate now owns a chain of bison ranches, and he is by far the single biggest bison rancher in the country. The Flying D, in the beautiful Gallatin River Valley of western Montana, has about 3,000 bison on 128,000 acres of wooded mountains and grassland. In drier central New Mexico, near the western edge of historical bison range, are two newer Turner acquisitions.

Individual bison often tolerate close quarters fairly well. This cow is in temporary quarantine at the Terry Bison Ranch. Photo: Christine Leefeldt.

The Armendaris Ranch, with 338,000 acres, is fifty miles long and has its own mountain range, though no bison as yet. The Ladder Ranch, not far away, comprises 300,000 acres, on which there are now about 2,000 bison cows and some 200 bulls. On unfenced properties of this scale, bison can live much as they lived historically—wandering over the terrain as grazing opportunities and weather conditions impel them. Most recently, Turner added the Spike Box Ranch, 31,700 acres in the Sand Hills region of Nebraska; this is in the relatively well watered heart of original bison habitat.

Turner was attracted by the low labor requirements of bison; on the Flying D, four men manage the herd, whereas a dozen cowboys were needed to handle the former herd of 3,800 cattle. The Turner operation expects to level out at sales of 6,500–7,000 animals per year. Since bison prices to ranchers are currently about $1.25 per pound, while beef prices have fallen steadily and are now down to $.65 per pound, the financial prospects appear excellent. As Turner is reported to have said, "Hell, this could be a business."

Bud Griffith, manager of the Flying D, has been in the livestock business in Montana for a long time. He is a working manager, and it is not easy to catch him in his office. Turner, Griffith told me, had a long-standing desire to do something with bison; he had collected buffalo nickels as a boy. He "kind of lucked out" in being able to buy the Flying D. The current herd has been built up with animals bought from a number of suppliers. The current plan is to keep the herd at 3,000 cows and 300 bulls, not counting the annual calves. Recent winters have been mild, so it is hard to tell how many bison the property will to be able to support in the long run, but the number ought to be somewhat larger. There is talk of putting Turner bison on public land that is part of a nearby national forest, which once had 150 Flying D cattle on it, but Griffith says the Forest Service is undecided about this. Although ultimately the ranches will all sell animals for both meat and herd stocking, at present they let go of very few and concentrate on building up their own herds. The staff of the Flying D interferes as little as possible with the animals, though they have done a little occasional winter feeding and will do more if it's necessary. The ranch has many natural sources of water, but a little well water is also pumped for the bison. As Griffith says, "it's all one big pasture," so the bison distribute their grazing impacts naturally, and he has not observed any problems with overgrazing—the land still seems to have plenty of unused capacity. Confirming observations at Yellowstone, he also has not noticed any impact on the bison by bears or other predators. The bison are rounded up once a year and occasionally twice, for vaccinations, using as few "buffs" (bison cowboys) as possible—just ranch employees.

The New Mexico ranches, according to Russ Miller, who is in charge of them, also follow the general preservationist goal that Turner has established. (Turner once said, "The best way to protect land is to buy it." He has a strong conservation ethic and has been working with The Nature Conservancy; there is a conservation easement on the Flying D, protecting it from future development.) The overall plan calls for some 4,500 bison cows, together with some bulls, on the two New Mexico ranches combined.

At this point, no significant acquisitions of new animals from outside the Turner operation are planned; Turner simply wants to let the existing herds multiply until they are numerous enough to fully occupy the available grazing land.

Miller said that though he knows that the short-duration, high-intensity rotation method used by some bison ranchers seems to work well for them, the Turner style is to stick to free range, at least as an initial approach; free-range ranching is light on personnel requirements, and he will see how the bison do when left to their own devices. Later, if the approach needs modification, he will think again. The Flying D does use fire in management: "It's one of the few tools that we have at this point to try and alter the movement of the bison herd." They do not plot herd movements systematically, as has been done in Theodore Roosevelt National Park, but they have a pretty good sense of where the bison are from day to day.

The Turner ranches may yet acquire further land, but even now they are unique in their scale. More representative of serious bison-raising operations is the Terry Bison Ranch, just south of Cheyenne on the Wyoming-Colorado line, with some 27,000 acres of former cattle land and about 2,500 bison. Dan Thiel, who runs the ranch with his father, Ron, says that 5,000 cattle were kept on it, resulting in serious overgrazing, which the Thiels are still trying to heal. Even in this dry, short-grass country, the ranch with its buildings and corrals cost the Thiels $2.5 million. They have been selling animals briskly—some 350 to Ted Turner for his new New Mexico ranches in one year, plus some excess bulls for meat. The economic prospects look good for the long term, but ranching of any kind is admitedly a treacherous business. When I quoted the former cattleman's remark about half the work and twice the money to Ron Thiel, he grinned and replied, "Well, that's half true."

Thiel got into the bison business after spending thirty-one years running a company that built electrical utility lines in twenty-seven states, including Alaska. He had owned a few bison, a couple at a time, but was never home enough to "deal with them right." So, he said, "I decided to sell that company to the employees, for $125,000 down on an $8 million sale, and then I went out and bought all this land and buffalo—very risky, because I have to depend on the income from the sale of the company to pay off the obligations for the land." Land purchase or rental costs are a major factor in bison ranching, of course, and cheap land is one reason why most of the major ranches are located in high, dry country. The bison cost Ron an additional $2 million. In addition, he recently invested heavily in tourist facilities, including a string of cabins and the large gift shop where we talked. "Kind of stupid, in a way. But I did it, eight years ago, and I guess we're about 40 percent paid off, so the risk is less every day. Plus I'm doing what I like to do! But you can figure it out—$6.5 million at

8 percent is a thousand bucks a day in interest. It takes a lot of ice cream bars and sacks of ice and buffalo burgers to pay for that. And that's just the interest." But at bottom, Thiel says, "I do it for the love of the animals; the economic part came later. I really just started it as a hobby. Then the damn thing got out of control. But I would not want to be doing anything else."

The Terry Ranch is situated on beautifully rounded hills, but it is bone-dry, virtually treeless grassland. Visible among the hills are railroad tracks, power lines, roads, and other signs of human impact. The old ranch buildings are snuggled down into a draw next to a creek, where they get protection from the winds, but the restaurant and gift shop are up near the interstate in order to be in clear view of passing motorists. It is clearly a working ranch—for example, a farrier shoes horses as tourists look on—and Ron Thiel says that sometimes this aspect of the ranch has profound effects on people. He has a basketful of letters about how a stay at the ranch has changed people's lives. "Thank you," wrote one woman, "for putting a little of the cowboy into my husband!"

Tourists can go for a horse-drawn wagon ride out in the hills, probably see some bison, and come back for an all-you-can-eat "chuck-wagon dinner," which, of course, features bison. A motorized bison-safari ride, reserved for groups, takes visitors farther out on the ranch. Dan Thiel, who is tanned and fit from a life outdoors, conducts these tours, and his public-address-system spiel is extremely informative.

"You cannot really herd bison," Dan explains. "What we do is lure them by turning off the water in the area we want them to leave and turning it on where we want them to go." (The ranch has a system of piped water, but the Thiels have left the original windmill towers intact, without blades or gearbox, in case of trouble with the pipes.) Bison have a very good sense of smell, says Thiel, "They can smell water for miles." Ranchers also use other methods familiar to animal (and human) trainers. As the fast-food chains have profitably demonstrated with humans, it is easy to manipulate mammals by utilizing their food preferences, and ranchers do the same with bison. "Bison cookies," also called ranch cubes or protein cubes, are made from grains that bison enjoy. Dan distributed some of these as he drove his tourist train around on early experimental rides, "to convince 'em that we were good guys." Strewing a trail of hay through an open gate can also persuade bison to follow it into a new pasture.

The Durham Ranch in eastern Wyoming is another major bison operation. A flyer issued by the ranch says, "Due to their independent nature, bison are handled as little as possible. They spend their lives in grass, much as they always have, and very little time in the feedlot." But the usual industry practice is to send most bull calves (except for a few kept for breeding purposes) off to feedlots—the owner's or others'—when they are 18 to 22 months old, along with heifer calves deemed to be poor breeding prospects, and to keep them there for at least three or four months, until they reach target sale weights. In an industry in which animals are scarce, ranchers are intensely motivated to get more weight on those they have before marketing them because acquiring new animals is expensive and difficult. Bison muscle does not marble, or accumulate fat throughout its fibers, which in the eyes of the U.S.D.A. raises the grade and hence the price of meat. So the added weight is mostly fat laid on between the hide and the muscles; it is lost in slaughtering, cutting, and trimming. But it adds to the sale price.

Feedlot bison bulls seldom reach three years of age, after which they are usually considered good only for burger and sausage meat. Life in a feedlot is stressful for bison, not only because their natural range of daily movement is restricted but also because being confined in close quarters interferes with their natural dominance patterns and leads to goring. This increases the ranchers' temptation to dehorn calves so that when they reach the feedlot, they are less likely to injure each other or their keepers. Dehorning is controversial in the industry. Some ranchers believe that it detracts from the naturalness and visual appeal of the animals, making them increasingly like cattle; they do not find that horns are a problem. One rancher observed, "A bison cow uses her horns like a man uses his hands, and if you took a man's hands away from him he would be much more agreeable." Some producers, however, routinely dehorn all cows and most bulls—except for those expected to develop into "trophy heads."

In feedlots, bison tend to contract parasites and diseases, often borne by manure-loving flies, so inoculations, worming, and mineral supplements are routine. One disease, enterotoxemia, or bloating disease, almost never occurs in free-range bison but must be vaccinated against in feedlots.

By their nature, feedlot operations cannot be sustainable. They pump up the bison through intensive use of feed that has been grown elsewhere with lots of fossil-energy inputs in fertilizer, herbicides, and pesticides, then transported to the lot at the expense of large amounts of diesel fuel. Because so many animals are kept in close quarters in feedlots, they also require elaborate watering facilities (heated in winter), manure-removal equipment, and so on.

Feeding on the range is a practice that ranchers would, at least in theory, like to avoid. Replying to my question, Ron Thiel says, "No, we do not feed 'em." But then he adds, "Unless Mother Nature deprives us. This year we've had a big drought, so just this morning I bought $20,000 worth of protein cubes, because the grass is so low in nutrition. As you saw out there, they look pretty good—but they do not have much to live on." It also turns out that he runs another ranch as a feedlot, thirty miles away. "We have to struggle to get fat on them. They'll only eat what they need—you could have this whole building full of corn, but they just want to eat what it takes to sustain them. I've been feeding them now, I guess, seven years, and we have not made any money out of it."

John Flocchini of the Durham Ranch reflects, "You know, it's sort of against what they're meant to do," but he still keeps about 1,300 animals in feedlots scattered across the country. "We try to get them into places where the climate is more conducive to conversion of feed [into meat], and there's also the factor of feed prices and availability, so we move them closer to a source of grain and hay." Many ranchers with low-quality grass also feed their animals hay or range cubes occasionally, especially in the winter, when grass quality declines. And it seems to be a virtually universal practice to supply salt blocks and sometimes magnesium, copper, and selenium.

Ranchers know that bison by nature are remarkably durable beasts. Still, in *The Bison Breeder's Handbook*, you can read flat assertions such as this: "Parasites must be controlled or the animals will never perform well." Elaborate veterinary practices exist, and some ranchers apply them extensively. Selective-breeding programs are afoot, based on blood typing, with a central registry of bloodlines. Such practices should help in the outbreeding needed to ensure that deleterious genes do not become concentrated in individual herds.

However, there is a downside to selective breeding. If breeders also select for docility, in a century or two such genetic manipulation could remove much of the wildness and vigor from the species—a prospect that wise ranchers know would be self-defeating. "We can damage our image and our pricing structure if we do everything just like beef producers and begin to produce bison meat which is indistinguishable from beef," says *The Bison Breeder's Handbook*.

The one cattle industry standard that has not found adherents among bison ranchers is castrating bull calves and raising them as steers. The temptation for ranchers here, as the *Handbook* puts it, is that "when you remove sexual thoughts and drives you remove a lot of violent and exhibitionist behavior from animals." But since castrated bison do not thrive and put on weight rapidly the way beef steers do, it appears that bison will remain free of this indignity.

Rotational Grazing

Ranchers may possess acreages that seem impressive to city dwellers, but even the Terry Ranch's 27,000 acres or the Durham Ranch's 55,000 acres is not large from a bison's point of view. Bison naturally range over hundreds of square miles, equivalent to hundreds of thousands of acres or more. Paradoxically, only an extremely wealthy landowner like Ted Turner (or the federal government) can operate on the bison's natural scale. As *The Bison Breeder's Handbook* puts it, "Pastures of 640 acres or less are too small because the bison would normally travel across the whole pasture in a single day. That results in little chance for places to have more than a day or two between grazings, resulting in overgrazing." Ranchers with limited acreage—and even some with quite large acreage—therefore have often adopted systems of rotation designed to spread grazing impacts. In some cases, they also hope to help degraded cattle lands to regenerate.

Many have adopted simple systems of rotation among a few pastures, going either by the calendar or by the rancher's judgment of pasture conditions. However, some have turned to the more sophisticated and complex—and initially more expensive—system advocated by Allan Savory, discussed earlier. It gets complicated. The Durham Ranch, John Flocchini said, has fifty separate paddocks ranging in size from 300 to 2,200 acres. But rotation units of one kind or another are almost universal, even on extensive parklands such as those in Custer State Park or at the National Bison Range.

It may well be that for limited terrains, such fencing and rotation are the only way to prevent overgrazing by bison. If they are confined in an area with insufficient space and grass, bison will certainly affect grasses negatively, just as cattle do. But this can be seen primarily as an argument for providing them with much larger unfenced acreage. In Yellowstone, with its undivided 2.2 million acres, bison distribute their grazing quite satisfactorily. The problem can then be posed not as "How can we best manage bison on small properties?" but rather as "How can we amass sufficiently large territories so that bison can be left to manage themselves?"

In a natural herd such as Yellowstone's, the numbers of bulls and cows begin at approximate equality, though there is probably somewhat heavier mortality for bulls. Ranchers, however, usually keep the ratio down to about one bull for every eight or ten cows, since the overall reproduction rate cannot be increased by the presence of more bulls. Ranchers also tend to keep only younger bulls, since older ones fight more, sometimes even killing each other. (On one tour at the Terry Ranch, I did observe a bull's carcass lying in a pasture.) At the Durham Ranch, John Flocchini said, "We're always looking for different ways to do things; we experiment a lot. So we tried a ratio of 1:12 and it seemed to work okay. Now we're at 1:14."

Handling Bison

The pens and corrals of the Terry Ranch look almost identical to those on a cattle ranch, though they are built a great deal stronger and have one special feature. Continuous metal panels about five feet high line the pens so bison cannot see out; if they can see through cracks, they often try to butt or kick their way out. The process of handling is inevitably traumatic for bison, even for animals that are accustomed to being in some contact with ranch workers. Basically, the bison are lured or herded into a series of smaller and narrower catch and holding pens and finally into runways or chutes big enough for only one animal at a time. A neck-gripping device then holds the animal in place to permit inoculations, pregnancy testing, and tagging or branding (the newest technology here is dry ice branding, which is thought to be painless and does not scar the hide). Even ranchers who do not intend to handle their animals need rudimentary corrals, if only for loading bison they have sold onto trucks.

Beginning bison ranchers soon learn to respect the power of their animals, whose charges have been known to put a considerable curve into a Jeep frame and who can stick a horn into an unwary horse with astonishing quickness. "Slow and easy" is the watchword for trying to get bison to do anything. Bison generally tend to move away from people unless you have roped them, in which case they will come "up the rope"—so attempts at roping are not advised. *The Bison Breeder's Handbook* counsels, "Bison are smart. It is wiser for the handler to outsmart the bison than try to force them to do anything. . . . Think like the bison think and you will find yourself working with them rather than against them." In chutes, people sometimes calm an excited bison by covering its eyes with a jacket or simply placing a firm hand on the bison's head above the nose—this works with many bison, just as it does with horses and dogs, but it obviously must be done with great care. Electric cattle prods infuriate bison; ranchers usually get them to move by using broom handles or sticks with little flags attached, by waving hats, and through other improvisations.

With good facilities, bison can be loaded onto a truck or trailer without harm, then shipped in an ordinary cattle truck. To avoid horn damage, mature bulls are usually shipped one to a compartment, but shipping poses few problems for young bulls. Truckers, in fact, like to haul bison, John Flocchini said. "They tell me they have better balance or something—maybe they lean into the corners!" Others report that bison being hauled sometimes lie down. Long journeys are rare, but a few bison have been shipped from Denver to Hawaii. They had to be tranquilized and given antibiotics, but most of them survived.

For some prize bison as well as surplus animals, their destination may

Left: For tagging and injections, bison are run into a "squeeze chute," where they can be briefly immobilized. *Right:* Bison are handled in corrals that are very similar to cattle corrals. Here bison are being moved along with noisemakers on sticks. Photos: Michael H. Francis.

be the Gold Trophy Bison Show and Sale held yearly in Denver. Complete with judges, prizes, and auction sales, this jamboree gets bison ranchers together to exchange information, look over each other's animals, and make deals. There are also video auctions, which have the great advantage of avoiding stress on the animals and trouble for the ranchers.

Both the Terry Ranch and the Durham Ranch have sold bison to Ted Turner in recent years. Ron Thiel has sold him about 900 animals, some shipped to New Mexico. John Flocchini said that Turner is no longer buying bison, however. "He was pretty smart. He bought for about five years and then quit, though he recently did buy a few more animals. Basically he's now building his own herds. We contracted with him for five years and sold him over a thousand animals. For the last two years, they went to New Mexico, and before that, to Montana. He bought when they were in the $800 range, and now you can't touch 'em for a thousand—"

Ranching Strategies

Their wildness notwithstanding, bison can be treated almost like cattle: rounded up in the fall and sometimes even twice a year, given full "seven-shot" inoculations, culled for meat or sale to other herds, and sent out to roam again. But it is also possible and, in the long run, probably economically preferable to rely on their natural hardiness. Whatever the origins of brucellosis, a disease that bison carry, most observers say that bison themselves do not suffer brucellosis-induced abortions as severely as newly bred beef cows do. (Because it is a prime focus of contention about bison's future, brucellosis is discussed more fully in the next section.) Moreover, bison can overwinter outdoors without attention from the rancher, who might as well be in Florida, whereas the delicate if highly productive cattle breeds raised on the Plains since 1890 have had to be fed and sometimes, in bad weather, brought in to shelter—operations that obviously require constant attention and significant labor and capital expense. In addition, modern cattle have been genetically manipulated to such an extent that they often have difficulty giving birth unassisted.

Cattle and bison are not necessarily an either/or proposition for ranchers; some who have switched primarily to bison continue to raise cattle, though not in the same pastures as bison. The ranch cycle for cattle is much shorter than that for bison, and new animals are cheaper. So in a drought year, ranchers can simply sell their cattle without significant loss and cancel their land leases—whereas drastically reducing a herd of bison can be extremely costly.

Brucellosis

When the European invaders arrived in what they called the New World, they brought with them many microorganisms unknown here—smallpox, measles, the virulent form of tuberculosis, scarlet fever, and many others—which killed off roughly half of the resident Native American peoples, leaving the rest in a state of social shock that facilitated rapid conquest. (Sometimes, as in what is now the southeastern United States, the diseases moved so rapidly through the densely populated waterway villages that they outpaced actual European occupation.) But the Europeans also brought with them, deliberately or accidentally, a menagerie of domestic animals, vermin (particularly rats), and their favorite plants, many of which have proved to be what ecologists call hardy invaders.

Sometime in colonial history, an animal disease called brucellosis probably came to the Western Hemisphere with the cattle that Spanish settlers imported to Mexico. Brucellosis is not a picky disease—it infects cattle, sheep, goats, pigs, elk, even yaks, and bison. It can affect humans as undulant fever, although no cases have been verified for years. Readily treatable with a thirty-day course of antibiotics, it is, I was told by several people who have had it, like a very severe case of flu. Untreated, however, it can cause crippling arthritis and other painful aftereffects.

But the reason why some cattle ranchers are disturbed about brucellosis and have no love for bison is that brucellosis transmitted from bison to beef cows could potentially cause costly abortions in the cows—although this has never been confirmed in the field. A beef cow has perhaps sixteen or seventeen pregnancies, and ranchers do not like the possibility of losing any unborn calves. Brucellosis among cattle formerly caused financial havoc, with losses estimated at more than $1 billion for the period 1952–1981. Some $1.3 billion in federal money in addition to state and private funds has been spent on an ambitious national program, in progress since 1945, to eradicate brucellosis. The northern tier of states is now considered brucellosis free, but the disease remains in a good many herds of cattle in Texas and Oklahoma and eastward into Florida; there is also a little in California.

One side of the brucellosis controversy is represented by Donald S. Davis, professor of veterinary pathology at Texas A&M University. As his critics are quick to point out, Davis is not a field ecologist; he works under highly artificial conditions. Davis and his colleagues contend that, in a paper published in 1990, they proved conclusively that strain 2038 of brucellosis can be transmitted from infected bison to uninfected cattle, at least in confined, two-acre experimental paddocks. They conducted parallel exposures of beef cows and bison cows, and about half of each caught the disease, though testing of the bison proved troublesome and a battery of tests had to be used. Examination of tissues established the presence of microscopic lesions in the bison's sinuses and lymph nodes that were not significantly different from those found in infected cattle. When I talked to him, Davis also mentioned a case in South Dakota in which an apparently brucellosis-free cattle herd was probably infected by neighboring bison who were initially believed to be brucellosis free but later tested positive for the disease; he also cited a similar case reported in Arkansas.

In 1991, Davis and his group published a second paper describing vaccinations with brucellosis strain 19, concluding that this vaccine could not eliminate brucellosis from an infected herd of cattle and, thus, presumably not from bison either. Cattle have lived with brucellosis for tens of thousands of years; bison probably have encountered it only recently. (A few researchers suspect that bison have always harbored a different variety of the disease.) Davis believes that bison are therefore much more susceptible—vaccinating them just gives them brucellosis. Thus, he concludes, "The only proven method to eliminate brucellosis from a herd of infected animals is to test and remove the infected animals." This prescription has in fact been followed in much of the country; the current pressing question is what, if anything, to do about the bison herds in Yellowstone National Park and in Canada. (A related problem, although it receives far less attention, is widespread brucellosis in other species, particularly the large elk herds in northwestern Wyoming.)

When I talked with Davis, he said that it would not be necessary, as some people think, to kill the entire Yellowstone herd in order to eradicate brucellosis in it. Eradication has been accomplished in Canada, he says, as well as at Montana's National Bison Range and elsewhere. The staff at Yellowstone, he says, "are under a misconception that you have to round up every animal and test every one every year to eradicate the disease. That's not true. For instance, in Custer State Park, they eradicated brucellosis, and they never eradicated more than about two-thirds of their herd at one time. They did it in about a four-year period. The only bison that are dangerous [as potential transmitters] are pregnant females, so you can either spay females that are positive for the disease or abort them if they're already pregnant, and then there's not a problem." However, a statistical study of the prognosis for a similar program in Grand Teton National Park is far less optimistic. Even in twenty years, its authors contend, current vaccines used in a removal program would be unlikely to lower brucellosis rates below 20 percent.

Brucellosis, along with bovine tuberculosis, has been prevalent in the large bison populations in Canada. C. Cormack Gates, who works for the Northwest Territories government, has found that these diseases debilitate bison enough to make them easier prey for the area's numerous wolves. In fact, wolves then function to regulate bison numbers, whereas healthy bison are regulated only by the availability of food. A government panel concluded that the diseases constituted "a small but finite risk" to other bison, to cattle, to other wildlife, and to people and endorsed elimination of all brucellosis-exposed bison, which would have meant many thousands. Strong public opposition stalemated this proposal.

Some ranchers have different views about brucellosis. Roy Houck, for instance, whose herd was quarantined by the U.S.D.A. in 1978, questioned whether antibody testing—which was then and remains an inexact science—could reliably guide management of bison. He had never observed ill effects of brucellosis on his own animals' pregnancies and believed that bison have strong immune systems, as do elk, deer, and antelope. After a series of fines, Houck was forced into testing and elimination of "reactor" animals and into regular vaccinations—which, he contended, actually give bison brucellosis and thus ensure that they, in turn, will have to be killed when later tested. Over the years, blood testing led to the slaughter of many hundreds of bison that Houck was sure were healthy. (After slaughter, he claimed, only 1 percent of his animals were reliably found to have the disease.) Such skepticism is fairly widespread; a symposium in the summer of 1994 brought together researchers, Indians, and ranchers, many of whom, as mentioned earlier, suspect that brucellosis in bison is actually a different disease organism from the brucellosis in cattle (and in vaccines).

I also discussed brucellosis with Margaret Meyer, former professor of veterinary medicine at the University of California, Davis, and a leading authority on brucellosis, who has recently been collaborating on bison research with Mary Meagher, Yellowstone's primary bison expert. Meyer is skeptical about the danger of bison brucellosis affecting cattle. "It's transmitted to calves through milk, but as far as other animals go it's not transmitted through feces, but through birth fluids. A bison would practically have to abort in a cow's face to pass it on." There is a remote possibility that birth fluids could contaminate the ground, but this is no problem in normal bison and cattle habitats, where the two species keep, or are kept, to themselves. Meyer regards as conclusive proof of her position the fact that, in the winter of 1991–1992, 900 bison wandered out of Yellowstone and commingled with eight or nine cattle herds in Montana. "This was during the peak of the [bison] abortion season, about halfway through normal pregnancies. A lot of the bison were shot, incidentally, because of property damage. And in the spring, not one single brucellosis reactor [among the cattle] was found!"

Davis's rejoinder to this is that the escaped bison had not been out of the park for more than a few days before they were shot, and he also maintains that usually it is young bulls, nonpregnant heifers, and the current year's calves that wander, so pregnant cows would have been the last animals to leave the park. Moreover, cattle ranchers near the park keep their cattle separated from any wandering bison, so he is not greatly impressed by the fact that no ranch cattle got the disease. People closer to the scene, however, discount this line of argument.

Meyer thinks there is a real brucellosis problem with elk, which gather in large numbers at winter feeding stations in the Grand Tetons area. Fifty percent of the elk are thought to carry brucellosis, and they even amble into cattle ranchers' barns. Contamination, then, would seem easy. "But still there are very few instances of transmission to cattle," Meyer says. Neither from elk nor from bison can the disease, she argues, be considered a major menace to cattle. The one legal attempt to prove otherwise, a lawsuit brought by a rancher named Parker in Wyoming, vindicated her position because Parker was unable to document transmission of brucellosis and lost in court. And as far as the reverse transmission possibilities go, "unless bison are around infected cattle herds, they do not get the disease," Meyer says.

In the coming decade, brucellosis may well be wiped out among American cattle, although, as Davis says, NAFTA-stimulated growth in trade with Mexico, where brucellosis is widespread, will make eradication difficult in the border states and perhaps elsewhere as well. But there are both ranchers and researchers who believe an attempt should also be made to wipe out brucellosis among bison. The eradication efforts, as tends to happen in such enterprises, have taken on the quality of a crusade—or, rather, a biggish business in which grants and government jobs are at stake. Meyer dislikes the prospect of the slaughtering of Yellowstone bison and also points out that accurate testing of bison for brucellosis is much trickier than testing of cattle—either milk must be extracted or the animal must be killed. Meyer says she is "all for disease control," but she does not think highly of the research standards of eradication proponents. In one case, she says, "they tested three animals out of a large herd and considered that was a sample large enough to conclude that two-thirds of the herd was infected! That's just irresponsible science."

It is possible that some degree of cooperation between the two sides may develop. Public outrage would be enormous if the Yellowstone herd were decimated. Further, ranchers would receive government aid if their cows were to contract brucellosis from vagrant bison, just as they receive government indemnities when they suffer damage from elk eating their hay—very likely, in the nature of such programs, more than the cows were worth. A proposal to establish winter-range overflow areas just outside Yellowstone's boundaries, where cattle would be kept off the government allotment lands at least until bison and elk calving are over, has gathered support. But the eradication movement has a life of its own. The Yellowstone bison thus will probably remain in jeopardy from humans, though they are thriving in spite of their natural enemies. The effect of brucellosis on bison, says Meyer, is negligible. So far, the National Park Service has been disinclined to sacrifice a substantial part of the Yellowstone herd in order to attempt eradication, and for all practical purposes the debate remains a standoff.

Bison-Ranch Tourism

The Terry Bison Ranch's "safari experience" resembles that at Custer State Park. From April through mid-October, Dan Thiel takes loads of visitors onto the bison range on his homemade people mover, or tourist "train," drawn by a 1962 army surplus Studebaker truck—the whole outfit painted bright red, white, and blue. Each car of the train has rows of wooden benches and a protective roof; visitors bounce along the ranch roads at a few miles per hour, with frequent stops to observe and take photographs. The trip takes about an hour on the way out and three-quarters of an hour on the way back, and it almost always brings participants into the midst of grazing bison groups. On one recent windy summer day, when I took the trip, three other safaris had gone out, for a total of about 400 visitors for that day. The wind was strong enough to make the trip a bit difficult for some. However, no hats went flying among the bison—though if they had, they would have been left behind because for safety reasons nobody is allowed to leave the vehicle. In spite of such precautions, Dan had some difficulty in obtaining liability insurance for the rides and ended up taking an insurance agent for a convincingly safe tour.

The Terry Ranch seems to be the only bison operation that has entered to such an extent into tourism, and a number of other ranchers are watching to see how the venture works out. The Thiels now call their place a "guest ranch." They have a six-cabin motel and a seventeen-room "bunkhouse" (both booked up long in advance), a restaurant, a substantial gift shop, and a small campground, complete with a bicycle rack and a video-game room for kids. There is a weekly amateur rodeo. All this, Ron Thiel says, required almost as much investment as did the ranch itself— and it appears rather more of a gamble. Regulations that protect public safety are unfamiliar to ranchers, and it was costly (and maddening) for the Thiels to deal with fire sprinkler requirements for the restaurant and treatment regulations for the sewage system.

Fortunately, the ranch is located between Cheyenne and Denver, a major and rapidly growing metropolitan area where bison meat has been on a fair number of restaurant menus for years. The ranch is easily accessible, located next to Interstate 25 just fifteen minutes' drive south of its interchange with Interstate 80. On the summer day I visited it, the place was crawling with tourists and the restaurant was jammed. The restaurant has a pleasant bar with a pianist.

The menu offers a bison sampler plate, which other restaurants would do well to emulate; it gives you the chance to try bison steak, bison short ribs with barbecue sauce, bison kabob, bison liver pâté, "prairie oysters"

Tourists are sheltered from the sun as they observe bison on the Terry Ranch tour.

(deep-fried bison testes with dipping sauce), and bison tongue Wellington (as the cowboy-style menu puts it, "that means in some fancy kind of pastry crust"). The regular beef, chicken, and bison meals were ample, service was good, and the atmosphere of the place—a large, barnlike room built in ranch-carpentry style—was very pleasant.

The "Terry Trading Post" gift shop is impressive, displaying a bison robe on the wall and offering tourists bison coffee mugs, T-shirts and vests, many books about bison (including *The Bison Breeder's Handbook*), bison postcards, carvings of bison and other wild species, tic-tac-toe games with bison on the boards, bison bolo ties and belt buckles, and quilts with bison on them—though not the dried-bison-penis canes or putting irons I once saw in Montana. There are also plenty of nonbison offerings such as cowboy paraphernalia, toy tomahawks, film, and maps showing the locations of Indian tribes at the time of white arrival. (The shop also has a "general store" section with camping supplies, RV repair books, etc., for people staying at the ranch.) The gift shop was bustling during my visit, but tourist operations, says Ron Thiel, have too much "leakage" for his taste—they require a large work force with varied skills and meticulous management.

The Terry Ranch has been working with an outfitting company to offer approximately seventy-five trophy hunts each year. However, since bison are not normally afraid of humans, some hunters do not find the prospect of hunting them very appealing. And there have been sharp criticisms of game-hunting operations involving "penned" exotic animals, in which the hunters' prey cannot escape and may become entangled in fences. Ron Thiel says, "Well, it can be made fun. We'll haul the buffalo out—we do not let the hunter stumble around, he's already in place and we bring the buffalo to him. And as soon as the buffalo gets out of the trailer he's all excited by the new surroundings. He's been in the feedlot and now suddenly he's out on the plains and does not know how to act, except to try and get away. He starts tearing around, and the hunter has to go after him and get him…. They're just after the head and hide. Maybe one out of fifty wants the meat, though they all want to buy back a little bit, maybe twenty pounds." He chuckles happily, and adds, "At retail price!"

Management, Genetics, and the Future of a Species

As noted earlier, the tendency of cattle-management practices to control and reshape bison in the name of profit potential has self-limiting effects. If customers and potential customers begin to believe that buying bison meat is not significantly different from buying beef, the market on which the present great expectations depend may be destroyed. Zoologists also caution that culling males before maturity is genetically risky. "In nature," says Jim Shaw of Oklahoma State University, "the older males are the dominant breeders—and they carry the traits of survival. Systematic culling for desired characteristics reduces genetic variety. Herds should be culled randomly. We should keep aggressive cows, disfigured bulls. Above all, we should not breed for pretty."

In the technological gambles undertaken by modern humans, it is usually impossible to tell during the process what the outcome will be. Genetic selection and manipulation particularly seem to be a one-way street; if wildness is bred out of bison, it will be gone forever. And on some deep, symbolic level, the taming of the last wild bovine would be the taming of ourselves. Indians choose wildness for their bison without hesitation. What the white ranching community will choose remains to be seen. The sentiments of many ranchers toward bison are on the side of letting them be bison. But when it comes down to actual management choices, only providing bison with access to land in much larger acreages than is presently the norm will realistically prevent a long downward spiral for the species. Biologists have pointed out that the deleterious genetic effects of intensive management would be counteracted to a large extent if bison had access to territories large enough to permit migration and mixing of herds, similar to their historical movement patterns.

Human pressure on animals under our control is steady and unrelenting, and the effects of management on wild species are a worldwide concern. In the New Zealand Society of Animal Production's *Proceedings* for 1993, for example, you may read about how managing New Zealand elk for meat and antler harvesting is expected to result in "rapid changes in genetic, physiological, morphological, and behavioral characteristics of animals." Any people that allows its splendid native animals to be reduced to timid captivity gives itself a dispiriting model to live by.

Today, there are even bison ranches on several of the Hawaiian islands, though bison there are bothered by insects and diseases unknown in their natural habitat. There are substantial numbers in Alaska. With few exceptions, bison throughout the country are popular with neighbors, with nearby townsfolk, with tourists, and with businesses that cater to tourists. Whether in small herds or large ones, bison are again making their presence felt throughout the territory that their ancestors once dominated, and in a few other places as well.

But the future of the species is far from secure. Because a large majority of bison today live on ranches, the way they are managed is supremely important. If consumers make it known that they desire bison-meat products from free-living animals, ranchers will listen. In the chapters that follow, we will examine ways in which bison can be given the expanses of land they need and deserve.

Part III Bison Future

The transformation of the Plains from a region inhabited by native plants, native animals, and the Native Americans they supported to one in which Euro-Americans determine what grows and what dies has been more profound than we can readily grasp. A few undisturbed fragments of land, mostly hidden in parks, hint at the wonderland the region must have been before the plow, before the European grasses, and above all before imported livestock and their keepers dominated the landscape. But there is no possibility of going back to that primordial scene. We have only the possibility of going forward, in ways that are informed by lessons from the past.

All cultures slowly evolve over generations, through exposure to new ideas, new practices, new technologies. It seems likely, though by no means certain, that our information-rich, mass-media society will prove more readily responsive and adaptable than earlier, slower-moving societies. In particular, we may soon come to understand that subsidized farming and ranching on the Plains must give way to a more economically and ecologically viable culture in which the Plains are once again bison country rather than cow country. But we are only beginning to have a clear vision of what that will mean.

Modern life estranges us from nature partly because living in cities and suburbs means we see so little of it. More fundamentally, Western peoples often consider themselves a special part of creation, separate from and above other living elements of the world. Whereas Indians and Buddhists regard all living beings as kin, we distance ourselves from other animals, treating them as subservient living machines. We quantify, set prices on, and make instrumental to economic development everything that lives and grows—including, it must not be forgotten, members of our own species. In short, we display, thinks David Orr, a biophobia that runs deep in our philosophy and religion as well as in our daily lives.

Orr regards this biophobia as a kind of collective madness. "Biophobia," he writes, "shrinks the range of experiences and joys in life in the same way that the inability to achieve close and loving relationships limits a human life." He goes on to envision a "biophilia revolution" that would transform our relationships with animals. "We need animals, not locked up in zoos, but living free on their own terms. We need them for our imagination and for our sanity. We need animals for what they can teach us about courtesy and what Gary Snyder calls 'the etiquette of the wild.'"

If Orr's vision can be realized anywhere, the Plains seem the first, best place.

The Plains population includes a relatively high percentage of people whose upbringing or current work has put them in close contact with aspects of the natural world. Even though much of this contact may have been aimed at exploitation and control, many have gained through it a knowledge of natural processes more authentic than that of city people, who experience nature mostly through books and television. Paradoxically, then, if their concrete familiarity with the natural world can be connected to new ecological perspectives, Plains people may come to understand the true needs of a sustainable future for their region more acutely than do people in densely populated regions, whose dependence on the natural order is distant, abstract, and impersonal.

Not only is the natural world more visibly present on the Plains, it is also clear to thoughtful Plains people that their present way of life depends on a long and vulnerable supply line from outside. Oil brought in from abroad runs their vehicles, produces their fertilizer and pesticides, heats their houses and barns, and transports their crops. Increasingly, their essential manufactured goods are imported from Asia. Financing for crops and equipment not provided by Washington comes from banks based far away.

Moreover, traditional American virtues of thrift, self-reliance, and simple living still prevail on the Plains. Plains people buy practical cars and trucks and drive them for a long time—practices that just happen to minimize the massive environmental impacts caused by the manufacture of new vehicles. Even the disinclination of Plains people to follow current fashion fads is an ecological plus: lowered consumption of clothing reduces the surprisingly heavy environmental impacts of both fiber production and fabric dyeing and printing.

As in other largely rural regions, we find on the Plains a noisy minority whose enthusiasm for the outdoors is limited to what they can shoot, steal, or destroy. These angry people often manage to set the public cultural tone in isolated places and thus sharply limit the development of stewardship or responsibility toward the shared American landscape. All who care about the future must surely condemn the actions of those, on the Plains or anywhere, who seek only to despoil and exploit nature. Knowing the land intimately should lead Plains people to support not continued destruction but reconstruction—a process in which bison must play a central part.

A future with less dependence on uncertain foreign energy supplies and more reliance on the real long-term productivity of sun, grass, and wind should prove to have a surprising appeal on the Plains. And transformation of the land back to bison country would not be as revolutionary or difficult as some might think.

Chapter Six
Bison Country

Americans love happy endings, and the story of bison puts one within our grasp—an ending that can be brought about through reconciliation and cooperation between ranchers, restorationists, and the general public interested in preserving the vitality of our American landscape.

The story offers tremendous drama: first, the great beasts thronging the Plains; then their near extermination through vicious killing; later, the painful preservation of the few remaining animals by dedicated souls; and now, at last, bison returning in splendor to their grassland home.

Yet bison have not thus far figured significantly in the ambitious plans to preserve America's dwindling populations of large mammals that are being worked out by conservation biologists, scientists devoted to the understanding and restoration of biodiversity. ("Biodiversity" refers to the presence of a full range of species. Natural ecosystems are normally very complex, with almost infinite interconnections and interactions, but human activities tend to simplify them drastically and make them ecologically unstable by destroying the habitat requirements of many species.) Big carnivores—grizzly bears, mountain lions, wolves—extinct or on the brink of extinction in the lower forty-eight states, have gotten practically all the attention. The case for preserving habitat for these precious species, who are under pressure even in Canada and Alaska, is, of course, overwhelming in its priority. Still, it is curious that you can read in *Wild Earth,* the journal of the conservation biologists, inspiring and impressively thoughtful plans to connect remaining wilderness areas with corridors suf-

ficient to ensure necessary range for these and many other species, yet find
only asides about the bison, who in their millions also inhabited many of
these areas. That bison belong in a vast tract of plains and mountains,
amounting to almost a third of the continental United States, is evidently
still difficult to imagine, even for biologists.

However, a few defenders of biodiversity are beginning to include
bison among species of interest. George Wuerthner, for instance, mentions
them several times in "Envisioning Wildland Restoration," an article in
which he argues that urban and even suburban development is relatively
compact. If we merely stop subsidizing marginal commercial activities that
impact broad areas, the land they affect will revert to conditions undisturbed enough to support a full range of species. He writes, "The present
causes of biological diversity losses over a large percentage of the landscape are not housing and malls, but marginal farming, ranching, and logging." Wuerthner's argument is significant for the future of bison and
should prove influential. He believes that farming and ranching, which
take dominion over virtually every square foot of open land, are what stand
in the way of restoration of bison and other species, not the small towns or
even the relatively isolated cities of the Plains and Rockies. Using Anchor-
age, Alaska, as an example, Wuerthner contends that limited urban development need not compromise an entire region's potential for wildland
restoration, including some that is very "close-in." Wildlife species, he
says, "can co-exist with humans if we show tolerance and give them the
space they need." Wuerthner is a Montanan, a naturalist and photogra-
pher who knows wilderness firsthand and prizes it passionately, so his perspective is intriguing. And he goes on to suggest, as I will do in more detail,
that agricultural subsidy money diverted away from ranching and farming could be used to employ displaced people on restoration projects—including the restoration of grasslands on acres they once plowed up.

There is already a natural alliance between restorationists, with their legions of hiking, camping, and nature-watching followers, and that growing portion of the American public sympathetic to bison. On any territory
where bison could be brought back to replace livestock, and where the de-

Left: Like the thousand-pound gorilla in the riddle, a bison bull sits or lies down wherever he feels like—in this case, right next to a road. Photo: Christine Leefeldt. *Right:* Bison and tourists' cars coexist on the roads of Custer State Park.

termined government and private efforts to extirpate any life that competes with livestock come to an end, a fascinating array of other species besides the great carnivores and their main prey species—elk, pronghorn, deer, bighorn sheep, mountain goats, ground squirrels, and so on—can come back too.

Take the black-footed ferret. This lithe little animal lives with prairie dogs, who are its main prey and who also construct burrows that the ferrets often preempt. As a side effect of the campaign to poison prairie dogs, ferrets have become virtually extinct, existing only in precarious captive-breeding populations. In the natural world, as the first law of ecology reminds us, everything is literally connected to everything else. Bison obtain essential salts by licking up dried urine around prairie dog holes. The wallowing of bison evidently helps to create and maintain prairie dog habitat; hence, it would help ferrets as well. In bison country ferrets would thrive, together with hawks and golden eagles, which prey on small mammals. Altogether, then, restoring a key species like bison leads to positive effects that ramify out through the complex interrelationships that make up the grassland ecosystem. Living in an area with such a vibrant, interlinked richness of life forms would be rather more satisfying to most people than living on a landscape managed for the sole benefit of cattle.

However, some people are alarmed at the prospect of the nation's present bison population multiplying mightily to fill the ecological niche being vacated where Euro-American–style agriculture is dying out. A few bison, they feel, we could live with. But millions? Bison and traditional ideas about boundary lines and fences may not always mix easily; what matters to bison is where the grazing is. Like any species, their natural tendency is to expand their numbers to utilize the available food and fill the available range. In theory, the available range is about a third of the land area of the contiguous United States. But only a fraction of that can realistically be expected to support bison again.

Land Availability and Bison Needs

"Forests decay, harvests perish, flowers vanish, but grass is immortal!"
—*Senator John J. Ingalls of Kansas*

Where could the land be found to provide millions of acres for bison? Much will come from the conversion of failing or otherwise available cattle ranches—the same process that has led to the establishment of existing bison ranches. In addition, as Daniel S. Licht has argued, some of it should come from the withdrawal of Plains land from uses that draw more in government subsidies than the land itself is worth.

American taxpayers have been laying out billions of dollars to pay farmers not to farm "set-aside" acreage—presently some 26 million acres in thirteen Plains states, plus lesser acreage elsewhere. The U.S.D.A.'s current Conservation Reserve Program (CRP), successor to a half dozen similar programs, has as its main rationale the protection of marginal land that is hilly, especially erosive, or unproductive. Some CRP acreage is replanted with native grasses, an ecological gain. However, CRP's basic function is to keep in business farmers of wheat and other export crops. Exportation of crops and of subsidized armaments is one way the government seeks to reduce our deficit in foreign trade.

Since the typical CRP recipient is a fifty-seven-year-old part-time farmer, the program also has a welfare component. The ecological benefits of CRP are limited: because of the mostly small and scattered tracts involved and the ten-year limitation of the withdrawal contracts, only a few species, such as pheasants, have actually benefited. Large wild herbivores, though their presence is crucial to the long-term health of grasslands, have been excluded.

What is tantalizing is that while taxpayers have been paying out, over ten-year periods, some $374–$814 per acre (ranging from poor land in Montana to rich land in Iowa), the per-acre value of the land itself ranges from only $138 per acre for Wyoming short-grass prairie to $358 for North Dakota mixed-grass prairie to $1,178 for Iowa tall-grass prairie. In other words, as Licht writes, the government "could have bought many of these lands (and the buildings on them) for less than the costs of the CRP contracts." He adds that these land prices are artificially inflated by the existence of the CRP bounty; without the expectation of its continuation, the land would be worth markedly less.

Hence, if Congress could be persuaded by ordinary arithmetic, it would spend our money more wisely through land acquisition, as in fact it did long ago in buying up the Dust Bowl properties that now constitute national grasslands and BLM lands. However, the farm lobby—now primarily representing large and corporate farmers—retains enough political clout that Congress will probably continue the CRP subsidies, spending another $21 billion over the next ten years. Agricultural subsidies, like those to industries, are kept in place through the trading of political support in Washington. In CRP matters as in any political arena, change to a rational policy of land acquisition will happen only when there is widespread and vocal national backing for the idea.

Part of such support for removing Plains cropland permanently from subsidized nonproduction could be galvanized by the prospect of the land becoming productive habitat for bison and a wealth of other species, large and small. As Licht proposes, the first priority for acquisition should be lands adjacent to large existing public tracts, whether national grasslands, national forests, or state or national parks. Then, as bison-friendly policies are increasingly adopted on those lands, the benefits would be multiplied by the combined acreages. In a hypothetical way, he describes two places where such ecological reserves might make sense.

One is a seventy- by thirty-five-mile area around Badlands National Park in South Dakota. Incorporating existing federal lands would make establishment of a reserve politically easier; 40 percent of Licht's proposed Badlands reserve, in fact, already is public land. The private land that would be needed amounts to only 940,800 acres. This land and the few buildings on it are worth only $140 million, so even if the land were bought at one and one-half times its value, the cost would be only $210 million, with a high, animal-proof perimeter fence, figured at $20,000 per mile, costing another $4.2 million. For perspective, Licht notes that in 1991 alone

the federal government spent $87.4 million on 2.1 million acres of conservation (unplanted) cropland in South Dakota, and it proposes to spend $800 million more. Impacts on the state's tax system could be avoided if some of the needed land were acquired through trading away to ranchers equivalent acreage in national grasslands elsewhere in the state. The new reserve, Licht proposes, could be managed jointly by the federal government and residents of nearby Indian reservations, who could serve as wildlife managers, tour guides, and service providers, gaining economic independence and stability. Virtually every species associated with the short-grass region of the Plains could be protected in this reserve.

Crested Wheatgrass

Licht also suggests a twenty- by twenty-mile reserve in the tallgrass prairie region of eastern Iowa. Outdoor recreation would be an important component here; the proposed reserve has two canoeable rivers and is near population centers that have few recreational resources. (Iowa has few tourist attractions of any kind.) Even here, where land prices are relatively high, Licht makes a strong economic case: set-aside programs in Iowa kept 2 million acres idle in 1992, and in 1987 federal subsidies were $1.2 billion, or about $16,000 per farmer. Thus, buying out farmers and creating a reserve would result in substantial net long-term savings to the nation's taxpayers. Meanwhile, the number of farms in the proposed reserve fell by 12 percent between 1987 and 1992; in 1992 alone, 554 farms went under.

The Needs of the Wild

Reed Noss, editor of the scholarly journal *Conservation Biology* and science editor of *Wild Earth*, writes in his "Wildlands Proposal" that "reserves of 10,000 to 100,000 hectares [24,700 to 247,000 acres] might maintain viable populations of small herbivores and omnivorous animals, but large carni-vores and ungulates require reserves on the scale of 1 to 10 million hectares [2,470,000 to 24,700,000 acres]." Yellowstone National Park, with its 2,213,000 acres, is on the lower end of this range, but private ranch hold-ings, even the giant ranches belonging to Ted Turner, do not even remotely approximate the needed scale. Although viable reserves need not necessar-ily be in compact blocks as Yellowstone is, only the federal government can operate on a scale that matches the natural scale of bison.

Sheer size of range is important; so is shape. As wildlife biologists in-creasingly realize, the land connecting protected areas is of supreme im-portance. Corridors, or natural areas linking core park or reserve areas, are essential to permit genetic interchange among populations of a given species. Recently a great deal of speculation has gone into trying to deter-mine just how wide corridors must be for animals of various kinds. Solid research is scarce, but it is most advanced, luckily, where it is needed most urgently, in the area stretching from the Canadian Rockies down through Yellowstone. Some reclusive and badly threatened animals like grizzlies seem to need corridors many miles wide if the corridor is at all long. Intre-pid and social species like bison may be able to get by with quite narrow ones, conceivably only a mile wide at narrow points if the corridor length is a dozen or so miles.

Sometimes, at crucial junctures, a society needs to set bold goals for it-self if it is to accomplish anything at all. In the Wildlands Project, a group of dedicated North American wildlife biologists and their supporters pro-pose to incorporate strings of wild areas totaling millions of acres into linked habitats to ensure survival for the original denizens of this conti-nent. Although the Adirondacks and other eastern regions figure in this overall plan, its centerpiece is the Northern Rockies Ecosystem, based on what is sometimes called Greater Yellowstone and including areas in Idaho, Oregon, and Montana. This area has a good deal of bison habitat, and its integration as wild territory would be a major advance in bringing bison populations nearer to their original levels.

But in addition, we should adopt a long-term aim of creating several major bison reserves, probably amounting to 10 million acres of public land in all, farther east on the Plains. These reserves would ultimately support more than a hundred thousand bison, enough to begin to make good on restoring their former majesty. Some protection can be achieved short of government ownership, but we must face the fact that acquisition of particularly vulnerable and valuable areas will be an ecological necessity. Moreover, new strategies now exist to make these bison reserves advantageous for all.

A Fair Mechanism for Government Land Acquisition

Beyond ensuring that present government lands are again hospitable to their original inhabitants, we must dedicate new lands to them if we are ever to have bison herds amounting to even a small fraction of their historical extent. Considerable new land for bison will become available through expansion of private ranches, but public lands must also be expanded.

People who take a dim view of government land acquisition might be somewhat mollified by learning of the process developed for the Cape Cod and Point Reyes National Seashores. As Superintendent John Sansing of the Point Reyes Seashore explained to me, the first and essential element of the process is for Congress to designate an area as, in a potential Plains case, a national bison reserve. Farmers, ranchers, and other residents within the established boundaries are then bought out at market prices but are not forced off the land. They may stay for twenty-five or fifty years or even for their lifetimes, essentially on a lease basis by which the "rent" they owe the government is deducted from the payment they get for the property. In cases implemented so far, the result has been that former landowners live on the property free for as long as they wish. On the damp, grassy Point Reyes Seashore, some cattle ranchers are remaining in profitable operation under this system, but on the Plains and prairies, where many farms and ranches are marginal or bankrupt, owners (at least in areas without potential for remunerative wind-power development) would presumably wish to retain only a house and homestead area. In any case, for Plains land, the market value of which is only a few hundred dollars per acre and would be significantly smaller if government subsidies were reduced or removed, the rent would also be small because it is fixed on a percentage formula. People should thus come out better than they would had they sold out or stayed on the land as owners—but after their death, their fences and structures could be removed to create new, lasting, and large-scale bison habitat.

This strategy pushes ideological polemics aside and would offer rural Plains dwellers what they want most—the chance to stay as long as they live on the land they love—though it could not, of course, bring their children back from Denver or Chicago or Minneapolis or preserve small towns when nobody is left to inhabit them. However, on the Cape Cod National Seashore, healthy towns providing tourist facilities and rentals of summer homes remain, and similar arrangements would surely develop in bison country. The plan offers dignity and continuity to the people involved. Taxes would continue to be generated by profitable enterprises within the reserve. And for the government, it not only makes the local politics of land acquisition manageable but also reduces net acquisition costs.

Thus, if Congress wishes to ensure an economically and ecologically sustainable future for the Plains, it should set the process in motion by establishing several trial buffalo reserve areas. If congressional delegations from the Plains states are truly devoted to the future of their region, they should begin cooperating to work out feasible plans and gather support for them in the Congress.

Plains people may be better prepared for the coming of bison country than government agencies are. Whether any existing agency of the federal government is really equipped for the new task of restoring bison is a troubling question. The Forest Service has been responding to protracted criticisms of its forest-management practices (and to a series of important lawsuits that the agency lost) with programs called New Forestry or Ecosystem Management. The Forest Service may yet become capable of true multiple-use management, in which there is room for other grazers besides cattle and sheep, but so far its ecological record is at best spotty. The Bureau of Land Management's record is equally discouraging. But both seem more likely candidates to serve future sustainability concerns than the U.S.D.A.

at large, whose notions of agricultural productivity would have to be expanded on a truly revolutionary scale to encompass the fostering and sustainable exploitation of wild animals. In land matters as in everything else, however, when a constituency for something exists, a way can be found to accomplish it.

Conflicts between Bison and Humans

Large numbers of bison roaming over free-range areas, whether private ranches, lands leased by grazing associations, or government holdings, would pose some new problems, but none of these seems particularly difficult. From a distance, a grazing bison herd presents a tranquil appearance. Still, as we have seen, bison are gregarious, highly mobile (indeed, migratory), intensely status conscious, and intelligent. To foolhardy or uninformed humans, they can be dangerous. Visitors entering Yellowstone Park nowadays are handed a flyer warning them to keep clear of bison (see next page). Nevertheless, foolish behavior by tourists still leads to an occasional accident.

Like humans, bison need water as well as land, and on the Plains water tends to be in short supply except along rivers. Coexisting with large numbers of bison would require minor adjustments in human access to water in some situations. But in other areas water is fairly plentiful—as in parts of the Sand Hills of Nebraska. Here, as in many other parts of the Plains, people draw their drinking and other household water from wells and would continue to do so. A surprising amount of water is also available in the Sand Hills in beautiful spring-fed ponds, which bison must once have used as their basic water supply, and would again.

Today, all over the West, ranchers have established water sources for cattle wherever possible on their own grazing lands by drilling wells and pumping water with windmills or, more and more frequently, electric pumps. The Forest Service and BLM, dominated as they are by ranchers' concerns, have readily developed water sources for the benefit of cattle on public lands by putting in wells, tanks, stock ponds, and so on. If you fly over ranch country on the Plains, you will often be surprised at the number of small water sources that have been provided for cattle. Because cattle will not venture far from water, these lure them to graze available range. Ranchers ask the agencies for more water sources because this reduces cattle impacts, especially on riparian areas, and can thus help the ranchers secure permission to graze more animals on a given allotment of land.

If large areas are turned back to bison, most of these artificially developed and expensive water sources could be left to a slow process of decay, and bison would come to use naturally available streams and ponds as they did in eons past. This will pose problems for humans only where we persist in plow agriculture, especially in bottomlands near rivers, and thus attempt to exclude bison from cultivated fields. A large herd of bison in need of water will be impossible to exclude, so if large bison reserves evolve, they will have to include access to water, perhaps every five miles.

WARNING

MANY VISITORS HAVE BEEN GORED BY BUFFALO

BUFFALO CAN WEIGH 2000 POUNDS AND CAN SPRINT AT 30 MPH, THREE TIMES FASTER THAN YOU CAN RUN

THESE ANIMALS MAY APPEAR TAME BUT ARE WILD, UNPREDICTABLE, AND DANGEROUS

DO NOT APPROACH BUFFALO

Let us imagine now that the processes we have studied lead to the presence of several million bison on large areas in reservations and parks and on both large and small areas of private and publicly owned grazing lands. On these parts of the Plains, cow country has given way to bison country. The condition of the grasses is steadily improving, and many other species are directly or indirectly benefited by the return of the bison. But what changes should we expect in the lives of humans, especially in the small towns that would remain scattered throughout the region?

Early towns were usually located on rivers that could be reached by boat, and those that survive and prosper are generally on waterways still. In areas that become largely bison country, such towns will have to be protected to some degree from wandering bison. The problem is not a severe one, however; Yellowstone Park functions perfectly well with large numbers of free-ranging bison everywhere, including the heavily used areas around the hotels. (Bison are fond of the lush grass found there.) Millions of annual visitors mix happily with thousands of bison without significant problems.

But bison could potentially interfere with town life in ways serious enough to necessitate fencing them out, rather as medieval towns and cities were walled to keep out animals and bandits. Residents of the Alaskan town depicted in the television program *Northern Exposure* easily tolerate the occasional presence of a moose who ambles through the program's opening shots. But real Plains people with vegetable and flower gardens would want to protect them, and streets and sidewalks, school playgrounds, athletic fields, picnic areas, and similar public venues would need to be kept free of bison.

On the basis of experience to date, this would not be a very difficult task, though it is harder than keeping out cattle or sheep. Ordinary roadway cattle guards, which measure about six feet across and keep cattle in bounds, are easily jumped over by bison. But double guards (twelve or even sixteen feet across) would suffice on roads coming into towns, especially if the ground under the guard rails is kept clear or covered with light-colored gravel. These work well at the entrances to the National Bison Range in Montana and the Fort Niobrara National Wildlife Refuge in Nebraska.

In public refuges established some time ago, like those just mentioned and some of Custer State Park's lands, the standard fence comprises five or six feet of woven wire with a couple of strands of barbed wire on top. (It is said that if a bison can get its nose over a fence, it may well decide to jump it.) However, recent experience by ranchers indicates that fencing requirements are actually much more modest so long as grass is ample.

One current tendency is to use a nonbarbed but very strong wire called New Zealand Wire, running in six or occasionally eight strands on wooden posts. A New Zealand wire fence costs about the same per mile as a five-strand, two-ply barbed-wire cattle fence and less than half as much as a woven-wire fence of equal height. According to Dan Thiel of the Terry Bison Ranch, unbarbed wire is better because bison like to scratch on barbed wire and thus will knock its fence posts down.

Ranchers love to tell stories, and there is a good fence story from the filming of *Dances with Wolves:* a bison got separated from the excited herd, thirty of whom had just broken through a stout woven-wire fence, and was trying to rejoin them by going through the fence in another place. As an onlooker reported, "The woven wire bowed in thirty feet as post after post

Bison crossing a river. Many rivers on the Plains are shallow much of the year, but bison are quite capable of swimming across them if necessary. Photo: Michael H. Francis.

broke. The wire zinged a mile up the ridge, but the fence held and catapulted that buffalo up the hill. Head over heels it flew past the cameramen. When it stopped rolling it got to its feet, shook its head, spotted the hole the others had made earlier, and shot through it at full speed."

No fence, however, not even high-strength woven-wire fence, can withstand a charging herd of bison, any more than it could a runaway truck—but bison herds very rarely pose that problem. In fact, electric fencing is becoming the first choice of bison ranchers for their internal fences, though they often use heavier fencing for their outside boundaries. Electric wire is the simplest and cheapest of all fencing to string, and it is easy to maintain as well. John Flocchini of the Durham Ranch, who has installed some seventy miles of fencing in recent years, says, "We educated ourselves to the fact that you do not need a physical barrier for the animal if you can create a mental barrier. If you saw the electric fence that we're building now, you would not believe that it would hold a buffalo." Flocchini reports that they have gradually worked down from three electric wires to two and, in some internal fences, to one; this is facilitated by the practice of rotating the animals from pasture to pasture every two or three days. "They want to move—they're ready to go," says Flocchini, "and if they're not stressed, you can hold them probably with one wire." (In the very dry conditions in his area, though, two wires work best—one serving as the electrical ground that the soil is too dry to provide.) As another example, electric fencing set about eight to ten inches inside six-foot-high barbed-wire fencing is used at The Nature Conservancy's new Oklahoma preserve.

Bison are intelligent animals; they get accustomed to staying clear of electric fences, though in introducing them it helps to make the fence wires easily visible, by attaching bits of rag, for instance. Homesteads located on the edges of bison ranches do not report any serious problems with bison breaking in and eating shrubbery or gardens. It seems likely, then, that the perimeter security needs of many small towns could be met with electric fencing around the town and highway guards on the roads into it. If special attractants were present, like water sources that bison might smell from a

Bison are not shy about using roads, which can help them economize on the effort they expend in getting around. Here, bison cross a bridge near Mammoth in Yellowstone National Park. Photo: Michael H. Francis.

distance, heavier fencing would be required. Ranchers tell of temporarily using bright orange plastic ribbon tape to keep bison from going through holes in fences. People forced to be observant of bison attractants and repellents would surely invent ingenious ways to protect whatever needed to be protected from free-roaming bison .

How much personal hazard would people experience if bison country were again full of bison? Experience suggests that having a lot of bison around is not significantly more dangerous than having a lot of cars around. Though very observant animals, bison are not much concerned with humans. In historical times, they often kept on grazing while outlying members of their herd were shot down by stealthy hunters. Such behavior earned them the adjective "placid" from some writers, but it is not a term that Mary Meagher would use. A widely published and respected scientist, Meagher has been Yellowstone's ranking bison expert for decades. A wiry, slight, but intense woman, she studied at the University of California, Berkeley, with the world-famous naturalist Starker Leopold and has spent most of her professional life at Yellowstone. A staunch defender of the park's bison, she is quick to point out misconceptions and pseudoscientific thinking.

Meagher passes some of her days sitting quietly with her notebook near a group of bison. The encounter, she says, is on their terms, so she never anticipates trouble, though even bison long habituated to interaction with humans can never be considered tame. They come up to inspect her, sniffing and listening and looking her over with their great, red-rimmed eyes. Bison are obviously in intimate and alert contact with what is going on around them, and they can be spooked into stampedes by what seem to humans negligible disturbances. They are also curious and fearless; Dale Lott, a biologist at the University of California, Davis, who has worked extensively with bison, reports that they may walk into your house to look around if you leave the door open.

When you watch bison quietly and attentively, you soon observe that groups of bison have dominance structures—some bison get out of the way of others—and the ranking system is enforced by butting if necessary. People who live around bison would have to understand the importance of proper deference in bison's eyes. This concern ought to seem familiar to us, since humans also display a wide variety of dominance behavior. On city streets, for instance, some people, regardless of physical size, insist on dominating others by keeping straight on their path, and others give way. We have conventions like keeping to the right that reduce and simplify our contentions for dominance, but dominance interactions occur in our lives many times each day—in speech, in gesture, in gaze, and with friends and family as well as strangers. Being highly social animals, bison are well attuned to dominance matters. Mature, experienced cows generally lead the herds, and a sort of pecking order prevails among the cows below them. Because of their larger size, bulls can generally exert intermittent dominance over cows.

It is small wonder, then, that occasionally a bison takes exception to some human action that infringes on its expectation of other creatures' giving way. A friend told me that he was driving his Volkswagen bug with headlights on through Yellowstone one summer at dusk when he approached a bison bull standing in the road, looking his way. My friend slowed down and prepared to drive cautiously around the bison, but the bison was not mollified. He charged the VW head on, stopping it cold and causing minor damage to the front end, then shook his head and sauntered away, having evidently made his point—perhaps something like "Get those goddamn lights out of my eyes!" At any rate, in some way the VW had apparently "disrespected" the bison, who undertook to restore proper relations of dominance and submission. My friend, shaken but unhurt, drove on.

To get some perspective on just how dangerous it might be to have a lot of bison around, we can compare recent Yellowstone statistics on fatalities and injuries from bison with those from cars. This is not an altogether fanciful comparison, since cars are, after all, bison size, bison weight, and bison fast. (Bison can run at thirty-five miles per hour for five miles. It is legal—but not always safe—to drive as fast as forty-five miles per hour on Yellowstone's roads.)

The people involved in these encounters—and, in fact, in all the encounters reported by the park since 1978, when figures were first kept—

were doing extremely foolish things, such as backing up toward a bison while being photographed by friends. One recent incident involved two men who approached to within ten or fifteen feet of a bison so that a friend could take their picture. As the friend prepared to snap, he noticed that the bison was beginning to charge, but his warning came too late. One of the men received a severe puncture wound on his thigh, which sent him to the hospital briefly.

The sole Yellowstone fatality, in February 1989, involved a forty-seven-year-old snowmobiler who stopped his machine at night and waved his companions on; when they came back for him later, they found him severely injured and bison hair clinging to his snowmobile. No bison were visible at the scene, and the nature of the altercation between man and beast remains unclear; bison usually tolerate the presence of snowmobiles on the winter trails shared by the two species.

A characteristic Park Service accident summary from July 1993 gives

YELLOWSTONE INJURIES: CARS VS. BISON

	Injuries from Cars	Injuries from Bison
Summer 1990 Season* (July and August)	3	0
Summer 1991 Season (July and August)	3	1
Summer 1992 Season (July and August)	7	1
Total	13	2

*Yellowstone does not keep all its statistics by month, so these are yearly figures. However, since virtually all of the park is closed to cars during the snowy months, it can be assumed that the auto accidents must have occurred during the summer. Source: Yellowstone National Park police records.

the flavor of most Yellowstone bison accidents: "A 50-year-old man from Jacksonville, Florida, was gored by a bull bison when he approached the animal within two feet. The incident occurred near the Madison off-ramp at the Old Faithful interchange. The man approached the bison, turned his back to the animal, and when he turned back the bison charged and gored him in the left shoulder and upper right thigh. A companion of the man drove him to the Old Faithful Clinic where he received initial medical treatment. He was later transported by Yellowstone and Grand Teton ground ambulance to St. Johns Hospital in Jackson, Wyoming, where he was treated and released." (And presumably swore never again to walk up to a bison.)

Aside from the luckless snowmobiler's case, injuries from Yellowstone bison have been painful but not fatal, even for tourists who surprise bison by accident and consequently get butted. The park's accident reports give the overwhelming impression that bison intend not to kill people but just to get them out of their way. It is known that there are occasional ill-tempered bison bulls, and I have heard a few third-hand reports about bison elsewhere that knocked people down and then stamped on them with their forefeet. However, the documented Yellowstone accidents involve people who were simply asking for trouble, such as the father with camera ready who sent his nine-year-old daughter within three or four feet of a bison, who promptly butted her, giving her minor bruises. Only once, in June 1992, did the Park Service decide that a bison was displaying unreasonably aggressive behavior and kill it; it had gored a seventy-year-old man who approached it too closely. Overall, bison display tolerance toward humans despite aggressive human behavior: teenagers in Yellowstone, for example, have been known to tease bison, and one adult has been arrested by park police for harassing the animals. Goring and butting incidents happen from time to time in other parks; Custer State Park in South Dakota, for instance, has had three goring incidents since 1987, none of them fatal or even requiring hospital care, with a bison population ranging from 900 to 1,500 and hundreds of thousands of visitors.

To continue our perhaps quirky quest to assess the relative dangers of cars and bison, we must know how many cars and how many bison frequent Yellowstone. The total numbers of autos for July and August of our three years are 405,805; 428,955; and 444,190. Since these cars remain in the park an average of forty hours, or 1.7 days each, the actual numbers present on any given day were roughly 23,870; 25,233; and 26,129. During this time, total daily bison populations were 1,625; 1,390; and 2,053. Hence:

WHO'S MORE DANGEROUS TO WHOM		
	Injuries per Car	Injuries per Bison
Summer 1990	.000126	0
Summer 1991	.000119	.00072
Summer 1992	.000268	.00049
Total	.000513	.00121

The danger in both directions is thus minute, though bison come out overall as roughly twice as dangerous as cars. (Incidentally, the extremely shy grizzlies in Yellowstone cause only one injury for every 1.5 million visitor-days.) A prudent person should watch out carefully for both cars and bison. As we have seen, bison presumably would be fenced out of towns and cities where pedestrians abound. But even in free-range settings, having numerous bison around would be essentially the same as having a lot of cars around. We have been living with that for some time now.

Although bison may be comparable to automobiles in hazardousness, large numbers of free-ranging bison would obviously pose some novel traffic problems. There would have to be, explicitly or implicitly, a new rule of the road in free-range bison areas: "Bison always have the right of way."

But since the act of getting into a car transforms even the gentlest of human beings into something considerably less nice—no longer a citizen but a driver—we can anticipate driver vindictiveness against bison similar to that which is sometimes visited upon bicyclists and pedestrians. When a car hits a bison, however, the mass of the bison is likely to damage the car at least as much as the bison is damaged, so the first time a driver deliberately aims for a bison will probably be the last.

Not that bison-car crashes would be entirely novel; in free-range cattle country there are plenty of close encounters of the bovine kind. A friend of mine was once driving along a deserted road in Nevada in the middle of the night when a dark-colored bull leaped from the shoulder. In the resulting collision, the bull hurtled onto the car's hood and the car was nearly totaled. My friend was battered severely, and the bull suffered unknown but probably not terminal damage, since he disappeared. Bison on the whole are bigger, heavier, and quicker than cattle, so encounters with bison are likely to be still more to the disadvantage of drivers than are those with cattle.

Interstate highways are even now, of course, protected by sturdy fences along their entire lengths, with a few breaks at exits and interchanges, so we need not imagine vagrant bison appearing often in their lanes. But if we ever get to the point at which bison inhabit tens of millions of acres of unfenced land, bison migrating across major highways would be a problem that would need to be addressed. We are most unlikely ever to have unfenced areas large enough to accommodate herds approaching the historically reported concentrations of animals, but herds could conceivably grow enough that they could take fifteen minutes to cross an unprotected road if they decided to do so, resulting in delays similar to those of construction projects.

Thus, in some areas it would probably be thought necessary to provide ways for large numbers of bison to cross interstates and a few other main roads without interfering with our precious right to get from point A to point B at maximum speed. One solution would be to construct artificial hills that are really overpasses for bison or, from the cars' point of view, tunnels over the tops of which bison could cross. These would have to be quite substantial affairs, perhaps several city blocks wide, so that a herd of bison would cross them readily. Like humans, bison are adept at following the path of least resistance. Since the mature cows that guide herds' movements have very good memories of the landscape and its resources, these overpasses would not have to be terribly numerous—perhaps one every ten miles or so. Moreover, they would not be unprecedented. In Florida, underpasses have been constructed to accommodate movement of the endangered Florida panther, and India may build wide elephant bridges over irrigation canals.

One clue about potential relations between cars and numerous free-ranging bison comes from Sweden. Moose are numerous in Sweden and wander freely. It is reported that someone driving 12,500 miles a year there faces lifetime odds of one in ten of someday hitting a moose. This may sound ominous, but it is far less than our chances of being involved in an automobile accident.

In bison country, people might well come to give somewhat less automatic priority to roads. Roads open remote areas to the risks of roadkill of wildlife, and to logging, mining, poaching, development, pollution, use of off-road vehicles, and other ecologically disruptive human activities. A case can be made—and is regularly and passionately made by an organization called Alliance for a Paving Moratorium—that we have far too many roads and that we would do the environment a magnificent favor by closing a lot of them. (In a delicious irony, the Alliance is headed by Jan Lundberg, son of the Lundberg who published a famous oil-industry newsletter.) The Wilderness Society, now a broad-scale environmental organization, was founded in 1935 to protect wilderness by fighting roads.

In areas where the Forest Service has for decades been extending subsidized road access for timber companies to practically every last stand of trees, conservationists aim at "putting roads to bed"—removing pavement or gravel surfaces, regrading the land to its original contours, and reestablishing natural drainage and vegetation. (The Forest Service sometimes claims to close roads after timber harvests, but a study in Oregon showed that only 21 percent of such roads were actually closed.) Totally roadless areas have become extremely rare in the United States and usually qualify for official wilderness status, which almost always prohibits road building.

The rolling Plains grassland habitat natural to bison has no such unroaded areas or wilderness, and few national parks, for that matter. However, since the region's rural human population has declined so drastically, many Plains country roads already see little use and would be taken over by vegetation if left alone for a century or so. We could help nature take its course, and in the short run save a lot of road-maintenance outlays for hard-pressed county governments, by eliminating roads that are not really needed or worth the upkeep. On those that remain, the situation would be rather as it is now—bison, like slow-moving tractors, require drivers to take it easy and use some common sense.

In sum, the risks of conflict between humans and bison seem minor, and well worth taking compared with enduring the long-term drain on the public purse of subsidized cattle ranching with its uncertain future. In bison country, we can share the rural land with bison and other grazers of the Plains in a relationship of mutual support. In doing so, we can regain a comfortable sense of integration with beneficent nature that has been sorely lacking in American life.

Chapter Seven
Real Productivity

"Not only does nature operate on 'current income,' it does not mine or extract energy from the past, it does not use its capital reserves, and it does not borrow from the future. It is an extraordinarily complex and efficient system for creating and cycling nutrients, so economical that modern methods of manufacturing pale in comparison to the elegance of natural systems of production."
— *William McDonough*

"Mining" is a term that is applied to water and soil as well as to minerals, meaning the extraction and loss of a nonrenewable resource. Thus, irrigation farmers with their high-powered pumps are mining the High Plains aquifer (of which the Ogallala is the best-known component)—an underground storage tank of fresh water laid down during hundreds of thousands of years, stretching from South Dakota to Texas. Everybody knows that the aquifer will in time be drawn down to the point at which pumping is no longer feasible, initially in those areas where the saturated layers are thinnest but in the end everywhere. Abandonment of irrigation is well under way in Texas and Oklahoma and is moving northward; Nebraska has the "thickest" water layers, so irrigation will remain possible there longer.

Monocrop, agribusiness-style farming, which leads to loss of soil fertility and to heavy erosion, is also a kind of mining and has a fixed time horizon. For example, it is seldom noted that the national doubling of crop production between 1945 and 1975 required a forty-fold increase in fertilizer use. Payoffs from fertilization have been falling, so this ratio has become still worse. Moreover, the layer of topsoil in which plants can grow is thin on the Plains, and nationally 54 percent of pastureland is overgrazed and subject to severe erosion. Even in deep-soil parts of the Midwest, like Iowa and Illinois, erosion has decreased topsoil depth alarmingly. In a devil's bargain, American agriculture's grain exports are earning foreign exchange by selling off, in effect, nonrenewable soil and water, and in return we are buying nonrenewable foreign oil. By one of those stunning ironies history sometimes presents to us, the amounts involved almost balance. In due course, a fearsome equity will prevail: we will be out of farmable soil and water and the oil states will be out of oil.

It is often argued by the technocratically minded people who preside over most current agricultural research that the destruction of traditional farming and its replacement by modernized farming (which usually appears, in gross terms, more productive per acre) is worth the social and biological costs, or at least that these costs are inevitable. However, current agricultural practices, unlike the solar-reliant traditions of the three or more preceding millennia, depend heavily on industrial inputs—essentially, on oil. They are net-energy-negative; that is, they use up more fossil-fuel energy, in the forms of fertilizer, pesticides and herbicides, equipment fuel, and so on, than they produce in food energy. According to the research of David Pimentel and his colleagues at Cornell University, we put about 300 calories of fossil-fuel energy into our agricultural system for every 100 calories of food energy we get out of it. (Other studies have arrived at still higher, less-favorable ratios.) In other words, we would be much better off if we could figure out a way to turn oil into some kind of porridge and eat it directly rather than running it through plants first. Although net-energy-negative agriculture may continue for some decades, its long-term prospects are grim.

The rises in output per acre (and, sometimes, in profitability) of which agricultural technologists are so proud are thus really an achievement of the oil industry. And oil is a finite resource; at current rates of consumption, its exhaustion as a viable energy source is predicted to occur in a matter of decades. There will always be some oil left underground, and as it gets increasingly expensive, more arduous and expensive drilling, extraction, and probably rerefining technologies will be worth bringing into play to keep some of it available for lubrication, plastics manufacture, and other high-priority purposes. But other energy sources will gradually displace it as a fuel—including sustainable solar technologies, whose "fuels," sunlight and wind, are free. Wider use of coal and liquid fuels made from coal is likely for a time, especially in China, but coal's contribution to global warming is far worse than that of oil or gas. In one way or another, the long drama of human exploitation of stored solar energy is coming to an end; before long, we must learn to live on current solar income.

It is remotely conceivable that some massive new source of energy might be developed that would not be impossibly expensive, or dangerous, or damaging to the environment. (Extensive use of nuclear fusion, for example, if it could ever be deployed at competitive costs, would generate immense amounts of heat and thus itself exacerbate global warming.) In that highly unlikely case, net-energy-negative agriculture could continue—unless climate change rendered it impossible. However, on the basis of what we now know, modern agriculture cannot be considered sustainable; it is limited by dependence on fossil inputs, and hence its support for the growing billions of earth's people is increasingly precarious.

A thoroughly sun-dried "buffalo chip" is durable and virtually odor free and burns with a slow, hot flame. Left on the ground, it provides a habitat for many organisms, from fly larvae to beetles. Decomposing, it sends nutrients back into the grassland life cycle.

In this perspective, the emptying out of farmers from the Great Plains is a signal that sustainability matters in the real world—that we cannot defy nature. Petroleum inputs and government subsidies combined have not been able to save farming on the Plains. Only new forms of net-energy-positive agriculture will survive there in the long run.

The appeal of bison is that they can utilize the fundamental solar productivity of the Plains, which creates the enduring wealth of grass, in a sustainable way. Nobody knows exactly how many bison could be maintained on the Plains without damage from overgrazing, but in light of the history of the species it is probably at least tens of millions, at practically no expenditure of fossil fuels—and, as we shall see in detail later, in combination with the generation of renewable, sustainable energy through wind power.

The lure of the Plains, then, is that we could begin to practice sustainable agriculture there, lighting a beacon to show that new ways of producing food are possible, practical, and profitable.

Far out on the fringes of modern technology, visionaries are beginning to devise "living machines"—complex arrangements of hundreds of organisms that metabolize the wastes of other species and produce a wide variety of useful products. In a related line of development, "zero-emissions" industrial clusters are being planned, in which the wastes of every industrial process become the feedstocks of others. Indians hearing of such developments may well smile, since these miraculous modern achievements have been accomplished since time immemorial by bison. Bison had the capacity to synthesize hard, durable bone; they supplied strong and flexible sinew; their bodily fluids were useful in many ways; their hides and hair could be manipulated into forms of a thousand uses. And yet these walking factories, if we may call them that, were nature-designed and self-sustaining. They required no husbandry by humans, did not befoul their surroundings with toxins or undermine the resources they depended on, and supported directly or indirectly humans and many other species. If we are looking for models of productive systems on which we might hope to rely for the long-term future of our species, then bison surely deserve our closest attention.

Economics and Sustainability

Our current economic notions put us fundamentally out of sync with long-term or even short-term biological reality. Under the institutions of modern capitalism, the time horizon within which we make decisions has contracted to well under a lifetime. This maladaptive limitation is formalized in our concepts of interest and discount rate. These may seem like arcane and specialized notions, but it is worth a brief digression to examine how they determine what we consider feasible and what we dismiss as an impossible dream. An informed citizenry concerned about its future cannot afford to be ignorant of their effects.

The discount rate is interest paid for an investment in advance rather

A herd of bison moves purposefully across the landscape, representing an incalculable richness of natural productivity. Photo: Michael H. Francis.

than periodically over the life of a loan, and it functions as a way for banks and other financial institutions to compare the present value of something with its future value. Thus, it has critical consequences for all human activity. If the discount rate is set at 6 percent, for instance, it is a way of assuming that half the benefits of an investment accrue during its first twelve years. At a 6 percent discount rate, building a cheap school and replacing it in fifteen years would appear more economically efficient than building a durable school designed to last a century. If central banks such as the U.S. Federal Reserve set interest rates high in hopes of averting inflation, an investment (as in terracing land, improving pasture, or planting windbreaks) must pay off quickly or capital cannot be found for it. It is only when interest rates are low, in the vicinity of 2 percent or 3 percent, that long-term planning becomes economically feasible. In low-interest periods like the Great Depression of the 1930s, socially ambitious projects such as the Golden Gate Bridge and Hoover Dam can get built. In such periods, which have been rare in recent times, farmers can realistically contemplate the sorts of property improvements that have traditionally been essential to sustainable peasant agriculture: houses and barns meant to last through the generations, wood-lots or coppice areas, fallowing and crop rotation, maintenance of banks of streams and lakes, and prevention of overgrazing on pastures.

A people whose decisions are economically correct but are systemati-cally incorrect biologically is likely to be indulging in suicidal behavior. As Gretchen C. Daily and Paul Ehrlich have written, "There are numerous sit-uations (sometimes called social traps) in which the immediate, local in-centives are inconsistent with the long-run, global best interest of both the individual and society, and with the maintenance of carrying capacity. . . . One of the most pervasive causes of social traps is the natural human ten-dency to discount costs that appear remote, either in time or space." In seeking sustainability, we will find it necessary to question currently ac-cepted economic doctrine, which has evolved to suit the priorities of ex-pansionist capitalism. We must find ways of financing the necessities of survival, even if that requires us to modify cherished economic conven-tions. New times require new ideas on every level.

Lessons from the Past

A few ranchers, mindful of the history of their business, think of bison in somewhat the same terms as the old longhorn cattle. For a period after they escaped the Spanish in Mexico and experienced a population explosion on the Texas grasslands, longhorns were almost entirely wild. Cowboys las-soed and branded them, then allowed them to roam free on open range, mixing with the animals of other owners. It is attractive to think of raising bison in this low-cost way, quite differently from modern cattle—with min-imal handling (or "working") of the animals and on extremely large, un-fenced acreages. To achieve these more efficient operating units, the hold-ings of ranches must be combined; as we have seen earlier, this can be accomplished through an expansion of existing grazing associations or co-operatives. Although grazing associations banding together to run bison would not amount to a true commons in the ancient sense I will discuss later, such arrangements could enable large bison herds to be managed through joint rather than individual ownership of animals. Similar possibil-ities on the reservations appeal to Native Americans; Euro-American ideas of private property do not mesh with Indian belief systems. And these are possibilities that the roaming nature of bison strongly encourages.

There are intriguing ramifications here that go back far beyond the adoption of settled agriculture, to prehistoric gathering and hunting cultures. Relying on bison roaming through vast areas could put us in contact again with our evolutionary past, and in surprisingly reassuring ways. Recent anthropological research on remnant Paleolithic peoples in Africa and Australia have shown that far from living lives that were starving and brutish, so-called primitive people who depended on gathering and hunting for their food had far more leisure than moderns do and an easy sense of abundance instead of our anxious sense of scarcity. They even ate a more varied and nutritious diet.

On the North American continent, European invaders called the Plains Indians savages. Yet, as historian Larry Barsness remarks, "These independent men and women lived far more comfortable lives, had far more time to devote to practicing their religions, more time for speculation and ceremony, more time to while away in gambling, in game-playing, in caring for the young and old—more time for doing as they pleased—than any European peasant, craftsman, or soldier."

Some researchers suspect that we have been going downhill ever since the gathering and hunting days. Noting that one-third to one-half of humanity regularly goes to bed hungry nowadays, Marshall Sahlins writes, "The amount of hunger increases relatively and absolutely with the evolution of culture." Our not-so-primitive predecessors seldom went hungry for more than a day or two, worked only three to five hours a day, and enjoyed frequent naps.

Like the bison-hunting tribes of the Plains, earlier hunters and gatherers moved around a lot and hence owned what seems to us few material possessions—everything of real value had to be portable. In warm climates, earlier peoples did not bother to store food, since it was reliably plentiful in one form or another. They kept their populations modest, practiced production for use rather than for wages or profit, and lived leisurely, comfortable lives. Ironically, the attachment contemporary ranchers have to their cattle-based way of life may reflect the deep satisfactions that our distant ancestors felt in their intimate dependence on the herbivores of their era. And Indians' desire to restore bison to a central place in Plains ecology may reflect more than their spiritual beliefs or a desire for culturally appropriate reservation enterprises.

Bison Productivity

Bison are a distinctly dryland species, and they have different ways from cattle of utilizing the biological productivity of the Plains. Like other wild animals, they make less intensive demands on the land than do livestock, and they are probably more productive per acre. It has been found in research on African grasslands, for example, that gazelle are three times more productive than cattle. Bison and other wild mammals even drink less water than do cattle; in the case of elk, in whom these matters have been precisely studied, cattle weigh about twice what elk do but consume three to five times the water. Cattle deposit fifty pounds of manure and twenty pounds of urine daily, usually near or in creeks, ponds, or lakes. As Lynn Jacobs observes, "Few other large animals evacuate their bowels and bladders directly into their own water sources."

It would be difficult to overstate the destructive impact of cattle on the planet. Some 50 percent of the earth's land mass is grazed by 1.3 billion cattle (plus 2.7 billion sheep, goats, and other livestock—goats being a primary agent of global deforestation and desertification). In addition, 50 percent of all freshwater used in America goes for livestock production, and livestock consume 70 percent of our total grain production. Cattle raising is extremely energy intensive. Cattle are normally kept on rangeland only until they are ready for "background" operations in which about 50 percent of their food is grain, and then for feedlot operations, in which 80 percent is grain. It takes six to eight pounds of grain to produce one pound of beef—but since only about half of a steer is edible, the pound of steak on your table took twelve to sixteen pounds of grain to produce. Such figures explain why meat eating as a cultural trait puts such a heavy burden on the earth and why ecological as well as health claims are now widespread for vegetarianism.

Learning the details of beef production has also been driving many Americans away from meat eating. "Agricultural by-products" fed to cattle include feathers, manure, and ground-up dead cows, and, of course, American cattle are routinely given large doses of hormones and antibiotics, enough of which remains in their meat to cause some fastidious countries to refuse to import it.

Because bison are more productively adapted to grasslands than are cattle, they will gradually gain partisans for both ecological and economic reasons. And because they naturally fit the land without requiring human management, we need to learn again to treat bison as wild but usable animals, just as the Native American peoples of the Plains did until little more than a century ago. This should be the direction of public-lands policy, as it is of Indian tribal policy. On private lands, we may also be able to move in that direction through a slow, steady increase in size of bison ranches that would permit minimal management. Ted Turner may acquire further ranches, and other wealthy individuals and perhaps even agribusiness corporations might follow suit. But more modest spreads, in the range of

Bison calf nursing. To start milk flowing, a calf gives its mother's udder a quick upward butt. Cows are intensely protective of their calves, and the whole herd also will cooperate to defend calves if necessary. In today's market, a bison calf is worth about four times as much as a beef calf. Photo: Michael H. Francis.

30,000 to 50,000 acres, seem likely to develop in great numbers, as well as cooperatives consolidating acreages into working ranges on the same scale—enough so that free-ranging bison could be expected to thrive in a highly productive and sustainably low-management way. A good bit of this acreage could and should be public grazing lands leased from government agencies with leverage to encourage the ranchers to work together.

Sustainable Farming

"There is no higher standard of your performance than the land and its natural community."

—Wes Jackson

The Farm Bill of 1990 called for a research program in sustainable agriculture and included a sidelong glance at conservation of fish and wildlife habitat. The U.S. Department of Agriculture has reluctantly investigated low-input mixed farming (sometimes called organic farming), and the recognition is growing that this approach may enable many farmers to survive if subsidies are cut or withdrawn, though at present farmers are forced to continue monocultures in order to benefit from price-support programs. A few state universities' agricultural schools are also showing interest in sustainable farming practices. However, for the new thinking that is needed to enable us to move toward net-energy-positive agriculture, we must look outside the establishment.

Wes Jackson, head of the Land Institute, a research station just outside Salina, Kansas, lives about seventy miles from the farm where he was brought up. He travels the world lecturing on his particular expertise, perennial polycultures: mixed perennial plants which, when all relevant costs are acknowledged, prove more productive per acre than the cultivated annual grasses human populations depend on (chiefly wheat, rice, and corn). Moreover, these polycultures protect the soil from erosion, one of the most intractable problems of monoculture farming. Jackson is a practical sort, with the hands-on resourcefulness that farmers need to cope with the unexpected, and a wry wit. But he also writes philosophically sophisticated and technically erudite books, appears at learned conferences, and strategizes with urban grant makers who support his Institute. He is also a poet; in one of his books, in a discussion of human-caused erosion, he speaks of "native plants and animals, the only assured guardian against the seaward flush of hard-earned soil to a watery grave." When I visited him, he was wearing his normal farmer's bib overalls. It was a hot summer day; he offered the traditional midwestern refresher, ice water, and aimed the room's fan to blow my way.

The Land Institute is situated just where the high Plains to the west descend to the wetter prairies that meet them from the east. The region was once bison territory, and there are bison there again. Several people in the vicinity are raising bison and marketing meat on local delivery routes, and the state's Maxwell Game Preserve, not far away, has a small bison herd. Even though Jackson is a passionate defender of farming, not a rancher, he believes that bison have a role to play on farms, here and probably farther east. His vision for the future is exemplified not only in the research work of the Institute but also in plans for a sustainable-farming operation out-

Bison cow wallowing. (Note the small size of her udder compared with a dairy cow's.) Because of their humps, bison cannot roll entirely over—they lie down and wallow on one side at a time. Dust and mud caked in their fur provide some protection from insects. Photo: Michael H. Francis.

side an almost-abandoned nearby town, Matfield Green. (Jackson has been buying empty houses in Matfield Green with money he received from a MacArthur Fellowship. The Land Institute has also purchased several properties, including the elementary school and the high school gym. Jackson hopes to revive the community on a new, permanent basis.)

One of the Land Institute's projects is its Sunshine Farm, which Marty Bender has been analyzing from an energy, materials, and labor standpoint in an ongoing nine-year research program. A quarter of its tilled acreage would be needed to support "traction"—hauling, plowing, threshing, and so on, done partly by draft animals and partly by a diesel running on oilseed oil. Another quarter would have to be devoted to nitrogen production through the planting of legumes; unless the ability to fix nitrogen from the air can be bred or transplanted genetically into food crops, they must be provided with a source of nitrogen, and commercial nitrogen fertilizer for them is made from natural gas. So only the remaining half of the farm's output would provide food for humans—either directly, as grains and vegetables, or indirectly, as meat.

I divulged my hunch that everything considered, it might be more energy efficient simply to turn Sunshine Farm over to bison and then eat the

A bull tends a cow, waiting for her to be ready to mate.

bison. "Well," Jackson countered, "do not forget there's a 9:1 conversion factor, so that would end up producing much less food. It might be okay if there were a lot fewer people, but eating lower on the food chain is still better—a diet really heavy in meat, on balance, is probably not as healthy. Remember, we evolved with the gramineae [the botanical family that includes grasses]—we're seed eaters."

The basic goal of the Land Institute's research is to prove several basic agricultural principles, rather in the way the Wright Brothers proved the basic principle of aerodynamic lift. That critical conceptual step was the hard part; after that, plenty of engineers could be found to develop better planes. Jackson believes that his carefully managed plots have proved that perennialism and high seed yield can go together; he is now working on the best combinations. As Jackson has written, "One species that fixes nitrogen complements others that are unable to fix nitrogen. Another species may do a better job of pulling up trace elements necessary for the nitrogen fixer and other species as well."

Remembering boyhood experiences of mowing and threshing, I asked precisely how we would harvest these polycultures and whether farmers would make hay in the traditional way. However, these are not problems that bother Wes Jackson. "You just use a combine and seed-cleaning equipment. The real problems are not mechanical; they're biological. Like how to get synchronous seed set on different species—though you can do two harvests if you have to. Plant breeding thus far has aimed for shatter resistance, not synchrony, and that's much easier—just a single gene may be involved."

The Land Institute now has ten longhorns and may eventually move to incorporate bison. On the rich, flat bottomlands along rivers, Jackson would keep plow agriculture, with fields fenced off from bison. On the rolling uplands and the rougher land that slopes down into the valleys, he would have bison and mixed perennial seed crops. He has been told that whereas cattle rip plants out with their sideways mouth motion, bison bite off the tops of plants instead, so modest numbers of them can coexist with seed plants grown for harvesting.

"You know," Jackson says, "when Coronado first explored this country, he came to one area that some modern archaeologists estimated had 25,000

Indians living in it. If you look at that same area today, it now supports only 10,000 whites—the young people can't make a living here." He cites a recent study of the history of one local farm through its fourteen successive owners as a depressing example of the heroic but failed individualism of the past. The positive vision he proposes instead must have come, he jokes, from his Methodist upbringing, though that also leads him to speak of our living after the Fall—by which he means the invention of agriculture, which first enabled humans to dominate the earth. Present doomed patterns can and must be turned around, and the region can support a vibrant culture again; as he puts it, a more sensible sustainable agriculture needs a critical mass of supportive rural community to flourish, and vice versa.

The necessary changes, however, may run deeper than an acceptance of perennial polycultures. Fencing, Jackson reflects, is a walling out of natural processes as well as an enclosure of property, in land and animals. Perhaps only farming coalitions of some kind can again spread the risks of this dry and difficult region over large areas—as the migratory bison once did.

What Wes Jackson and the Land Institute are doing in their scientifically elegant yet homespun way is the research needed for "security agriculture." They are weaving a safety net for the day when present net-energy-negative agriculture has run its oil-dependent course. In exploring the neglected biological potential of prairie plants, their research is patiently demonstrating how we could maximize and utilize the long-term productivity of the whole midwestern region once covered with native grasses. Thus, even though bison are not as central to the future here, the principles of sustainable farming being demonstrated at the Land Institute run parallel to what will be needed in the primarily bison country farther west.

Chapter Eight
Bison as a Food Source

Not only are bison an undeniably essential component of a healthy Plains ecosystem, they can also provide meat for humans that is low in fat—a marked advantage over the meat of domestic livestock species. Thus, bison should play an increasing part in the American diet. Americans, of course, have long been big meat eaters, and our habits are now spreading throughout the world—a situation widely recognized as unfortunate for both people and planet.

Universal medical opinion holds that eating fatty meat contributes to heart disease, cancer, and various other maladies and malfunctions. Nonetheless, the quantity of meat consumed per capita is sometimes still used by economists (not a profession notable for being in close touch with ecological or public-health realities) as an index of a country's welfare. But as the steady drumbeat of public-health advice goes on, the recent displacement of beef by lower-priced poultry in American diets may continue or perhaps accelerate. The long-term decline in beef consumption has lately turned upward a bit, but it seems likely that this reflects the recent relative prosperity of the top fifth of the population—people who, if they choose to, can afford to eat bison as a healthy choice. Most Americans, whose real incomes have been declining since 1973 and will almost certainly continue to decline because of global economic competition, are likely to turn increasingly to poultry and fish for animal protein and only later to bison, if its price drops sufficiently. (At present, bison prices run at least 25–50 percent higher than beef prices, because of a shortage of supply.) Bison, of course, will never interest the vegetarians among us, whose numbers are likely to increase, driven by both household budgets and health concerns; a recent British study found vegetarians' death rates from heart disease and cancer to be markedly lower than those of meat eaters.

Diet and Health

Whatever the role of economic considerations, it is likely that many Americans will want to eat bison instead of beef if they become convinced of its relative healthfulness. And some people even give bison eating an ecological twist: as Harold Danz, executive director of the National Bison Association, has observed, "To preserve buffalo, the best thing we can do is eat them. Animals that people eat do not become extinct." (Danz's optimism must be qualified, however, remembering the fate of the passenger pigeon. Moreover, many ethnohistorians believe that the mammoths, ground sloths, camels, and horses originally occupying North America were exterminated by early Indian hunters arriving on the continent after crossing the Bering land bridge.)

There is already a certain cachet in the eating of bison, strongest in the Denver area, where the Fort restaurant has been serving bison to a faithful clientele since 1963. The Denver Buffalo Company restaurant has bison soup, salad, burgers, and tenderloin on its menu. (In its first six months of operation, its sales of bison amounted to $1 million. The parent company's mail-order sales of bison meat rose from 15,000 pounds in 1990 to 600,000 pounds in 1992.) Chicago's Prairie restaurant offers buffalo burgers for lunch and buffalo steak for dinner. In New York, An American Place serves bison, and in San Francisco, Tommy's Joynt has been serving bison stew since the 1950s. (Tommy's is not a gourmet establishment, but the stew is delicious and popular, and the bison in it is very tender.) In Montana and other sections of prime bison territory, buffalo burgers are offered on many menus.

Even a militant organization called Beyond Beef, whose goal is to convert 50 percent of Americans to vegetarianism by the year 2000, is enthusiastic about bison. Howard Lyman, a stocky, ebullient former rancher who until recently was executive director of the group, agrees that bison are easier on the land than cattle and could fit in admirably with what he calls permanent agriculture, a system of grazing that would require neither fuel-intensive cattle nor government subsidies.

Although Lyman describes Beyond Beef as basically a tax-revolt group aiming to end subsidies to ranching, he also views meat eating as a major health menace. "You are what you eat" is, in the context of meat consumption, an ominous saying. Lyman quotes the U.S. surgeon general to the effect that "70 percent of U.S. deaths are related to diet, particularly the overconsumption of beef and other foods high in cholesterol and saturated fats." Beyond Beef has picketed McDonald's as one of its responses to this situation, but it also tries to change the fact that so many of the surplus food products distributed to schools by the U.S. Department of Agriculture have been high in fat: butter, cheese, and ground meat, for example. As a consequence, schoolchildren have been fed meals in which more than 30 percent of calories are derived from fat. Several generations have thus been trained in high-fat eating habits, setting off a new round in the national tendency toward obesity and early death that is heightened by our sedentary lifestyles. Meanwhile, both the Pritikin and American Heart Association fat-restricted diets include venison, and bison would certainly qualify too. The *University of California Wellness Letter*, a source of carefully checked information for people watching their health, recently noted that "game does fit nicely into a healthy diet and provides a pleasant alternative to chicken and fish." Wild animals, as the newsletter puts it, do not get fat. Some enthusiastic cooking suggestions are provided, including buffalo meat loaf and buffalo-strip stir-fry. It appears, then, that health motives should give bison meat a bright future in the American diet.

Eating and Being Eaten

"There is no death that is not somebody's food, no life that is not somebody's death. . . . Eating is a sacrament. . . . We too will be offerings—we are all edible."

—Gary Snyder

To the Indian mind, the question of whether humans should eat bison is unaskable: at the creation of the world, bison were given to humans to be eaten, as well as to be made into a hundred different artifacts of Plains tribal life. Indeed, bison were symbolic of the beneficence of the universe. To the ordinary carnivorous American, such a question has a simple answer: if you can find it in the supermarket, eat it. But vegetarians and animal-rights advocates today take a dim view of eating animal flesh. Reservations are sometimes expressed even by conservationists, such as the Sierra Club staff member who said to President Clinton at the 1993 Northwest forest summit conference, "We do not hunt buffalo. We should not cut down the last 10 percent of our ancient forests." For such persons, the idea of bison's becoming part of the American diet raises ethical issues. Before assessing the nutritional virtues of bison, therefore, let us review some positions on this matter.

Western religions, resolutely human-centered, approve of meat eating. Among the great world religions, only Hinduism espouses vegetarianism—and many nondevout Hindus do eat meat. Talmudic law assumes that meat will be eaten and focuses on precise instructions for humane slaughter. To the ecological mind, conscious of the fact that all life is an ineluctable cycle of eating and being eaten, the question of whether humans or coyotes or microbes are the immediate consumers of bison is not a matter of grave consequence in itself; the real question is whether the creatures eaten have lived lives appropriate to their ecological niche and nature.

This criterion, which is interpreted by some to mean that hunting is acceptable (and perhaps morally preferable to assembly-line slaughtering of feedlot steers) is actually much more stringent and far-reaching than the humane kosher rules, for it would ban livestock breeding and raising as they are practiced today: systematic genetic manipulation, captivity in cages or restricted pastures and feedlots, castration of males, artificial insemination—the whole regime under which animals are reduced to being at every moment of their lives subjects of human control. Obviously, this criterion also runs parallel to Indian attitudes, which do not condone tampering with nature and regard all "two-leggeds and four leggeds" as having natural rights.

The animal-rights movement among whites has had many positive effects in securing better treatment for animals, in laboratories and elsewhere. Much of it, however, operates on a philosophical level focused on definitions of consciousness, and hence remains basically human centered; it also tends to seem abstruse. As the naturalist David Quammen remarked, it may be better to respect all living beings: "Life is life." Some animal-rights advocates show a perplexing distaste for biological realities. They object to predation itself, one even going so far as to propose—perhaps inspired by Isaiah 11:7, that "the lion shall eat straw like the ox"—that carnivorous animals like leopards should all be put into enclosures where they would be fed, presumably, vegetable-based cat food.

As Buddhists recognize explicitly, we are all quite literally caught up in the great karmic wheel of reincarnation. You, gentle reader, when your turn comes, will be consumed by the billion microbes even now waiting on your skin, in your gut, on everything you touch. Thereafter, your component nutrients will recycle through food chains innumerable. Even cremation will only detour this ultimate recycling, reducing your remains to their mineral minima. There is a fierce and terrible beauty in this process, as well as much suffering, but it also has a humorous side—as is recognized both by Buddhists, who have a sense of cosmic irony, and by a recent country and western song about a cowboy returning as a pile of horseshit and thus "not changed much."

The Ecology of Bison in Our Diet

From both health and ecological perspectives, American meat consumption is far too high. For people wishing to diminish their personal impacts on the earth, eating less meat of any kind probably is, aside from driving less, the most important option available. However, it seems clear that most Americans, like the citizens of many other rich countries, are going to go on eating meat in unhealthy and ecologically damaging quantities.

Even if we had huge numbers of bison on the Plains, they could not conceivably support our meat-eating habit at anything like its current level. As it happens, however, most American beef is actually produced in the wetter climates of the East, where bison restoration is extremely unlikely. The United States also participates in the international beef trade with places like Argentina and Australia; moreover, our extensive importation of cheap hamburger beef raised on what used to be rain forests in Latin America has led to boycotts of fast-food chains by environmental groups.

If we made enough land available for them, we could theoretically have 33 million bison by the year 2011. Their natural increase annually thereafter would produce a harvestable surplus of about 13 million bison each year. But our current annual beef consumption amounts to the equivalent of about 36 million bison. Thus, the bison theoretically available a decade and a half from now would be enough to replace only a third of the beef we now eat, and the U.S. population is rising sharply. Even if we further reduce our consumption of meat, at the utmost bison are not likely to account for more than a third of our consumption of red meat.

MONTE QUADE: BISON ENTREPRENEUR

On a gray, threatening Montana day in June, Monte Quade stands outside his little house in Deer Lodge wearing a buffalo coat made by his wife, Colleen. Monte is brown haired, lively eyed, and friendly; he seems about thirty-five, and sports a battered, stained, edge-rolled western hat. The coat, which weighs ten or twelve pounds, has a heavy, curly collar (made from the thick bison "cape" fur) that seems to give a slope even to his sturdy shoulders. Monte says the coat would keep you warm in subzero winds. Colleen made it on commission; such coats can bring in a tidy sum. This matters in Montana, a low-wage state where one job may not be enough to support a family.

My wife and I met Monte, who is a butcher, at the meat counter of the local IGA supermarket, where someone had told us buffalo meat could be bought. As indeed it could: we found roasts, steaks, and ground meat, all looking very lean and surprisingly dark red. The color, we learned later, is due partly to bison's high iron content and partly to the virtual absence of fat marbling. Monte came out with a tray of pork chops and we got to talking; when he realized we were serious about bison, he invited us to come home with him on his lunch hour.

A fundamental if hypothetical ecological question arises: would harvesting 13 million bison annually deplete the Plains and prairie grassland soils on which the bison grazed? No one really knows for sure. Our present practice of extracting some 45 million cattle carcasses annually from feedlots is difficult to compare, since much cattle feed is grown by farmers elsewhere—particularly through highly net-energy-negative monocrop corn planting, which entails heavy damage to soils.

Currently, stocking rates, or numbers of animals (whether cattle or bison) kept on a given area, are theoretically set with the goal of maintaining the long-term health of the range. But there is a tendency to set stocking rates near the maximum, a major reason why so much leased public land is rated, even by the agencies presiding over it, as being in poor condition.

The small house where he and Colleen live with their daughter and two twin boys is full of stacked buffalo hides ready to be made into robes, coats, and, on demand, other bison artifacts. A commercial heavy-duty sewing machine stands in the living room, where several coats are nearing completion. While Monte showed us one of the old buffalo guns that he collects and reconditions, Colleen rustled up lunch for him and the kids. He also makes Indian-style arrows and other items and would have worked as a consultant on *Dances with Wolves*, except that the local Safeway happened to be on strike at the time and IGA's meat business was booming to such a degree that Monte could not take time off for movie work.

Butcher Monte Quade of Deer Lodge, Montana. He is also part owner of a bison herd in nearby South Dakota and sells bison meat in the supermarket where he works.

(Much privately owned land is in no better condition.) The problem is not a technical one; there are plenty of experienced people around who can recognize when rangeland is degrading. What will be needed is careful study, over a substantial period of time, of large herds of bison in large areas, measuring the effects on grass productivity as animals are removed. Sustainability in this respect is more likely the more bison occupy richer prairie grasslands—leading us to hope that their range can be extended eastward into the former tallgrass areas.

Filling city dwellers' bellies with bison is not comparable to Indian uses of bison, which, before whites provided a market for hides and tongues, were entirely local and rigorously sustainable: all elements of the bison remained in the region. Even the bones were ultimately recycled through natural decomposition, until whites began hauling them east for fertilizer. Moreover, Indian populations were modest and their needs for bison as food were limited. Modern harvesting of bison, however, would remove millions of carcasses to the cities and suburbs, where most people live, and their digested remains would, like the rest of our urban sewage, be largely wasted or destroyed. Nature will set limits to this process, and we will need good research to learn them.

The Bison Meat Market

In most places, bison meat is still hard to find. But in the Denver area ordinary supermarkets stock it, and some small supermarkets around the country have begun to offer it as well, usually ground for burgers and available only frozen. Outside bison-producing areas, you have to order it by mail or find it in specialty stores supplying venison, antelope, and other game to restaurants.

Not only is the total U.S. bison population little more than the daily 125,000-animal slaughter rate for cattle, slaughterhouses and distribution facilities have developed slowly. But in New Rockford, North Dakota, the largest bison-processing operation in the country has recently gotten under way—a $1.6 million cooperative set up by the bison ranchers themselves. It slaughtered 950 bison in its first six months of operation and is capable of handling 5,000 per year. Exportation to Europe has begun, but most of the meat is sent to American distributors who serve stores all over the country.

However, there is a great gulf between the present vigorous but limited market for bison meat and a future distribution system purveying enormous amounts of meat to millions of customers. Because bison cows only have one calf yearly, there are limits on the speed with which bison could displace cattle. And distribution is also a factor. The complex system of slaughterhouses, chilling plants, refrigerator trucks, distribution warehouses, and meat counters must adapt to bison, and this will inevitably be a slow and gradual change. It took many decades for the beef industry to evolve to its present scale, and it may be decades before bison becomes widely available.

However, at least in cities with sophisticated tastes, bison should be a familiar foodstuff within a decade. After all, the present American enthusiasm for fish is a relatively new phenomenon. It began in restaurants and in ethnic neighborhoods and only afterward spread to general home consumption. The same factors that brought fish into wide national consciousness will also favor bison: gourmet tastes and a desire for low-fat foods, abetted by better refrigeration and transportation technology. It is a favorable sign that some supermarket chains in the West have recently started offering bison, betting that diet-conscious customers are ready to begin switching.

Bison is butchered into all the cuts familiar in beef; steaks and roasts are what people usually try first. Each of these comes in a wide variety of forms, and there are also ribs, stew and kabob meat, ground meat, tongue (not favored, of course, by those avoiding fat), and several flavors of jerky. A delicious if fatty pâté can be made from bison liver, but liver can be obtained only from a dealer in fresh meat or directly from a rancher.

Strong claims are often made for the healthfulness of bison meat, and its present sales depend substantially on its being marketed as a healthful gourmet delicacy, though if it is to become a major part of the American diet its price will obviously have to drop somewhat. Since there is very little waste, however, before or during cooking, even present costs are often reasonable. Bison burgers shrink negligibly in cooking, making their cost per final pound not enormously higher than that of ground beef. Fanatical fat trimmers find that bison top sirloin roast at $6.95 is actually cheaper per eatable cooked pound than lean pork loin at $3.95.

Bison is chilled, frozen, and shipped just as beef is. If you would like to try bison and cannot find it in a local restaurant, look for a meat broker or meat jobber in the Yellow Pages or ask a local butcher for advice. Dealers in exotic meats or game can often supply bison; they usually operate out of a freezer plant with a small showroom. Most major coastal cities now have such sources, but it takes some looking to find them. Bison dealers are accustomed to shipping.

Advice on cooking bison can be found in *The Great American Bison Cookbook,* published by the National Bison Association (see the Notes for the Association's address). Here you will find recipes ranging all the way from Hobo Dinner to Grilled Medallions of Bison with Jalapeño Glaze and Jicama Relish. But you can easily adapt any of your favorite beef recipes to bison. As the National Bison Association comments in its booklet *Buffalo: A Health Food You Can Sink Your Teeth Into,* "Fat is an insulator that heat must first penetrate before the cooking process begins. Buffalo, with its low fat content, does not need to be cooked as long with as high a temperature to get the job done." Just remember that restaurant chefs will not take responsibility for bison ordered well done—and neither should you.

Claims are sometimes made that bison is more tender than beef. In my experience, bison is usually tender, but not infallibly so, just like beef. (Nobody who prefers meat well done is likely to be happy with bison. Heavy cooking definitely ruins it, even for people who regard a certain amount of chewing as desirable exercise for their jaw muscles.) Here, as with nutrient content, it is likely that "range effects" are significant: animals living active open-range lives, whether cattle, bison, elk, or antelope, are not likely to be quite so tender as animals that have been standing around in feedlots.

Following the Notes are some basic bison recipes you could try in your own kitchen.

Fat and Cholesterol

Anyone interested in bison as food soon runs into sales pitches enthusiastically pointing out that it has more protein, less fat, and less cholesterol than beef. Many people, of course, like bison simply because it is tasty. If they can get hold of it readily they eat a lot of it, and we will probably see this preference spreading widely. But at present, health appeals are a major factor in the expansion of the bison market.

The National Bison Association issues a lavish four-color brochure, *Today's Naturally Healthy Red Meat*, which is quite up to date about health and fat issues. There is wide agreement that bison is much higher in iron than beef. It also contains no antibiotic or hormone residues, and buffalo sausage products contain no nitrates or nitrites. The claim is often made that people allergic to beef or to substances injected into beef can eat bison without difficulty. These factors certainly appeal to health-conscious eaters, whose numbers are growing.

Bison cuts on sale in a Montana supermarket.

The currently prevailing view among health experts is that cholesterol, a fatlike substance necessary to all animal cell membranes and nerve fibers (but never found in plants, though coconut and palm kernel oil are high in saturated fats), is not the main dietary villain; fat is. Cholesterol and saturated fat are distinct and independent substances, but they are linked by the paradoxical fact that eating saturated fat raises blood cholesterol levels more than eating cholesterol-laden food does. To confuse matters even further, some foods high in saturated fat, such as sour cream, butter, and lard, have little cholesterol; on the other hand, liver and eggs have a lot of cholesterol but only moderate amounts of fat. However, the moral of the tale is simple: eating a lot of fat of any kind—even unsaturated vegetable oils—increases various health risks. Hence, seriously health-conscious eaters today tend to stay away from red meat, though they usually allow themselves some chicken and fish. All such folks would be just as well off—maybe better off—eating bison.

If you are going to eat meat, here are the relevant numbers. A half pound of raw bison muscle contains almost five grams of fat. This figure comes from the research of Martin Marchello at North Dakota State University, the most careful and consistent so far, which focused analysis on a single muscle (the longissimus, comparable to the breast muscle in chickens) and also examined the effects of cooking, which removes some minerals, protein, and cholesterol. By comparison, a half pound of choice beef contains more than eighteen grams of fat—more than three times as much. A half pound of chicken comes in at less than two grams of fat, or half as much as bison, and has a trifle more protein than either bison or beef. The U.S. Department of Agriculture has studied the nutrient content of foods for many years, issuing the results in frequent revisions as better data come to hand, and it includes bison and other game animals in its *Agriculture Handbook* series. The latest edition rates bison at 1.8 percent fat, with beef at 6.2 percent and chicken at 3.1 percent.

Cooking methods and cuts make some difference in the final fat content of a dish, of course, but taking all these figures together, the upshot is clear enough: bison, chicken, and most fish expose you to less than half the health risk of eating beef. As for cholesterol itself, only pure vegetarians really avoid it. Bison, beef, chicken, and dairy products all contain cholesterol; bison has only a slight advantage here.

Displacing Beef

As we are frequently reminded, the present American high-fat, high-salt, low-fiber diet is a major cause of our national pudginess, our disease rates, and our early mortality. Yet meat eating probably will not diminish much from its present level. The realistic question, then, is how much of current beef consumption bison meat is likely to displace.

Some bison products seem to me to be indistinguishable from beef, and if their prices approach parity with similar beef items, I believe that people will switch. Bison burgers are a good case in point; their popularity seems to be rising sharply. Claims are sometimes made that ground bison is "all lean." Monte Quade, however, strives to keep his ground bison at about 10 percent fat—in Montana this is considered low-fat, although among health-conscious city folks even ground chicken breast, with 3 percent fat, now seems marginal. Frozen ground bison I obtained recently in California was rated at 15 percent fat by its producers; that is enough to permit grilling over charcoal without much hazard of overcooking, but of course it defeats the health reasons for eating bison. Bison burgers you buy at roadside cafés that are made mostly or entirely from fresh meat are undoubtedly delicious, but they sometimes contain beef suet, mixed in to make them more suitable for high-temperature broiling.

For a future mass market, storage factors will be important. Meat scientists have been evaluating how well bison meat holds up under frozen storage, which is the fate of meats used by fast-food chains. In one research study, bison and Hereford cattle scored similarly on various phospholipid measures likely to affect quality after storage. A "McBuff" burger may not be far away.

Whether there will be a market large enough to support bison raising on a massive scale is still hard to determine, but as we have seen, there are plenty of ranchers willing to bet on it. Assuming that economies of scale develop in slaughtering, butchering, and shipping, the price of bison meat should decline toward that of beef and might even beat it. "People really want to eat red meat again," said an executive of the Denver Buffalo Company. He also thinks that *Dances with Wolves*, especially its bison stampede scene, "reintroduced the country to the American bison." Moreover, eating bison may well take on a certain éclat, perhaps a little like the fanciful view still propagated by the Beef Institute, that beef gives strength. Sizable numbers of people may find it reassuring or entertaining to believe that eating bison gives even more strength. As an article in *Adweek's Marketing Week* predictably urged, a major ad campaign along these lines would help bison achieve a bigger market presence.

Antibiotics and Public Health

The fact that range bison are not injected with growth stimulants, hormones, or subtherapeutic drugs or given antibiotic-laced feed is a great comfort to health-conscious bison eaters. The beef and poultry industries stoutly maintain that the residues of such substances in their products are negligible, but some scientists are not convinced. Widespread public doubt persists, encouraged by the fact that some foreign countries refuse to accept American meat. As in human medicine, much misprescribing of cattle drugs takes place, according to a 1992 General Accounting Office report; in fact, 40–85 percent of prescriptions for dairy cows are for drugs not even approved by the Food and Drug Administration for the diseases they are being used to treat. Nobody has the remotest idea what human hazards may be involved in eating the resulting dairy or meat products, but the overall picture does not inspire consumer confidence. Moreover, some members of Congress are seeking to remove livestock drug regulations entirely.

The issue of drug dosing of domestic animals is important in far more than an individual-health perspective. From a long-term ecological view, animals given "precautionary" antibiotics are millions-strong walking incubators for antibiotic-resistant bacteria. Bacteria evolve rapidly, and when they are steadily exposed to antibiotics, especially in low dosages, they quickly develop strains that can survive in the presence of the drugs. As a recent issue of *Science* pointed out, "In the last 50 years bacteria have shown a remarkable facility to develop resistance to every antibiotic that has been developed, often by quite unexpected mechanisms." Consequently, we are now precariously near to losing our ability to cure tuberculosis and several other serious diseases, and only one single antibiotic remains capable of controlling all common hospital disease organisms. Like indiscriminate prescribing of antibiotics to treat viral infections, which in fact they cannot touch, the widespread use of antibiotics in food production endangers our dwindling ability to secure our bodies, not to mention our hospitals, against uncontrollable infections. Mixing low doses of antibiotics into cattle feed may save bodily energy the animals might otherwise lose in fighting off diseases and thus enable cattle to grow faster, but it also provides a nationwide reservoir for the development of bacterial strains with antibiotic resistance—which, when people eat beef or drink milk, can be transferred to human-inhabiting bacteria. Deriving a substantial part of our meat supply from bison, which are not fed antibiotics, would greatly decrease this increasingly ominous problem.

Ideally, we would be better off eating less meat of any kind. Short of that, however, even though bison will never completely replace cattle, fostering and eating significant numbers of bison will mean a major contribution to the public health of the nation as well as to the sustainable productivity of its grasslands.

Chapter Nine
A Buffalo Commons

People hold as strong convictions about land as about anything, especially in the West, and it is conceivable that the return of the bison will entail conflicts over land use reminiscent of the land wars, familiar to us from dozens of Western movies. These were fought between the cattle and sheep barons, determined to preserve millions of acres of open range, and the flood of settlers, whose ideal was 160 fenced acres, a reliable water supply, and an impartial legal system. This war appeared to have been won, as the century turned, by the settlers, whose numbers increased in the Plains until the 1920s and whose plows tore up endless acres of prairie sod. As historian Frederick Turner declared in 1893, the frontier was closed.

But then nature reasserted itself, through frequent dry years and the winds that created the Dust Bowl; farming began to dwindle. Some areas of the Plains still go on producing large quantities of dry-farmed wheat and sorghum, and irrigated agriculture is hanging on where water can be pumped up from the Ogallala aquifer. But in recent years, for a large part of the Plains even subsidized ranching and farming have weakened to the point at which, as Frank and Deborah Popper have argued, the frontier has returned under our noses—or perhaps, in some areas, it never really closed after all. And in a frontier Plains ecosystem, bison have a natural role to play.

The Poppers and Their Plan
Frank and Deborah Popper, who invented the term "buffalo commons," are experts in demographics—changes in population levels. Their aca-

demic field is not generally considered news, although its scope includes (for a relatively dramatic example) the slow, inexorable process that is gradually changing California into something that Joel Garreau, in his *Nine Nations of North America,* considers part of "MexAmerica." In 1987, the Poppers recognized that a great swath in the middle of the country, including parts of ten states, had been drastically declining in population. For many rural Plains counties and their small towns, population had been decreasing steadily since the 1920s. Kansas now has hundreds of ghost towns, the Poppers noticed; Nebraska has five to ten thousand deserted farmhouses. Perhaps, they suggested, creating a buffalo commons—bringing back the bison and encouraging bison-oriented tourism—could help reinvigorate the region. In proposing this notion, they did not attempt to specify which areas might be devoted to bison, who might hold rights to harvest bison from the commons, how those rights would be limited, how the government might manage lands that constituted the commons, or any other details. Into this void, as we shall see, many fantasies promptly rushed.

Frank Popper comes from a background in planning and is still active in the field; he has been chair of the Rutgers University Department of Urban Studies. He is of an intellectual generation that was confident that government programs could solve major social problems. When America confronted the decline of an entire region like Appalachia, the Tennessee Valley Authority was created to halt widespread gully erosion, turn winding valleys into power-producing reservoirs, and bring in jobs. Lowly urban neighborhoods were cleared and rebuilt wholesale through urban renewal programs. Many of Frank Popper's professional journal articles deal with land-use regulations. Now that their Buffalo Commons proposal has made them famous, the Poppers travel together on frequent lecture and research tours, on the Plains and elsewhere.

Moved by the stark beauty of the Plains, the Poppers pondered the region's future. At one point, they were talking about the matter while tied up in traffic on the New Jersey Turnpike. They knew that Burt Wallach, a geographer at the University of Oklahoma, had made a bold suggestion that the Forest Service move beyond current U.S.D.A. subsidy programs.

Wallach's idea was for farmers to be paid salaries for fifteen years to phase out their operations almost entirely while they worked to restore native grasses, animals, birds, and other life forms. (He seems not to have specifically mentioned bison.) At the end of the fifteen years, the farmers would be bought out but would retain forty-acre homesteads. Also, Robert Scott of the Institute of the Rockies had been proposing a massive "Big Open" plan for turning about 15,000 square miles of eastern Montana into a region of game ranches capable of supporting, he estimated, 150,000 deer, 75,000 bison, 40,000 elk, and 40,000 antelope. Moreover, although the Plains region had never been particularly sympathetic to parks, some faint stirrings had begun among a few venturesome park advocates.

At the point when they broached the buffalo commons idea, the Poppers had never dealt with bison firsthand; they simply shared the common American respect for the great beasts. Mulling over ideas for a viable future for the Plains while they crept along in traffic, Frank reportedly said playfully, "A buffalo homeland." (That phrase has, of course, a resonance with the establishment of Israel as a Jewish homeland.) Deborah rejoined, "A buffalo commons."

Recently I asked the Poppers what the term meant to them at that time. As they now remember it, they had in mind biologist Garrett Hardin's famous article, "The Tragedy of the Commons," to which we will shortly return. They felt that the occupation of the Plains by whites—cattle barons and settlers alike—had recapitulated the sad parable of self-destructive waste that Hardin tells—offering a vivid contrast with Indians' shared uses of the region's natural resources, which had been sustained successfully for ten thousand years. The term might, then, suggest a rehabilitation of the commons. In any case, the Poppers intended it to have a provocative edge, and despite the storm of criticism the term has brought them, they have no regrets.

Planners tend to be public-spirited souls, hoping against all sordid political realities that they can devise and secure acquiescence to reasonable schemes for land use, transportation, and so on. From outside the profession, and even from some perspectives within it, planners appear to lead painful lives, since the government bodies that most of them work for, whose actions are dominated by developers and other large campaign contributors, systematically reject, undermine, and go around the best-laid plans.

It seems normal to planners, then, that they should propose plans—sometimes even daring ones—for debate and discussion. They do not expect easy adoption; we live, after all, in a country where it is often a matter of hot and lengthy civic controversy whether or not to put up a stoplight. So the Poppers, in December 1987, published a rather playful piece in *Planning* magazine. With the allegorical bent that was to get them into a great deal of trouble with Plains dwellers, they titled it "Dust to Dust." It reviewed the demographic and economic decline of much of the Plains region and suggested that perhaps the government should set up something like the TVA to help out. More land could be bought to fill out the national grasslands acquired for soil conservation purposes during the Dust Bowl, and bison could be put back on it. There was lots of land there not usable for much else; the history of agriculture on the high Plains had been one of brief booms followed by long busts.

The Poppers are not biologists or agriculturalists, but they had a perfectly reasonable hunch that repopulating Plains land with bison, some way or other, would be more reasonable than plowing it up and letting it blow or wash away. (Erosion, as we have seen, remains severe on the Plains. In addition, it is probable that global warming, largely brought on by industrial-era carbon dioxide emissions, will result in even less Plains rainfall and drier soil.) The Poppers also suspected that bison might constitute a world-class tourist attraction that cows could not. They did not make a great point of this, but it is a fact that many German and other European as well as Japanese tourists are enamored of the present and historical American West; German is the most frequently heard language in some places around the Grand Canyon.

The Ideological Context

Bringing back the bison was an idea that the well known Indian writer Vine Deloria Jr., among others, had been thinking over too. But the Poppers, through the term Buffalo Commons, touched a nerve. Many people in the

Plains states, not normally concerned with demographers' opinions, saw these eastern city intellectuals as telling them what to do—a most unwelcome thing in a region where unasked-for advice, especially from outsiders, is frowned on. In the frontier culture that still persists on the Plains, needing help from somebody else can easily be pride destroying—especially, perhaps, if the help offered is that troublesome urban product, an idea. Worse still, the Poppers' idea set Plains dwellers to imagining massive government land grabs; they suspected plans to euthanize their culture and undo their political control of the region. To this day, there are outraged Plains people who believe that the Poppers were saying that all humans should be forced to abandon the Plains. Although evidence was all around them, some questioned the Poppers' statistics about population decline. Predictably, the Plains response to the Poppers was quite bison-like: its overriding theme was "Butt out!"

Plains culture remains exceedingly homogeneous compared with that of most other regions, and it tends to resist anything or anybody from outside. Take Kansas, for instance, where the Indians from whom the state takes its name were utterly destroyed in the space of about ten years. (There are no reservations in Kansas.) Later, Kansas nobly if narrowly declined to become a slave state at the time of the Civil War, but its recent opposition to establishment of a Tallgrass Prairie National Park in the middle of the state relied in part, according to William Least Heat-Moon, on the fear that the visitors drawn to the park might include African-Americans. The fact that the park would have attracted tourist dollars and revivified a considerable area economically was to no avail. Ultimately, park advocates had to turn their attention south to Oklahoma.

The Poppers hardly expected the storm of outrage that their modest proposal generated. In their eyes, they were just trying to help, suggesting a way for people of the region to avoid increased destitution and to survive with dignity. But their proposal plunged them into violent public controversy. There is now a book about their work, giving an account of a recent lecture tour on which armed guards were sometimes provided, by a *New York Times* reporter who followed them around the Plains.

Demography as Destiny

The 1990 census gave the Poppers convincing new evidence that the trends they had identified earlier were continuing. Cattle and wheat—lots of wheat—were still being produced on the Plains but by a sharply dropping number of people. By then, 133 counties comprising an astounding quarter of the contiguous United States had reverted to frontier population sparseness—fewer than two people per square mile. Using the common but less-rigorous standard of six people per square mile, this new internal frontier—mostly lying in the area from North Dakota to Texas and westward to the Rockies—amounts to 40 percent of the country but has only 1 percent of the national population. Moreover, it is expanding from the "empty quarter" mountain states onto the high Plains to the east.

Bison are, in fact, only a minor aspect of the Poppers' overall campaign to revise what they regard as the false consensus that the American frontier disappeared before the turn of the century. It has never gone away, they say. In fact, it is enormous and it is growing. Attention must be paid to it and some new thinking done; the doling out of larger subsidies is not enough, and in any case agricultural-state politicians may soon lose the power to procure them. The new era's priorities must be seized: "Preservation will shape the 21st-century American frontier, and it will refocus the nation's attention on a land heritage it thought it had lost."

The Poppers work on a county-by-county scale, and their maps are mind altering. A large part of the decline they document is due to abandonment of farms, a process that is continuing. In 1990, 26 percent of farmers with Farm Home Administration loans were delinquent in North Dakota, 42 percent in South Dakota, and 28 percent in Nebraska; production loans were more than 40 percent delinquent in all three states. Some of the decline is traceable to the relentless long-term decline of wages in the extractive boom-and-bust industries of mining and energy. (Our image of the Plains as nonindustrial is belied by the oil wells that are everywhere in Oklahoma, Kansas, the Dakotas, and eastern Wyoming, with their pipelines, access roads, and other impacts.) Some of the decline also flows from mere remoteness, which in this age of deregulation raises the costs of trucking, railroad transport, buses, public services, even telephone service. This is not cowboy country anymore. What thrives now is an economy of isolated enclaves in which extractive energy or timber operations come in for a time or high-tech agribusiness finds a temporary source of irrigation water.

But in arid sections of the country, even for some of the currently prosperous city centers, nature has begun to draw limit lines. Desertification is occurring in areas near El Paso and Albuquerque, from which city water supplies are drawn. The whole area between Amarillo and Lubbock in Texas has been dried out. In 1982, the Kansas Water Office estimated that by the year 2020, 75 percent of the state's irrigated acreage—most of it using center-pivot systems that draw water from the Ogallala aquifer—would be lost. Altogether, say the Poppers, an area 200 to 700 miles wide is affected. Although some towns and small cities in this area are growing, as we will see below, their populations will be limited by available water.

Another Popper map shows those areas that would make greatest sense as bison habitat because they are most distressed on a set of different indicators—not only steep and long-continued declines in population but also high population ages, high poverty levels, and low construction investment. This map resembles the one reproduced below. There are 110 counties highlighted on it, constituting a total area about as large as Montana but with only 6 percent of the total Plains population. The Poppers say

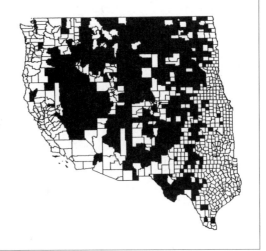

The shaded area shows counties with fewer than six people per square mile (1990). Roughly speaking, the eastern half of these counties fall into original prime bison range. From Robert E. Lang, Deborah Epstein Popper, and Frank J. Popper, "'Progress of the Nation': The Settlement History of the Enduring American Frontier," *Western Historical Quarterly*, Autumn 1995.

This highway sign's optimism was belied by reality: in mid-1994, all but one of the listed businesses in this small town had closed. Many county-seat towns, however, are surviving in Nebraska.

that these counties "tend to be distant from interstate highways, irrigation projects, large rivers and big cities, and to lack middle-sized settlements of their own. They are, in short, possible candidates for becoming part of a huge reserve we have called the Buffalo Commons."

This set of criteria defines those parts of the Plains that are outside still relatively successful sites of Euro-American habitation: dry-farmable areas in wheat or other crops, irrigated areas along rivers or in places where the aquifer's water layer is thick and easily accessible, and, of course, the region's few significant cities. The map thus indicates those areas where, if large numbers of bison returned, people would not find themselves in serious conflict with bison over access to either land or water, as happened when people on the Oregon Trail crossed the trails by which thousands of bison habitually went to drink in the broad Missouri River. The rural and depressed counties encompassed by these criteria could in theory easily provide room for millions of bison. However, the land in these counties is still being used for cattle operations, marginal though many of them may be.

A few towns in these counties, however, and even a few small towns, are thriving—and Deborah Popper's research now focuses on how they manage this. On the Plains as a whole, certain towns, Indian reservations, and cities are experiencing population growth, while in the remote rural sections of most of the region people are still clearing out despite government subsidies. Even the network of nuclear missile bases scattered across some areas of the Plains—an economic benefit of an unsettling kind—is being phased down. Many alternative ideas for "development" (like building casinos on Indian land or leasing land to faraway cities for use as dumps) have proved illusory, socially problematic, or ecologically unacceptable.

Fiber-optic technology, however—not something we would ordinarily associate with the Plains—is helping to keep certain towns viable. Nebraska, unpredictably, is a pioneer state in deploying "the fiber" to county seats and some other small towns. Better communication links help businesses in remote places keep in touch with markets and suppliers; they also enable doctors to tap into metropolitan medical expertise and offer high schools access to specialized teachers in bigger school districts. Given a suitable local work force, they even make possible computer "barns," in which people can serve distant corporations as mail-order takers or airline reservation agents. Although telecommunications advances have also led to the closing down of local banks and insurance offices, they facilitate the relocation to small towns of mobile professionals like accountants and stockbrokers, whose business can be conducted by modem and telephone. Some rural Plains counties that shrank during the 1980s are now growing, on the renewed strength of their towns.

In their very first article, the Poppers wrote, with a cool scientific detachment that was not appreciated by Plains people: "The most likely possibility is a continuation of the gradual impoverishment and depopulation that in many places go back to the 1920s." They sound a little more optimistic now, but Frank Popper told me recently, "Well, we would not step away [from that position] entirely." Sometimes cultures prefer to die rather than change, and this still, after the passage of a decade and a half, seems a distinctly possible scenario: as the people attached to the old culture die, the land will empty out further except for a scattering of towns and a few small cities, which will share the media, attitudes, economic base, and business practices of the country's metropolitan economy. But later generations will probably feel neutral about or perhaps even favor some government land acquisition, and many of them will probably see bison, on either government or private land, as an unquestionable natural resource. But whatever happens to the land itself will be governed, ultimately, by the twin bedrock realities of the Plains: the sea of grass and the winds that sweep over it—to which we will return.

Refinements

In recent years, the initial hostile reactions to the Poppers have mellowed somewhat. Plains academics have addressed the questions the Poppers raised. Stephen E. White, a Kansas geographer, thinks the region has been unfairly treated as if it were one uniform disaster area. The picture, he argues, is less bleak if you look, on a finer scale than the Poppers use, at what is happening within counties. Scott has identified a number of "Ogallala oases" in western Kansas—towns in pumped-irrigation districts where water is still ample and easily reached—that are prospering and even adding a little population, though the western Kansas countryside elsewhere is continuing to lose people. White also notes that on the Plains as elsewhere, big places tend to get bigger—an effect that he finds even more important than the availability of water—and he predicts that this dynamic can help develop nonfarm-based jobs in areas where the aquifer begins to falter.

The Poppers, too, have been refining their approach to the persistence of the frontier, emphasizing that current developments are a continuation of very long-term trends. In the rainy East, farmers settled from state line to state line, with towns and cities scattered throughout. By contrast, in the arid West, cities have always been isolated amid vast unsettled areas, and even as state populations have boomed on the strength of pockets of city growth, frontier population densities have persisted in rural areas. Paradoxically, thus, the West is more concentratedly urban in population than the East. As the Poppers say in a new paper written with Robert E. Lang, "Even Colorado-style growth need not shrink the frontier. A state can at once become more urban and more frontier." All major western city sites except Las Vegas were in place by the late nineteenth century. But the frontier areas—places with fewer than six persons per square mile—around them have actually grown slightly, from 388 counties in 1890 to 397 in 1990, with a strong expansion on the Plains that is only partly offset elsewhere. The overall prediction: "Much of the West will remain settled and keep growing, but in other places the frontier will reemerge, as it is now doing in the Great Plains." And this frontier may receive new kinds of environmental attention from urban westerners, who tend to show a strong concern with water and range conservation as well as logging and mining practices.

For his part, White endorses what he calls planned depletion of the Plains aquifer water and predicts that irrigated agriculture will continue in some places for generations to come. But whether his farming-based oases remain prosperous for two, or three, or four generations—and much depends on world food and energy price levels as well as water-conserving irrigation practices—in the end they will have to either find some new means of support or shrink. In practical terms, Scott endorses a kind of "triage": policies should be adopted to help marginal towns that show signs of surviving as regional centers while ignoring places that are either already successful or hopelessly in decline. Such an approach is indeed likely for towns, and the Poppers would probably endorse it enthusiastically. But in rural areas like the northwestern corner of Kansas, as farming goes bust, ranching grows more perilous, and small towns continue to die off, the shadows of returning bison will grow stronger on the land—initially on private ranch lands, but gradually on bankrupt ranches that should be bought up for federal bison reserves.

The flexible, innovative, and enterprising public initiatives that have resulted in our national seashores and other new public lands may be a long time coming in the cultural and political context of the Plains. But though a limited number of towns may thrive, it remains true that much rural land will be abandoned, and for some of it the most sensible future use will be for bison and other wild grazers. On parts of the Plains, it has already become respectable to consider that bison will someday have an important place in the future of the region. A small sign of this transition is the fact that bison steaks have found their way onto the menu of Rick's Café, the unofficial meeting place for locals in Mobridge, South Dakota.

Still, their heavy symbolic import makes bison hard for even Plains townsfolk to accept. Their return seems to signify the defeat of long-held dreams and a drift back into the past. People may no longer fear that bureaucrats will seize their homesteads and bulldoze their towns. But dreams die as hard in small communities as they do in larger ones, maybe harder, and the American country small-town dream is so closely connected to our national self-image as rural folk that giving it up seems impossibly painful. Even as we have become a nation of urbanites or suburbanites living so functionally isolated from one another as to hardly constitute communities at all, we yearn for the lost vision of the small town—the site, as the city-based television networks remind us each Christmas season, of Frank Capra's movie *It's a Wonderful Life*.

Decline of a Culture

In ranching areas where the farms and small towns have mostly withered away, current population levels are probably lower than those supported in Indian days by the bison and the native edible plants. What we are witnessing on much of the Plains is the undoing of a Euro-American settlement of the landscape so precariously and laboriously achieved that its loss, by whatever process, seems unbearable to the people still resident there. They say of the Poppers, with deep resentment, "They do not take into account our struggle and hard work." The idea of bringing back the bison strikes me, an Appalachian country boy gone urban, as an inevitable turn of the great circle of life, an acknowledgment of nature's ways, a promise of future sustainable habitation—for as long as we can see ahead, until the glaciers come again. But to Plains people of Euro-American descent, it seems an acceptance of the death of their culture—and possibly even an admission that trying to settle the Plains for agriculture was a mistake.

Ironically, thoughtful Plains whites may now feel exactly as the Indians did when the whites' forebears were displacing them. Something is ending on the Plains—has already ended, in many places. But nobody knows what is coming, and the thundering hooves are not much consolation in places like Hayes Center, Nebraska, county seat, where only 231 residents remain.

Bison Tourism

Although they did not propose details, the Poppers suggested bison-based tourism as a future enterprise on the Plains. Tourism has grown to be a massive global industry—indeed, it may now be the world's largest industry—and communities all over the planet are avidly seeking to make themselves profitable tourist destinations. Even in areas like the Pacific Northwest, where clear-cutting has laid waste to most of the ancient forest cover, tourism is growing rapidly and taking up some of the slack left by the export or mechanization of timber jobs. Tourism is reportedly the fastest-growing industry in the West and the largest private employer in seven of the eleven western states. State tourism-promotion efforts on the Plains are developing especially rapidly in North and South Dakota, but they are definitely under way all over the region.

In the future of the Plains, tourism seems bound to become much more important than it is today, and bison will be a strong attraction. As our urban and suburban populations grow, people will yearn even more to visit open spaces, to see wild animals, to experience scenery not cluttered with fast-food outlets, gas stations, and parked cars. Tourists, like retirees, bring substantial sums of money into rural communities. In many attractive areas, the economic input of tourism already greatly outpaces that of the local agricultural (or forest) economy. Argument on tourist issues sometimes involves hot resentment of outsiders, with their fancy four-by-fours and money to burn. But as Denzel Ferguson, author of *Sacred Cows at the Public Trough*, puts it, "Tourists are nonconsumptive. . . . Tourists do not shoot up signs with their twenty-twos or overgraze or clearcut or drive up hillsides on their four-wheelers. Local people do that. Tourists do not take the resource away with them."

Among the tourist attractions of the Plains (and, of course, of Yellowstone Park), bison already rank high. And touristic attention, because of the vigorous publicity machine of the tourist industry, has a way of multiplying and concentrating, so the process seems to be accelerating. Towns near bison herds issue flyers about refuges and ranches. Tourist shops situated next to ranches mention the presence of bison as a reason to venture off the interstate to visit them. Commercial "nature parks" with drive-through viewing roads from which tourists can see bison, elk, deer, antelope, and prairie dogs are proliferating.

The Dakotas have extensive Indian reservations and some of the nation's largest bison herds, as well as tribal powwows and other events that are increasingly open to outsiders. Even tourists interested mainly in Indian gambling casinos get some exposure to Native American culture. A group of tribes, in cooperation with the South Dakota Department of Tourism, has issued a sophisticated booklet for tourists about the museum resources and Indian cultures of the state that includes some etiquette tips for observers of powwows and information about how visitors can view the Cheyenne River Sioux's bison herd.

State tourist offices on the Plains work hard to attract out-of-state visitors. So far, bison tourism seems likely to expand in two basic ways. In the bison-rich area surrounding Rapid City, South Dakota, for instance, you can visit several bison ranches as well as the Custer State Park and Wind Cave National Park herds. At a reconstruction of the Fort Hays set from *Dances with Wolves,* you can view a video about the film's production, eat lunch, and buy bison-oriented souvenirs. Park visitor centers in the area offer a wealth of information about bison, including video showings and books. Museums devoted to western history often feature extensive bison displays. Other attractions include buffalo jumps, or *pishkun,* especially in Montana, some of which are sites of active archaeological studies. Jamestown, North Dakota, has not only a live bison herd next to a reconstructed old western town but also a museum dedicated to the history of the bison. A local landmark is a gigantic concrete bison monument— twenty-six feet high! Perhaps significantly, this thriving town is located on the intersection of an interstate and a major north-south highway.

A second trend might be called the dude-ranch approach, but it also has connections with what has come to be called ecotourism. We know well the destructive effects of heavy visitation in some of our most crowded and popular parks. Experience in remote, fragile environments like Nepal's has made us aware that masses of visitors can degrade landscapes and cultures and actually endanger rare species. In response, ecotourism companies have been devising tours and other experiences specifically designed to minimize visitors' ecological impacts. Getting tourists out of cars and onto trails, along with patronizing modest existing lodging facilities, reduces the physical effects of tourism. Respecting and utilizing local people's knowledge of their environment by employing them as guides and teachers rather than merely as service personnel leaves money in the local communities and reduces the deleterious social effects of tourism. Such ideas are proving remarkably popular the world over and can also be applied on the Plains.

Many city dwellers have learned to relish the experience of staying awhile at working cattle ranches. People with children (including teenage children) especially find dude-ranching a healthy and restorative—if sometimes physically arduous—way of vacationing. Some dude ranches merely entertain their guests, take them horseback riding, show them where the swimming hole is, and feed them enormous quantities of cowhand food. Others involve them in the ongoing work of the ranch.

Bison being much more impressive animals than cattle, bison dude ranches should have an inherent tourism advantage. The hayrides that are a standard feature of dude ranches would be an extremely attractive way to give an ecotourism component to ranch life if they took tourists into close contact with bison herds. Imaginative ranchers might reenact pioneer wagon-train camp-out experiences on their bison grasslands. There is already a precedent for this: the Oregon Trail Wagon Train outfit in Nebraska takes tourists on up to five-night treks in modern versions of the Conestoga wagon, letting them help drive the teams, make camp, and cook. Some ranchers already allow bison hunting, and it might be made part of "pioneering" activities. While it would not be to everybody's liking, observing the slaughtering, dressing, cutting, and cooking of bison meat for the ranch table would have an educational appeal for many.

The prospects for industrial development on the Pine Ridge Reservation are slight, but bison-oriented ecotourism could be an economic boost there. Visitors could observe the bison herds and other reservation wildlife, familiarize themselves with tribal life, and, as the tribe's tourism director, Tommy Tibbitts, said "maybe come and stay a night with a family, give them a little money and go on their way." Pine Ridge is also attractive to tourists for two other reasons: it lies in the middle of the biggest fossil bed in the world, and surprising numbers of tourists are even now drawn to the not yet developed massacre site at Wounded Knee—Germans, Californians, midwesterners, and many others turn up there.

The mass grave where the bodies of several hundred Sioux men, women, and children were tossed in 1890 after the troopers killed them, in the next-to-last atrocity committed by the U.S. Army on Indian land, has an air of terrible melancholy hanging over it. Flowers and ribbons festoon the fence that protects the grave; a simple obelisk monument honors the dead.

Wounded Knee has a direct connection to bison: the Ghost Dance religion, which spread among Indians after they had been herded onto reservations, predicted that the buffalo (who had returned to their origins underground because they were not respected) would come back and whites would go away. The excitement of this shared vision terrified whites, and with the army on hair-trigger alert, a minor scuffle became a massacre. But not all the area's history is bleak. A hundred miles to the west, tourists stare at the great white fathers carved into Mount Rushmore—including Theodore Roosevelt, whose liking for the hunt led him to establish five national parks, eighteen national monuments, and fifty-one federal bird refuges. And a few miles beyond Mount Rushmore, a monument to Sioux chief Crazy Horse, which will dwarf the white faces, steadily emerges from the granite.

Bison-related tourism enterprises can be expected to appeal to Americans not only through the inherent interest of the bison themselves but also through their central, symbolic role in western history; they are part of America's roots, part of the legend of the West. European and Japanese tourists too will be eager to experience bison as novel aspects of the romantic West.

History and Modern Prospects of Commons

Some of the hostility of Plains dwellers' reactions to the Poppers' buffalo commons term comes from its "socialistic" sound. Americans are not terribly enthusiastic about sharing, at least not after kindergarten, and the fact that Boston and most other New England communities were established around grassy commons is not widely known elsewhere in the country. For some people, moreover, the very idea of a commons has been discredited by the powerful parable enunciated by Garrett Hardin in "The Tragedy of the Commons," which appeared in *Science* in 1968 and has been endlessly reprinted and cited ever since. The Poppers were correct to believe that the tragedy of the Plains had important parallels with Hardin's essay, but whether bison restoration could reconstitute a real modern commons outside reservation land is highly uncertain.

Hardin's parable is actually aimed at the contemporary human population problem and has nothing at all to do with the historical commons by which humans have successfully and sustainably regulated their shared use of resources for, at the least, tens of thousands of years. Before capitalist notions of property arose, villagers enjoyed commons in both pasturelands and forests. Robin Hood's refuge, Sherwood Forest in Nottinghamshire, was a common forest until local dukes managed to seize private possession of it—indeed, part of it is now known as The Dukeries. Villagers all over the planet shared use of common resources intelligently and fairly enough to make the system work for millennia. Incredible though it may sound to moderns, who are convinced that humans have an innate tendency to pillage and ruin, these "commoners" sought and achieved mutual long-term sustainability, not individual profit.

It is clear from Hardin's text that he was not aware of all this. As scientists sometimes do, he relied on clarity of logic in the absence of historical facts to argue that "mutual coercion mutually agreed upon" could reduce the runaway population of humans to something approximating the planet's carrying capacity. What the fable section of his article describes so succinctly is really the ethic of capitalist appropriation, and it is thus diametrically opposed to the whole concept of the commons. "Picture a pasture open to all. *It is to be expected* [italics added—no participant in a historical commons would have expected any such thing] that each herdsman will try to keep as many cattle as possible on the commons." And the herdsman's neighbors, noticing his success, supposedly would follow suit. Soon the total number of cattle would be so great that the common grassland would be destroyed through overgrazing, and ruin would befall all the herdsmen. Q.E.D.

What Hardin assumed in the italicized phrase is that all people are interested in profit, not survival, and the fatal defect in his parable is the fact that real commons did not work at all the way he described them. Historically, village commons were restrained by networks of mutual obligation, age-old traditions of careful management, and a profound sense that survival was paramount. Far from leading to the prompt ruin that Hardin imagined, commons arrangements were so durable that they persisted in England, even against vicious attacks, well into the nineteenth century. (Their origins lay at least as far back as Neolithic villages.) As a recent magisterial study has established, English commons produced a great array of products, including food, grazing, construction materials, bedding, matting, clothing, fuel, toys, and knickknacks. A year's milk from a single cow on the commons brought in the equivalent of six months of grueling wage labor; it is small wonder that commoners were disinclined to seek factory jobs and had to be forced off their land. A traditional English rhyme expressed their resentment:

> *They hang the man and flog the woman*
> *That steals the goose from off the common*
> *But let the greater villain loose*
> *That steals the common from the goose.*

Nonetheless, Parliament relentlessly expropriated the common areas, and by 1876, 98.5 percent of English agricultural land was owned by 2,250 people—only .6 percent of the population. The result created the first modern proletariat: a mass of dispossessed workers huddled around what the poet William Blake called "the dark satanic mills." The situation has not improved much over the years. In England, more than half of all private land is owned by 1 percent of the population.

Resistance occurred sporadically. The Commons Preservation Society in 1866 began ripping down enclosers' fences, and this direct-action tactic managed to save Berkhamstead Common, Epping Forest, the New Forest, and numerous other natural areas whose existence is now taken for granted. In Scotland, where a new movement is trying to recapture for tenant-farmer communities some of the lands owned by absentee "lairds" (lords—now including oil sheiks and Swiss bankers) but used only for hunting, a tiny .08 percent of the population (4,000 souls) owns 80 percent of private land and, indeed, thirty-five families or companies own one-third of the Highlands. Similar concentrations of ownership are a bone of permanent political contention all over the world.

The ethic of private profit has led since the fifteenth century to a still-continuing process termed enclosure, so called because it was first practiced on a massive scale when the English nobility forcibly fenced off previously common grasslands, seizing them for the purpose of raising sheep—wool being a highly profitable commodity. Enclosure occurs in the modern world whenever governments and corporations seize and exploit rain forests inhabited for millennia by tribal peoples. As the Poppers recognized, it happened in U.S. history when whites seized Indian lands held in common. It happens in India today when a dam drives hundreds of thousands of people from their village homes, woodlots, and pastures. It happens, in a bizarre new legal twist, when corporations patent plant seeds or plant products that may have been used by indigenous peoples since humans first became human. Corporations are even seeking to patent genes, as in the human genes inserted into pigs. A profoundly sinister possibility thus comes into view: that components of human bodies might become "enclosed"—and thus become corporate property.

Gary Snyder, who has written cogently and at length on the commons, points out that "the commons is both specific land and the traditional community institution that determines the carrying capacity of its various subunits and defines the rights and obligations of those who use it, with penalties for lapses. Because it is traditional and local, it is not identical with today's 'public domain,' which is land held and managed by a central government."

Modern competitive capitalism, founded on an entirely different ethos and with entirely different principles of decision making, does work in the destructive way that Hardin describes. It has operated, of course, in agriculture as well as in most other recent human enterprises. Its depredations have been so catastrophic that we have been forced to try to reinstitute some of the ancient principles by which real commons achieved sustainability. In fisheries, for example, although Hardin tries to blame a residual "philosophy of the commons" for such problems, deep declines in catch produced by overfishing have led to the setting out of fair shares for different nations' fishing fleets, the limiting of total catch, and even, most recently, the prohibition of fishing in certain areas, all in the hope that fish populations will recover. Given the impersonal scale and awkwardness of modern bureaucratic management, however, this approach has not worked very well, and fishery catches are continuing to decline everywhere. Nor have attempts to defend the common seas against marine pollution and waste dumping been successful; the London Dumping Convention was argued over from 1970 to 1993, and its implementation by the industrialized countries that do most of the dumping is, to say the least, uncertain.

In other enterprises, like lumbering and grazing on public lands, we have adopted enclosure strategies whereby public goods are conveyed into private hands by means determined by market forces and politics. Anomalies inevitably occur when the rigid categories of property law are applied to natural processes such as shifting rivers or water tables driven down by well drilling. Nonetheless, this tendency has prevailed in the United States for a hundred years, during which time forest cover has steadily shrunk or been monoculturized and lands have degraded. The prospects of widespread sustainability over a long haul are dim—with the sole exception of the Plains.

The possibility of reconstituting a true commons in bison, such as the one that existed in precontact Indian days, seems remote except on Indian land because of the unlikelihood of whites restoring the kind of limiting community institutions of which Snyder speaks. Capitalism is the most powerful social corrosive known, and once it dissolves the traditional bonds among humans and between humans and the environment, these bonds are almost impossible to reconstitute. Only cash relationships remain, restrained solely by feeble government playing rules. In fact, in some areas where commons practices have persisted (ownership of underground minerals, allocation of radio frequencies, trade in plant seeds) we are now witnessing a rush to privatization—a new name for enclosure, though some prefer to call it looting.

And yet, and yet . . . When you watch a herd of bison moving across the land, the sight raises the prospect of other ways of thinking—ancient ways, tested over millennia of human survival. Our first impulse now is to subject bison to the familiar rules of private ownership and industrial-style management. But these strategies, with their burdens of capital investment and labor intensity, are in the long run less efficient than tapping the resources of a commons directly. We may, then, be forced into looking for older, more cooperative, and more natural ways to deal with bison and other wild grazers. In the long run, we may have to reinvent the commons in some new form that will not tragically fall prey to the destructive tendencies of human acquisitiveness. The commons sets two ineluctable rules for sustainability. First, people cannot take from the commons more than its natural productivity; it requires us not only to ascertain that productivity but also to honor it by limiting one another's greed. Second, the proceeds of the commons must be distributed fairly to all the people, so that all have a strong motivation to preserve and defend it. In teaching us to live again by these ancient imperatives, a buffalo commons might in time reinvent us.

Chapter Ten
Bison and Wind Power

Bison and wind power offer us strikingly parallel opportunities—ways to utilize the endlessly renewable resources of grass and wind that can preserve the Plains ecosystem and support its human inhabitants indefinitely. They are thus not at all the unrelated subjects they might at first seem. In the great test case that the Plains present to us, if we learn to honor and use the bison and the winds we will have made a fundamental transition in attitude from reckless exploitation to respectful coexistence with the great natural forces of the planet. Both bison and wind are there, waiting to teach us the imperative lessons of sustainability.

Only two generations ago, windmills were the normal power source for wells throughout agricultural America. Windmill, water-storage tower, and house constituted the basic image of the isolated farmstead, imprinted on our minds through a hundred Western movies. Spinning day and night, the faithful windmills pumped up life-giving water, the creak of their gears providing reassurance that all was well. Even today, amazingly durable old-fashioned windmills provide cheap and reliable pumping to many farms and ranches. Finding and rebuilding an old windmill, in fact, has now become the pride of former city dwellers moving to the country—a sign of nostalgia for a time when it was universal for farmers to draw energy directly from sun and wind and live sustainably on the land with their animals. But wind power is poised to return to the Plains in a new, highly sophisticated, modern-technology form.

As in any region, people on the Plains use energy for many purposes.

Transportation, heating of dwellings and other buildings, refrigeration and air-conditioning, lighting, and water heating are the biggest direct ways in which energy is consumed—most of it in the forms of gasoline, electricity, and natural gas. Plains coal is used in large quantities to produce electricity. But overall, the Plains depend on (as does the United States as a whole) imported fossil-fuel energy—a regime that cannot be maintained indefinitely.

A basic criterion for a society's sustainability lies in its material and energy "throughputs"—everything that passes through the industrial system. Mining and smelting of metals, casting and stamping, refining of oil and molding of plastics, painting and finishing—all the processes of manufacturing cause substantial environmental impacts, as do the combustion-driven shipping and distribution of products. Such are the scale and intensity of contemporary industrial activity that these impacts are overwhelming the capacity of the earth's natural systems to absorb them. Thus, either a scale-down of industrial production will have to be accomplished voluntarily or nature will enforce it. For instance, executives of major global insurance companies are beginning to think that increased floods and other weather-connected disasters may be due to carbon dioxide–driven global warming. Higher disaster risks translate directly into higher insurance costs, which feed back to reduce risk-exposed human activities.

Similarly, energy-intensive farming and ranching convert imported fossil-fuel energy (turned into fertilizer, herbicides and pesticides, equipment and its fuel supplies, animal feed, and so on) into beef and wheat. The unsustainability of this situation is increasingly manifested through the rising operation costs experienced by farmers and ranchers.

On the Plains, the transition from fossil fuels to renewable energy (solar, both thermal and photovoltaic; wind power; and existing hydroelectric development) will actually be easier than in other regions because of the Plains' sparse population and rich resources of grass and wind. Whereas solar installations will probably not become widespread until the middle of the next century, wind power is on the verge of wide deployment now.

It is sometimes argued that the transition to a sustainable-energy system, on the Plains and elsewhere, can be postponed indefinitely or avoided through reliance on coal and natural gas. The discovery of new large reserves of gas, in particular, has been welcomed by some as a sign that fossil fuels can power a century of continued economic growth. New supplies of carbon fuels, however, are in fact a curse rather than a blessing, since they will encourage the already industrialized nations (and rapidly developing larger nations like China and India) to avoid adopting renewable energy systems. However, burning up the planet's fossil fuel reserves will almost certainly exacerbate global warming to disastrous levels. Though gas produces somewhat less pollution and carbon dioxide than does coal, it can only serve as a transitional fuel to the renewable era.

A few scientists have begun to suspect, incidentally, that natural gas is a geological product still being created deep within the earth and not, like coal and oil, a fossilized biological product. Even if this turns out to be true, the long-term picture does not change; the gas-formation process, if it exists, must be enormously slower than human use of gas. Gas can serve, to some extent, only as a "bridge fuel" between the fossil-fuel era and a renewable-energy future.

A Plains Resource

Writers have often described the Plains winds as overwhelming—indeed, a character in O. E. Rølvaag's *Giants in the Earth* goes mad because of them. But wind, like grass, is a fundamental, permanent resource on which the Plains can draw for a sustainable future. And, as we shall see, wind and bison make an elegant combination.

Generated by differences in solar heat distribution over different regions of the planet, winds blow most strongly where they are unobstructed by trees, buildings, or rough terrain. Thus, the strongest and most constant winds are found at sea, along seacoasts, and in relatively flat country like the Plains, which are sometimes called the "sea of grass." The energy available from wind is proportional to the cube of wind speed. That is, wind three times as fast has twenty-seven times the energy, so wind installations are most efficient in high-wind locations. Many places qualify on the Plains.

Bison have always lived in harmony with the wind, and they survive winter weather so cold that ice forms on their beards. They face into blizzards, not away from them as cattle do, so they never crowd up against fences and freeze to death. When winter winds thin the snow on a rise, bison go there to nose down and find the underlying grass.

Wind and bison have fit together in the ecological past, and they have a sustainable future together as well. They are both dominant features of the original Plains landscape, and we can learn to rely on them both.

Our daily experience does not equip us to grasp the massive energy potential of the winds. But North Dakota's wind alone could provide 36 percent of today's total national electric demand; the state has more wind-energy potential than California, heretofore the nation's leader in wind power. The Great Plains as a whole could meet the nation's energy needs many times over. And wind installations, including the narrow service

Using their massive shoulder muscles, bison brush aside snow with their muzzles to reach grass beneath it. They will also eat snow for moisture if necessary, whereas ranchers must keep water sources open for cattle in winter. Photo: Michael H. Francis.

roads they need, occupy only a fraction of the land's surface, leaving plenty of room for bison. Well-designed "wind-farm" roads and towers do not cause soil erosion; wind-farm transmission lines can and should be placed underground wherever scenic values are important. And an important economic appeal of wind power is that leasing land for wind farms can provide much-needed supplementary income to ranchers, helping to preserve open space that might otherwise be developed into condominiums and strip malls.

World Wind Power Today

The Plains need not play a pioneering role in wind power; they can merely follow along behind striking developments elsewhere. A wind farm may soon replace one of the reactors at the Chernobyl nuclear plant, and there are twenty thousand wind turbines spinning worldwide. Northern European wind-power installations are expanding rapidly, but projects are also under way in Argentina, China, India, Mexico, New Zealand, Spain, and other countries. In New England, the United Kingdom, and Poland, among other places, wind turbines producing large amounts of energy are being planned for mounting, like oil-well towers, in shallow offshore waters. Some energy experts believe that wind power will come to supply 20 percent of the world's energy.

In the past, public and media perceptions of wind power, along with the decisions of U.S. utility executives, were colored by a series of spectacular failed experiments with giant wind machines by Boeing, Pacific Gas and Electric Company, and the U.S. Department of Energy. The blades of some of these early monsters were as long as football fields, and, predictably enough, they vibrated dangerously. But the learning curve in developing more modest-sized and easily managed machines has been steep. Three or four technical generations of design experience in California and, more recently, in Europe have led to much more efficient blades and to more responsive, electronically controlled turbines. Wind is now a thoroughly proven technology.

Moreover, the maintenance and repair of wind installations is a nondemanding, medium-tech business for which the Plains could easily supply the work force. Working on wind machines does not involve the heroic precautions for radiation safety or drastic interruptions to service that nuclear plants are subject to; when a wind turbine needs repairs, hundreds of others nearby keep right on working. In certain damp locations, like Vermont's Green Mountains, wind machines are subject to occasional icing up in winter. But otherwise wind has become a reliable, almost humdrum source of power. It will be right at home in the American heartland, along with bison.

By its nature, wind power is irregular—some days, even on the Plains, winds drop off—so heretofore it has always been used in conjunction with other power sources. But the peaks and valleys of wind generation will soon be smoothable by the deployment of a new generation of storage devices, including high-tech flywheels as well as new types of batteries. Sophisticated flywheels that store impressive amounts of rotational energy are a still-unfamiliar technology but one nearing commercial application. Essentially high–tensile-strength and virtually zero-friction motor-generators, they come in sizes small enough to supply power for cars or houses and also big enough for use by power companies. They will be particularly useful in regions like the Plains, with thin and dispersed populations. Meanwhile, wind is a natural complement to the new natural gas–turbine generators, which turn on and off quickly and can thus make up for drops in wind output.

Although Kansas, Nebraska, and the Dakotas have sometimes been referred to as the Saudi Arabia of wind energy, to this point wind power in America has developed on a commercial scale only in California and Hawaii. The Altamont Pass area, in fact, supplies enough power for the city of San Francisco's 700,000 people—about the population of Montana. Strong, consistent winds produce even more power near the Los Angeles metropolitan area. Like many other American industries, the intensive wind-power development in California since the 1970s has been encouraged by accelerated depreciation allowances and other occasional incentives, but its development now relies on sheer profitability.

The costs of building and installing wind turbines have dropped steadily and will certainly continue to drop. Some observers feel that Belgium and Germany have now surpassed the United States in wind technol-

The old and the new: modern wind-energy technology, which has made wind power virtually the cheapest source of new electrical generating capacity, will gradually spread to profitably windy sites throughout the country.

ogy, and the Japanese are also actively in the race. The authors of a recent study of American competitiveness in environmental industries note: "As is the case with other renewable technologies, wind power's early significant advances in this country have led to a worldwide technology development effort that far surpasses current domestic expenditures. In Europe, seven countries and the Commission of European Communities are each spending as much or more on wind energy research, development, and demonstration as the United States."

But in America, wind power has made its striking advances despite the fact that government support still flows overwhelmingly to the oil, gas, coal, and nuclear power industries. According to the Congressional Research Service, nuclear power has so far received some $97 billion (in 1990 dollars) and soaked up 65 percent of all federal funds for energy research and development from 1948 to 1992—not including the future subsidies that will be needed for decommissioning of closed nuclear plants and for disposal or storage of wastes and, conceivably, accident disaster relief.

Through advanced turbine design, wind power currently costs, on the average, about 5.3 cents per kilowatt-hour (kWh) to generate. This is roughly competitive with other types of newly built power generation—even with coal plants or natural-gas turbines—and markedly less expensive than nuclear power, which comes in at 10–12 cents per kWh, not including government subsidies and decommissioning costs. It is also less expensive than solar-thermal energy—produced by long reflective troughs heating fluid in a pipe to drive a generator—in sunny regions. Within a decade, wind power will probably be the cheapest known way to produce new electricity. It should cost 4 cents per kWh by the year 2000; if moderate tax incentives are provided, around 3 cents. A recent round of competitive bidding for power generation in California showed that wind turbines are already more economical than gas-plant repowering. They are also built very quickly, so when wind power really gets going on the Plains, it is likely to develop with surprising speed.

To assess wind power fully from a sustainability standpoint, a net-energy analysis should be carried out according to the same logic used to assess petroleum-based agriculture. How much energy goes into a wind farm's construction and, later, maintenance, versus how much comes out? A careful study along these lines has been done of photovoltaic cells—the devices now used to generate energy for roadside emergency phones, lighted buoys, and many other remote applications. Thin-film photovoltaic modules pay off in six months' to two years' time. It is almost certain that wind turbines pay off their energy investment in the first year of operation; thereafter, for the twenty or thirty years that an individual wind machine lasts, it generates net positive energy. Its maintenance causes hardly any environmental degradation, and it requires no mining or drilling, transportation of fuels, emission controls, or waste disposal.

Thus, wind power, as is recognized by most continental European countries and by the British, must be a substantial part of any long-term, sustainable national energy policy. It certainly should come to play a major role on the Plains, as it will in much of the world.

Over the next decade or so, the only way to acquire energy substantially more cheaply than through wind power will be to invest in installing more efficient motors, lighting, heating, and air-conditioning, thus creating "negawatts"—newly available power achieved without the building of new generating plants. Such conservation investments can make saved power available at a cost some 24–44 percent lower even than that of wind power—something that should have strong appeal to thrifty Plains people. U.S. energy use per capita is so high that conservation is now and will be for some decades the best energy investment we could make, and some state public utility commissions have found inventive ways to motivate utilities to help their customers improve efficiency. Many state regulatory agencies have yet to act on these long-term benefits for their economies, however, so the national pace of change has been regrettably slow. Yet in Iowa, a switch to renewable energy has been adopted as an official state goal, and six wind-power projects are planned or under construction. If the saying "As Iowa goes, so goes the nation" still has validity, this is good news.

Wind Power on the Plains

For the Plains, wind has a great many specific advantages over fossil-fuel power. It blows most strongly in the daytime and in the winter, when power needs are highest; it would thus be especially desirable for customers—businesses, farms, or householders—that presently pay stiff rates for peak-period power. Wind installations are highly compatible with ranching operations, whether of cattle or bison. From a jobs standpoint, residents of the Plains, which have suffered boom-and-bust employment in oil and coal, should find particularly appealing the fact that wind development creates about fifteen jobs for every million dollars of investment, slightly more than coal does,while hydroelectric power and natural gas are only half as job productive. Residents of rural southwestern Minnesota, aware of these figures, have lobbied their state legislature to push for wind development. (One site there is named Buffalo Ridge, and its present small wind farm will be greatly expanded by 2002.)

If current consumption trends continue, it is likely that the United States will depend entirely on foreign sources for its oil within fifteen years.

But wind power is not subject to fearsome swings in international fuel prices—no OPEC could ever block the winds from blowing. Nor could wind power ever incur the equivalent of the costs we would bear in the event of new Persian Gulf warfare: we spent tens of billions of dollars in military costs defending Middle East oil fields against Iraq—equivalent to a public subsidy to the oil industry of about $100 per barrel.

Plains resources of biomass could also furnish massive amounts of energy through the burning of crop wastes and the cultivation of fast-growing fuel crops like switchgrass and coppiced poplar. Putting biomass and wind together with an aggressive energy-efficiency program could make the region self-sufficient in energy and result in long-term net savings to the

Settlers experimented with different types of windmill blades to cope with extreme wind conditions. This model has been restored at Kauffman Museum in Newton, Kansas, which also boasts a small plot of tallgrass prairie.

regional economy of trillions of dollars—dollars that would no longer flow out of the region to the stock markets of New York or Tokyo or London.

Translating this potential into reality will, of course, take time. Even in Nebraska, which has a publicly owned utility system, there is as yet no renewable-energy development aside from the encouragement of ethanol production, mostly as a gasoline additive. However, small rural electric cooperatives can sometimes be individualistic and innovative, and a few may begin wind-power development soon. Only in Minnesota is rapid deployment in progress, since the legislature there mandated that the state's biggest utility bring renewable energy on line by December 1996.

Extensive wind-power development on the Plains would be a natural match with an increased presence of bison, and some ranchers are beginning to understand the financial possibilities involved. Entrepreneurs active in the field are not usually avid for publicity, probably because a key element in developing wind farms is obtaining rights from landowners to build towers and access roads; too much public awareness could lead to a "wind rush" and a rise in leasing costs. In windy parts of Wyoming, a hectare (2.47 acres) sells for around $100 but could yield $25,000 worth of electricity yearly. If Plains landowners received royalties similar to those in California, it would mean average annual payments of around $40 per acre on top of earnings from grazing or farming—enough, for many, to make the difference between bankruptcy and survival. In fact, since yearly cash rents for land range from around $30 per acre to $140 in rich-soil farm country, leasing land for wind turbines could greatly increase a landowner's income. Moreover, many prime wind-power sites are in elevated, poor-soil areas—exactly the areas where bison make special sense for ranchers. Income from leasing land to wind-power companies also has the crucial advantage for a rancher or farmer that once the wind-power installation's output is established, payments are made according to a long-term contract and thus provide security that volatile farm-commodity prices cannot offer. Some landowners could, in fact, grow rich, just as Texas ranchers did when oil was struck on their properties. Leasing to a 100-megawatt wind plant might reap earnings in the neighborhood of $400,000 per year.

The conditions for cooperation between landowners and wind-power companies are thus increasingly favorable, and some news has surfaced about upcoming developments. Kenetech, the parent company of U.S. Windpower, which was one of the major developers of the wind-power installation at California's Altamont Pass and now operates internationally (and is also active in biomass-energy production), recently announced a contract to build a Windplant™ in southern Wyoming for a utility called PacifiCorp. This is among the first wind installations to be sold directly to a utility; most are operated by smallish private companies. The site is in Carbon County, so the plant's power can be routed to the fast-growing Denver metropolitan area, not far away. It is, of course, a delicious irony that a county named for its coal reserves should become a pioneer in wind power. Texas, which is within original bison range, also has some quite windy areas. Four wind farms are currently planned in western Texas. One, for a utility company, is not far from El Paso and will feature a dozen newly designed turbines whose blades are 130 feet across.

Indian reservations on the Plains include a lot of windy territory, and Indians are interested in the bison–wind power combination too. In South Dakota, Fred DuBray has had the eastern half of the Cheyenne River Sioux reservation mapped for desirable turbine sites, according to Mark Heckert. The Indian perspective on current energy issues is a bitter one. In the beginning, of course, the tribes tended to live along the rivers, until whites pushed them back into arid lands. The whites then proceeded, in the 1930s, to build hydropower and irrigation dams and flood what were the best low-lying wildlife habitats. DuBray literally watched his own house float away as a reservoir was filled, so alternative energy sources are not a theoretical concern for him. Now, like all the inhabitants of the region, Indians must pay electric bills for power—power they see as coming from dams on their land. So to Indians—although finding the investment capital will not be easy—wind power on a small scale, decentralized on the reservations but perhaps also sufficient to allow them to sell surplus power to the grid, beckons as a means toward self-sufficiency and independence from economic exploitation. Needless to say, this is a scenario that would fit in well with bison.

It was not only Indians who were affected by the dams. The U.S. Army

Corps of Engineers created lakes that extend virtually across the Dakotas, flooding out many bottomland farmers and ranchers in the process. These happened to include Roy Houck, who was forced to move the ranch operation on which he later pioneered bison raising. It is an intriguing energy footnote to Houck's story that his new ranch has hot-water artesian wells that not only provide water for his animals but also heat his houses, slaughterhouse, and shop. Unfortunately, such geothermal energy is not a significant factor in the future of the Plains.

Time has not been kind to the irrigation agriculture the dams were supposed to promote; nearly all the farmers who got into irrigation have gone bankrupt because of high power costs. Some have reorganized and are irrigation-farming again, but the low costs of bison raising are likely to prove more appealing over the long run.

A New Model for Utility Planning

A careful analysis by the Union of Concerned Scientists, using computer modeling to isolate the top-quality sites for wind power in Kansas, Nebraska, North and South Dakota, and several neighboring states to the east, found that wind power could be installed in these areas in the near future for very attractive rates.

But in the deployment of electricity, access to transmission lines is actually a greater problem than is generating cost, and this has special implications for the thinly populated Plains. Like any large, central generating plant, a sizable wind farm must be located near existing heavy-duty transmission lines, since constructing new, long transmission lines is more expensive than constructing the power source itself. Unfortunately, the best Plains wind sites do not happen to lie near existing major transmission lines. However, wind power, like solar power, lends itself without economic penalty to smaller-scale plants. Thus, it seems likely that in the long run much wind-power generation, and not only in regions like the Plains, will provide electricity to relatively small areas over already existing power lines.

In fact, planners' increasing recognition that transmission and distribution costs are greater than generation costs has led to the concept of a "dis-

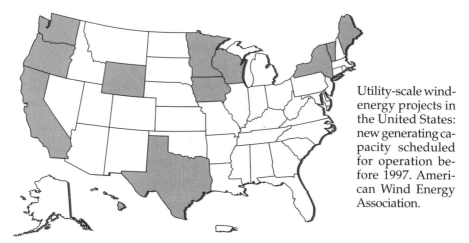

Utility-scale wind-energy projects in the United States: new generating capacity scheduled for operation before 1997. American Wind Energy Association.

tributed utility," with many small-scale generating facilities rather than a few massive central plants. This idea has been gaining ground for traditional plants in densely populated regions, but it makes even more sense for a region like the Plains, with a light and dispersed population. Moreover, it favors sources of renewable energy such as wind, sun, and biomass, because plants utilizing these sources are modest in size and can be modular in design—hence easily, quickly, and gradually built. Integrated resource planning, a basic criterion for maximum long-term efficiency that enlightened public utility commissions have gradually been adopting, also welcomes such systems because they may deliver power to users at a price lower than a centralized system would; furthermore, they have advantages of reliability and flexibility.

We may even see utilities or service companies offering individual isolated ranches wind-power installations to meet their own needs, entirely separate from the grid. There is an intriguing historical irony here because rural electrification was a major program of the New Deal, aiming to lift farmers out of their Depression-era isolation and poverty. To bring refrigeration, electric lighting, and even radios—on which farmers could hear FDR's presidential fireside chats—to farms at the end of the line, hundreds of cooperative electric companies were organized. Wires were strung to virtually all the scattered, lonely farms in the Midwest and on the Plains—a tremendously expensive undertaking. With present technology, it turns out, it would often be cheaper to give unserved farmers or isolated homesteads small wind-turbine and energy-storage installations and forget the wires.

Wind-power enthusiasts sometimes envision very large wind farms on the Plains that would be capable of providing power to urban areas—for instance, to replace the aging nuclear plants that ring Chicago when they begin to have accidents or are decommissioned. But to build new heavy-duty transmission lines over long distances would require billions of dollars in investment. Privately owned utilities thus will probably continue for some decades to build massive fossil-fuel generating plants near metropolitan areas. So wind power on the Plains is likely to develop for some time as a relatively rural matter. This may be to the good, however; a region with its own ample supply of local energy, not committed to distant buyers, is in a solid position for the future. And selling power back to the utility, a process that occurs whenever a wind installation has a surplus of power and "runs the meter backward," would certainly appeal to the thrifty instincts of Plains ranchers and farmers.

Perhaps most important of all, the political appeal of wind power will come from the fact that it keeps money within a state rather than exporting it in exchange for fossil fuels. It thus generates jobs indirectly as well as directly. Moreover, wind power provides a hedge against future rises in natural-gas prices.

Utility planners concerned about the reliability of wind and solar power (while living with nuclear plants, whose down time is often almost as great as their operating time) may find that one of their first compelling needs for wind-power installations is to meet fluctuations in demand in remote parts of their grids—a factor even more important in servicing the thinly dispersed populations on the Plains than elsewhere. Building local wind farms would be markedly cheaper than building more central generating and transmission capacity for the whole network.

But old ideas die hard, and the logical leap to realizing that the most important number is cost at the customer's meter, not cost at the generating plant, is not an easy one. If it were, all the Plains utilities would already be busy building modest-sized wind-power plants strategically placed to obviate the need for building bigger transmission lines. Indeed, where wind plants are situated near consumers, wind power may even now cost only 3 cents per kWh, all expenses taken into account—around half what most conventional power costs. When devices like flywheels become capable of storing wind-generated power overnight or longer, in both household-scale and industrial amounts, wind power will be used as "baseload" as well as peak-period power.

We might expect that such factors would earn very broad acceptance of wind power among utilities. However, because regulatory bodies customarily allow utilities to pass on fuel costs to their customers, they are not strongly attracted to the free-fuel aspects of wind and solar power. State regulatory bodies thus need to provide financial incentives that will lead utilities to diversify their energy base. Wind power's general benefits for society have led Congress to create tax credits for projects established before the year 2000, and this may spur Plains states into action—though many of them have yet to establish state energy offices.

Sustainable Energy from Many Sources

Other renewable-energy resources exist in the Plains states and will be developed in time, although wind will lead the way. Hydropower, at dams on the Missouri and other rivers, is already fully exploited and provides the region's cheapest existing electricity. In some areas, like Wyoming, with its cold but relatively cloud-free climate, solar-thermal and photovoltaic possibilities will open up, as well as direct solar power for space and water heating. In areas of the Plains with substantial rainfall, biomass burning, using either crop wastes or specially grown crops, could yield substantial power without a net addition to atmospheric carbon dioxide, and ethanol production for fuel use is already a major enterprise in Iowa. Wind, however, is the only renewable energy source that leaves the land surface free for grazing—a synergistic relationship that should greatly appeal to landowners.

The American energy system is in a period of flux and volatility. Deregulation is threatening the previously guaranteed profits of utilities; expectations are clouded. And generating technologies are changing. Despite billions of dollars expended annually in federal subsidies, nuclear power is effectively dead in the United States; it is simply not competitive, even aside from the unsolved—and enormously costly—problem of what to do with its radioactive wastes. Plants that burn natural gas will remain attractive for a decade or so, but coal plants now carry such heavy costs in pollution cleanup that they too are becoming financially unattractive. Thus, by economic default, as well as by the attractiveness of their pollution-free, durable, no-fuels technologies, solar and wind power have a solid future as parts of America's energy supply system, and the Plains in particular are in a fine position to exploit wind power.

Biomass energy in the form of ethanol already helps to power our vehicles, and we can envision a sustainable Plains world of humans deriving nourishment and economic support from grassland bison and driving vehicles powered by prairie biomass fuels. Wind also may come to power cars indirectly. Because automobiles and trucks are our greatest users of energy, transportation alternatives to imported oil are a fundamental long-term concern, both nationally and regionally, and wind-generated power will be one component in a future transportation system utilizing mixed energy sources. Our present transportation system gets more than 97 percent of its energy from petroleum—a dangerous dependency.

In the long run, electric vehicles have a bright future because they are much simpler mechanically than internal combustion vehicles, are capable of astonishing acceleration, and have a lower per-mile energy cost, especially when regenerative braking systems capture braking energy and put it back into the battery or flywheel. Electricity for cars can come as easily from wind as from fossil-fuel plants—with great savings in air pollution over internal combustion engines—though it can also be generated by compact internal combustion on-board engines. Unfortunately, the recently developed and otherwise promising nickel-metal-hydride batteries use toxic nickel, while lead-acid batteries involve some atmospheric pollution in their production and recycling, so flywheel energy storage will probably become very attractive for vehicles. In the distant future, hydrogen will be used for cars and many other purposes since it is a pollution-free fuel and can be piped and stored rather like natural gas. Wind and solar power will ultimately be used to produce hydrogen by dissociating the hydrogen and oxygen that make up water.

Battery-driven electric cars and vans are now becoming common for delivery and other short-haul use. California has required major car companies to sell substantial numbers of electric vehicles in the Los Angeles air-pollution basin by 1997, and pollution-plagued eastern states are adopting similar measures. If electric vehicles prove cheap and reliable, Plains dwellers will begin using them too. Nevertheless, fossil fuels will undoubtedly continue to provide a good proportion of our transportation energy, even if the government becomes less determined to subsidize the car-highway-oil complex through road building, police and court services, military expenditures to ensure control of the Middle East, and so on.

Living with Wind Power

Nothing and nobody is entirely innocent. Blades of wind machines take some toll on hawks, owls, and eagles who try to fly through them, though highways cause roadkills of immensely greater numbers of animals and birds. To combat bird losses, designers of wind machines are experimenting with slower-moving blades or a more visible and avoidable set of fixed vertical vanes in a star-shaped pattern around a vertical rotor—a system of this type is now in place on a property in Wales belonging to the Queen of England. Wind machines pose no known problems for other animals, particularly large grazers similar to bison—indeed, much experience in California has demonstrated that livestock and wind-power installations coexist very comfortably.

Wind machines make noise—a persistent swishing sound that most people would not enjoy living right next to; it is similar to the wind and tire noise generated by a highway. Luckily, however, the strong winds on hills that attract wind-farm designers also discourage residential siting. On the Plains as elsewhere, few people like to live on hillsides exposed to the strongest winds, so noise exposure should not be a significant problem.

And bison would probably love wind-machine towers for one special bison reason. In the spring, when they are shedding their heavy winter coats, bison like to scratch on vertical objects. On the Plains, this originally

Cattle graze placidly beneath thousands of wind machines at Altamont Pass, California. Such scenes, with bison replacing the cattle, will become common on the Great Plains. Photo: Kenetech Corp.

meant occasional trees or stumps or rare big rocks, which were polished smooth over centuries and were called "buffalo rocks" by the pioneers. Wind farms would be bison rubbing paradise. On ranches, bison rubbing can do substantial damage to fence posts. But the bison on Catalina Island have not been a nuisance to the wooden-pole power line crossing the island; nor has the herd at the National Bison Range in Montana damaged the steel power-line towers crossing its territory. So it seems very unlikely that even the most enthusiastic bison rubbing would affect heavy steel wind-machine towers with concrete footings, which are built to withstand severe winds.

To me, the sight of a field of wind machines dancing their intricate differential rhythms with the wind is a joy; it always makes me smile. (On Tehachapi Pass in southern California, some of the blades have red-painted tips, and they look positively festive as they spin.) The grave vertical-axis turbines, their great, curved blades revolving slowly like some space-alien eggbeater, fill me with awe. The whishes and swooshes of wind turbines as the wind direction varies sound reassuring to me, and windy grasslands with thousands of bison happily grazing among wind machines seem to me a delightful prospect. Nonetheless, there are a few people who find wind machines ugly or intrusive on the landscape.

It is hard, of course, to argue about impressions of beauty; as has often been said, beauty lies in the eye of the beholder. If displeased viewers of wind farms go out to observe a remote wind-farm area on foot or bicycle, and at home use only wood power for their heating and cooking and tallow candles for light, their aesthetic criticisms would rest on a purer footing. But it is hard to take such critics seriously when they approach by car over six-lane highways that are far more visible infringements on the landscape than a wind farm—besides being substantial contributors to atmospheric pollution. Moreover, unless the critics are very unusual indeed, they are (like all of us) heavy users of natural gas, oil, and electricity generated by burning of fossil fuels or deployment of radioactivity. A visit to a refinery, coal mine, or nuclear plant (not notably hospitable to bison or other life forms) should be a prerequisite before disparaging a relatively benign, life compatible, and sustainable technology like wind power.

There is, after all, no way we can make the world perfect. We can only try to choose wisely among available alternatives. In the interests of international competition as well as ecological survival, we need to use much less energy overall, but we will need energy from somewhere. On the Plains and elsewhere, we can increasingly choose wind and other renewable energy sources. Together with vigorous energy conservation, these new technologies offer us the chance of a sustainable future in which we and the bison can survive indefinitely.

Chapter Eleven
Bison Politics and Cowboy Culture

About two thousand years ago, at a time when tens of millions of bison were roaming the Great Plains, a Greek philosopher ruminated on the nature of human beings. "Man," declared Aristotle, "is a political animal." Nothing that has happened since has challenged his belief, so it is not surprising that the fate of bison today is in many respects a political question.

Or, more precisely, it is a series of political questions, most of which must ultimately be answered by Congress, although wildlife biologists, range scientists, and agency officials will play important roles in framing the answers. Since politics is always constrained by culture, all these players will operate within a general public context of greater or lesser sympathy for bison and other wild species. If bison receive the special symbolic status in our cultural life that this book argues they deserve, growing public concern with the welfare of bison could prove politically powerful. It would be a welcome sign of this political clout, and an opening to other issues, if bison were officially designated our national animal and given due honor and respect.

The Political Issues

Political questions are always answered within a dynamic of specific political forces driven by money and power and votes—though votes today are a secondary and, to a growing extent, manipulable factor. We will turn later in this chapter to some of the broader issues involved in a transition to a culture more hospitable to bison. Here, I will try to bring together the major directly political issues affecting bison that will be confronted in coming years; they have already, of course, been foreshadowed in previous chapters.

1. Shall public grazing lands continue to be used exclusively for cattle and sheep? If not, should the government agencies that are the custodians of these lands encourage ranchers to raise bison on them—or perhaps, in time, even require them to do so? As we have seen, an established cattle culture presently dominates the agencies, in terms of both official policies and the preferences of local personnel. This emphasis on cattle will gradually be undermined in the field if bison continue to prove more remunerative than cattle, and in the long run such changes in local perspectives will be reflected in Washington. But it is, after all, the public's land. If the public, through its elected congressional representatives, orders the agencies to change course, the process of change will be greatly accelerated. Through new legislation or by amending their governing acts, the Forest Service and the Bureau of Land Management should be directed to build bison herds on all public grazing lands, beginning with those comprising more than 5,000 contiguous acres. Many ecologically aware agency employees would be happy to carry out bison-friendly policies. But even new and strong policies do not always have quick results. In political life, tenacity is all. During a transitional period, allotments suitable for bison, either individually or joined with neighboring allotments, should be identified and ranchers using them given the choice of switching to bison or being bought out over time so that bison reserves along the lines described earlier may be created.

2. Shall fees paid by ranchers for the use of public grazing lands, whether used for cattle, sheep, or bison, be raised to approach market rates? Urban editorialists may deride low grazing fees as a cowboy welfare program, but they have a strong western political constituency. An attempt by the Clinton administration to raise fees ended in defeat in late 1994, and the political composition of Congress now makes it unlikely that the issue will be raised again for some years; although the newly dominant Republican ideology is theoretically antisubsidy, action is not likely against subsidies for political allies.

From a bison perspective, this situation cuts two ways. Keeping grazing fees subsidized will aid ranchers economically, enabling many of them to continue cattle ranching, at least for a time, despite declining beef prices and rising ranching costs. They will thus be less motivated to switch their operations to bison. On the other hand, profits will be significantly greater for those ranchers operating on public land who do switch to bison, probably enabling them to purchase or lease additional land on which to graze additional bison—and, in time, persuading fellow ranchers to switch as well.

3. Shall bison (along with elk, antelope, and deer) be restored to their native ranges in parks and on other public lands not classified as grazing lands? As public affection for bison widens and deepens, park managers will come under increasing pressure to bring back bison to areas where they formerly roamed. But in addition, constituents must persuade Congress (and some state legislatures too) that restoration of wild herbivores not only is ecologically desirable but also will result in savings of public funds. Congress sets basic policies for the National Park Service, the Forest Service, and the Bureau of Land Management, and these policies should be revised to give top priority to bison. On game refuges where cattle are now present, a changeover to bison should be immediate.

4. Shall new bison reserves be established? As we have seen, there is a fundamental need to establish a prairie grassland national park—which, of course, would contain bison as part of the ecosystem it is designed to preserve. But Congress should also establish several experimental bison reserves—ample areas located where they can be expanded later, composed of economically marginal Plains range land and farmland that is currently kept in agricultural use only through subsidies. We have seen earlier that there are now mechanisms for such land acquisition that are fair both to the current inhabitants of the land and to the taxpaying public.

5. Shall nongovernmental organizations, including Indian tribes and nonprofit groups, be given incentives to foster bison? Indian reservations seem likely to lead the way in devoting large new free-range areas to bison; they need political and financial support for these programs. Their offer to help operate a model bison reserve should be taken up forthwith. And nonprofit organizations, not limited to The Nature Conservancy, should be helped to push ahead with acquiring refuges and carrying out the experimental work needed to fully understand grassland ecosystems.

6. Aside from setting leasing fees at market rates, shall we reduce or end other subsidies that distort the value of agricultural land? As we saw previously, these take many forms, from range improvement and predator control to direct payments for land banking, price supports for commodities, and purchases of surpluses.

This question is obviously the most far-reaching of all, since it raises the possibility of a reversal of federal policies dating back many decades. However, we seem to be entering a period of reconsideration of many government activities, from which few federal programs will be exempt. And as it happens, there are some notable possibilities for reducing subsidies while at the same time promoting bison, the health of our rangelands, and the long-term security of ranchers. Federal assistance notwithstanding, ranchers claim that they clear on average only about $28,000 a year, slightly below the average American man's income. Many ranchers, like farmers, are part-timers these days and make their living primarily by their other jobs. Some basic rethinking can improve their situation and also restore sustainable productivity to the Plains.

Changing the Economic Base

As matters now stand, the economic base of the ranching economy consists only in part of land or livestock; almost as important a source are the taxable incomes of urban and suburban taxpayers. (Corporate taxes are now a minor source of federal revenues.) If government transfers of wealth from metropolitan areas to agriculture were simply stopped, cattle and sheep ranching as well as farming would undergo profound changes—including more bankruptcies. Some of these changes would probably benefit bison, and some might benefit public rangelands ecologically. But it is also possible to envisage new government policies that could improve the federal budget, keep ranchers on the land, and also foster bison and other ungulates while restoring grasslands to healthy ecosystem status.

Lynn Jacobs, who has probably given more consideration than anyone else to the salvation of western public lands, has proposed that the government buy out ranchers' privately owned "base" acreages (and remaining stock) and even compensate them for what they call their "possessitory" interest in long-term grazing leases on adjacent public lands. (Landlords of commercial office buildings would be astounded to hear that long-term tenants could count on renewing leases because of a possessitory interest in their buildings, but this is politics, not real estate law.) Jacobs suggests that the purchases be phased in gradually, to wean ranchers gently from their psychological and financial dependence on government and to allow easy replacement of the 2 percent of the American meat supply that comes from the public lands. The money needed to purchase the 22,000 base properties in the ten westernmost states would be around $11 billion—which would be saved in about a decade by ending ranching subsidies. Even if taxpayers footed the whole bill themselves, this would amount to around $44 per U.S. citizen for what Jacobs calls "perhaps the greatest environmental restoration program in world history."

But I suggest another alternative, one that would take advantage of the fact that many ranchers are devoted in more than monetary ways to the land. There is an honorable way in which they could stop the degradation of public lands by non-native livestock, join in the noble task of fostering bison and other native wildlife, and restore a sizable chunk of the country to its former glory as a truly American landscape. This can be done by using only part of the public money presently spent keeping cattle-ranching operations afloat. It would represent, of course, a great ecological advance. It would also greatly simplify and clarify the federal budget, accomplishing substantial savings compared with the present situation—a clearly defensible goal in terms of national politics.

I am proposing a plan with bison and the Plains in mind, but the principle involved is not limited by geography, and many ranchers farther west, outside bison range, might well be interested in variations of it too. If Plains grazing land constitutes roughly a third of the ten-state west, it has around 10,000 permittees. Allotting a third of Jacobs's dollar total to the Plains, we confront this tantalizing possibility: if we stopped subsidizing Plains cattle and sheep ranching and began bringing back bison and other species to help the land recover from the ecological mayhem of the past hundred years, we could easily afford to pay the permittees $28,000 per year in salaries as bison- and wildlife-restoration rangers. This might seem like a loss of independence to some of them, but in reality it would be an honest acknowledgment of their present dependence on federal subsidies. Ranchers could continue to occupy their base properties adjacent to restored publicly owned scenery. Since most of the government activities on behalf of ranching which we have reviewed earlier are counterproductive for wildlife, they should simply stop. We would instead pay the 10,000 new rangers a total of around $280 million per year—saving $20 million annually on the deal. Moreover, if a number of Plains ranchers were available only part-time, the savings could be still greater.

Obviously, it would take many years—probably a generation—to complete this transition from subsidized permittee grazing operations to subsidized restoration of bison and other wildlife. Individually or culturally, one does not progress overnight from the industrial approach that presently dominates the cattle industry to the attitude that the interconnectedness of nature is beautiful and all living beings have their own reasons for existence. But money talks; indeed, some would argue that in the current condition of American society, it is about the only thing that does. In any event, humans are a flexible species. We respond to incentives. We would give close attention to the recovery of native grasses and the numbers of resident bison and other species of interest if we were paid for doing so and penalized for not doing so. We would even more readily recognize profit potential in the harvesting of bison from public lands, which could be done on a bid basis, with careful supervision of the sustainable take. But the main tasks would be to remove feral stock; to dismantle fences, corrals, and water tanks; to close and revegetate ranch roads; and to restore riparian and other damaged vegetation. Some ranch buildings would remain useful as ranger dwellings and offices, while others could be removed. This is all work that ranch managers and employees are already ideally trained and equipped to do and, indeed, should get increasing satisfaction from doing. As we will see later in this chapter, the work of fostering bison is more physically and mentally challenging than cattle management; it deserves to take on heroic (perhaps even mythic) stature in the public eye.

In the eastern part of the Plains, and in bison country farther east in the prairies, cattle ranchers have access to less public grassland, but the subsidies supporting them in other ways are still substantial. In some places, a restoration program would probably have to employ former ranchers rather as county agents traditionally have been employed by the U.S. Department of Agriculture—as hands-on specialists who can provide information and advice to bison ranchers, slaughterhouses, and distributors. And in a transitional phase, we might subsidize landowners to raise bison just as we now subsidize them to let land lie fallow in conservation reserves; this program's prospective $21 billion in funding over the next decade could persuade quite a lot of people to work on behalf of bison.

Two dangers face all efforts to bring back the bison. One, whose history goes back to the beginnings of agricultural society, is the human tendency to try to subdue and domesticate wild species. Some people manage to tame bison to a degree, at least for a while. But bison have never been domesticated, and though people may try to modify the character of the species by selective culling and breeding, this will not achieve domestication.

As Jared Diamond has written, to be candidates for domestication animals must have specific characteristics: reliable dispositions, lack of the tendency to resort to panic flight, and a social order producing automatic submission so that humans can take over the top dominant position. None of these applies to bison, who are unpredictable, tend to stampede, and remain disdainful of humans. Like gazelles and cheetahs—both species that humans have tried to subdue—bison are inalterably wild. Thus, successful public policy and successful ranching will both have to incorporate new lessons in relinquishing control and recognizing mutual interdependence. In a word, we will have to learn to respect bison in a way that we do not respect chattel animals like cows, pigs, and chickens.

A second danger is that restoration might become captive to powerful private interests. History teaches us, after all, that Americans have been unable to control land-management agencies in the overall public interest. Recent events indicate that the historical pattern is weakening a bit, but it is still basically unchanged. Early in the Clinton administration, for instance, Jim Baca was appointed director of the Bureau of Land Management. Baca said he planned to revise the way his managers were rewarded: whereas they once were evaluated by the numbers of cattle they fed and miles of fences they built, he planned to ask them, "How many stream banks in your district are healthy? How many upland areas are improving?" But, as environmentalists are quick to remind us, talk is cheap in Washington, and opposition, as was apparent when Congress quickly squelched a modest attempt to raise grazing fees, is fierce. In February 1994, the political heat generated by the governors of Colorado, Wyoming, and Idaho, among others, was great enough to force Baca's resignation. His boss, Secretary of the Interior Bruce Babbitt, remarked that Baca might have been too "confrontational" but promised that the administration's drive for land-use reform would be continued through a more consensus-building approach. Advocates of market-based grazing fees observing all this were not encouraged. Six months later, in a parallel development, the mining lobby beat back an attempt to begin charging corporations for the hard-rock mineral wealth they extract from public lands. Hopes that the Clinton administration might defend public lands more staunchly than its predecessors faded, though revolt from below continued to simmer within the Forest Service, in which an organization called Forest Service Employees for Ethical Environmentalism continued to raise issues of responsible management.

On balance, we can hardly expect that historical patterns will change briskly. A long campaign will be needed to render government agencies hospitable to bison and their companion species. If the pressure is kept on long enough, agency policies and internal cultures can be changed.

There is another, more sweeping policy alternative. As Congress steadily pared down the Indian reservations from their original scale, the argument was always made that Euro-American farmers would put the land to "higher" use. But if whites cannot utilize a given area for farming or ranching without government subsidies, there is a strong case for giving it back to the Indians, from whom it was originally taken—leaving the nation as a whole better off economically and opening up new reservation lands for bison.

Transforming Cowboy Culture

As America industrialized, the cowboy myth ran strongly through movies and dime novels. Restive youths could dream of running away from boring eastern towns into the expanses of the West to find a freer home on the range; there they could confront real danger but also experience real comradeship—and, sometimes, bittersweet loneliness. Sleeping under the stars rather than in a slum tenement, they might learn independence, self-respect, even simple nobility. The original poet of this myth was the cowboy movie-maker William S. Hart, whose films survive as sentimental but engagingly heartfelt monuments to an earlier time.

In the 1930s, 1940s, and 1950s came singing cowpokes, glitzy costumes, fancy saddles; a cowboy's feeling for "girls" could now surpass his feeling for his horse, though Roy Rogers correctly perceived that it was Trigger, not Dale Evans, who was his real costar. Rogers had a 50,000-member fan club in London. I myself, at age eight, was a dedicated fan of the Lone Ranger—from whose programs I learned, among other things, that classical music existed. But these innovations were as nothing compared with what modern media have done to the cowboy myth, which is now overwhelmingly an urbanized, Hollywood-produced entertainment. We have people who have never been on a horse wearing expensive and impractical cowboy costumes. We have cowboy poetry declaimed to large gatherings. We have a major urban industry producing billions of dollars' worth of country and western music, which actually derives from Southern, hillbilly, black rhythm-and-blues, and urban working-class roots. (I like it, by the way.) And, of course, we have rodeo.

Even though the earlier Westerns, with laconic, individualist heroes like *Shane,* gave way years ago to stories of quasi-corporate male groups like *The Professionals,* the cowboy myth continues to have power. The reason it does may lie, however, in familiar origins: images of "life on the open range" offer a refuge from the urbanization, regulation, corruption, and corporatization of contemporary America.

Not all of the myth is suspect. As Sharman Apt Russell puts it, in her examination of the West's future in *Kill the Cowboy: A Battle of Mythology in the New West,* "We need every man, woman, and child who has found a way to slip into the land that rolls past our car windows. As our last frontier urbanizes, we need the psychic ballast of people who make their livelihood directly from soil, grass, and water. We need people who understand, rather more than the rest of us, that our society—our houses, our VCRs, our cereal boxes—depends on a base of natural resources. We need cultural diversity. We need dreams." The livelihoods in question actually derive substantially, as we have seen, from government subsidies to farmers and ranchers. Nonetheless, the genuine rural culture of America has had many virtues as well as shortcomings, and the virtues need to be preserved.

On a broad, cultural level, then, can we envision the transformation of cowboy culture, which has been centered on livestock for generations, into something compatible with, or perhaps even welcoming toward, bison and their wild companions? The very fact that so much cowboy culture is produced by urban corporations may actually open up some new possibilities. Cowboy culture nowadays is moving swiftly into a fantasy, media-centered *Urban Cowboy* world. Chain stores selling western-style clothing, hats, and other items are common even in metropolitan areas where no cows have been seen for generations. Advertising, particularly for four-wheel-drive sport vehicles, continues to use western imagery in its appeals; one of these days, it will dawn on a smart New York television-commercial producer that a background containing bison would be more attention grabbing than yet another shot of cows. The urbanites and suburbanites who make up so much of current cowboy culture are, on the whole, more sympathetic to the preservation of wildlife than are their country cousins; media cowboys who heroically coexist with bison, elk, and antelope might fit in well with their tastes.

But at least as important is the question of whether cowboy culture as it exists among rural people, and especially among landowners and other powerful figures, can be transformed. Change will not come easily. For one thing, the cowboy myth persists partly because it is such a useful political tool, feared as well as detested by critics of the current ranching dispensation. Every news story addressing the possibility of raising public-lands grazing fees or questioning "animal control" begins with an obligatory paragraph about some ranch family and its love of "our land." Yet, as Lynn Jacobs reminds us, only about 15 percent of grazing permits are "ancestral," and 3 percent of the permittees control 40 percent of the public land;

on BLM land, only 10 percent of the herbage goes to small operators. In addition, though journalists often wax lyrical about the intimate knowledge of the land possessed by ranch people, it turns out that a good many of them cannot even recognize the grasses their livestock depend on. The spread of more scientifically sophisticated knowledge, which could serve to prevent the degradation of grasslands, whether publicly or privately owned, will inevitably be slow.

Ranching communities, of course, include many people besides ranch operators: cowhands, veterinarians, feed suppliers, truckers, teachers, journalists, storekeepers, mechanics, lawyers, doctors, and so on. Many of these are still dominated by local ranching interests, but the isolation of rural communities is breaking down and the culture of small towns is changing. Gradually, many rural dwellers are becoming aware of new issues and new possibilities. These forward-looking individuals include people working in the local offices of land-management agencies—often former ranchers or people who come from or married into ranch families—who are making

This café in Montana explicitly links bison with a political theme.

crucial decisions about the future of public lands. If there is to be a sustainable future for our grasslands, they too must see the need for it.

Is it possible, then, that at least some people whose livelihoods have depended for several generations on government support of imported livestock could come to appreciate and work diligently toward the restoration and sustainable management of native vegetation and native animals? The future of the Plains depends on it; as far as restoring public grazing lands is concerned, there is no real alternative.

This is a question that Sharman Apt Russell has addressed in a context of present landownership and leasing patterns. Russell grew up in the West, and she feels that some ranchers have a genuine respect for nature; she interviewed a number of them, and she also talked to people who are trying, slowly and devotedly, to find common ground between ranchers and their critics. She takes comfort from a few places where local environmentalists and ranchers have learned to tolerate each other and to understand that they have overlapping positive goals: the environmentalists do not merely want to get rid of cows, and the ranchers do not merely want to sacrifice wildlife. It is unacceptable, she feels, for the community of subsidized ranchers to simply be deprived of their livelihoods, as ardent kickthem-off-the-public-lands partisans advocate. After all, she argues, even bad ranching is ecologically preferable to condos and vacation homes.

Russell agrees that the photographs and patient observations that researchers and opponents of grazing have accumulated prove that much public land, especially along streams, has indeed been so degraded that it must be withdrawn from cattle or sheep grazing. She knows the work of Allan Savory, though she does not address the argument that if cows and sheep are removed, bison and other grazers must be brought in. Russell feels that suitable incentives can turn most ranchers into good stewards. She accepts that the mythical cowboy must go, and that cattle should be "slowly and honorably phased out of most wilderness areas, wildlife refuges, and national monuments," but she makes a case that people who live on the land, truly love it, and want it to last should stay: "reborn" cowboys who can combine their intimate knowledge of place with new insights from ecology. (Russell frequently mentions elk and deer as wildlife that share the public lands. She also discusses wolf restoration, pointing out that if wolves are successfully reintroduced in Yellowstone, they are predicted to consume about 10 percent of the bison, approximating their probable predation rate before whites occupied the region. Otherwise she shows no interest in bison or antelope.)

Russell does not provide prescriptions for how her incentives might work in practice, but she quotes a proposal from Jim Corbett, a rancher-environmentalist in the Southwest. Corbett argues that whatever the legalities, the grazing allotment system operates as if grazing permits were private property—de facto, ranchers buy, sell, and sublease permits among themselves. Thus, it would be possible to establish fair market prices for these permits. Paying the government for them outright—a good deal more than ranchers now pay out over time in permit fees—would put money into a federal range program rather than, as now happens, into banks that finance ranch purchases. This would, Corbett thinks, give ranchers a new motivation not to overstock. It is a semiprivatization solution that many ranchers might ideologically welcome—and many economists and environmentalists deplore. Whether ranchers newly endowed with permanent grazing permits would be more likely to switch to bison is unclear.

Cultural change takes generations, but it does happen; and on that timescale there are signs of hope for bison. Young people from ranch families have been going away to college and taking courses that bear on ecological issues, and some of them do come back to the ranch. Television and other urban mass media have penetrated remote ranch country thoroughly; these days, every real ranch house needs a satellite dish. So new ideas about ecological responsibility and sustainability have become known, if not widely embraced. Some of the former cattle ranchers discussed earlier have, in fact, switched to bison because they agree that bison belong on the land—as well as offering the ranchers a way to provide a good life for their families with less investment and less work.

It may surprise anyone who last attended a rodeo long ago, but the rodeo National Finals are now held in Las Vegas—and televised—with all the media flash that venue might lead you to expect. The performers in rodeo may have begun as working cowboys (a lot of them come from families that have lost their ranches), but the rodeo circuit today resembles professional golf or other prize-centered sports. Except on the highest levels, the life of a rodeo performer is a hardscrabble existence of constant driving, cheap motels, and meager earnings. Rodeo is, of course, a dangerous sport; events like bull and bronc riding can cause crippling injuries. But the only common rodeo events that directly reflect practical ranch jobs are bareback bronc riding and calf roping. Relevance might also be argued for steer wrestling ("bulldogging"), in which a cowboy drops from his horse next to a running young steer, grabs its horns, and attempts to throw it to the ground—though few, if any, working ranch hands would attempt this. In short, rodeo has become a mass entertainment.

Handling bison is in another universe. Bison's wiliness, power, and quickness make them a formidable challenge; trying to herd them pushes the limits of the most skillful riders. And nobody wishing for a long life would try to mess with a bison calf if its mother is around. Managing bison demands not only the strength, determination, and resourcefulness under dangerous conditions of the old cowboy myth but also alertness, quick thinking, flexibility, and a keen sense of observation. Compared with bison, cattle are tedious and unchallenging. Bison handling, then, has the potential to replace the cowboy myth, which, now commercialized and cheapened, awaits rebirth in a new form.

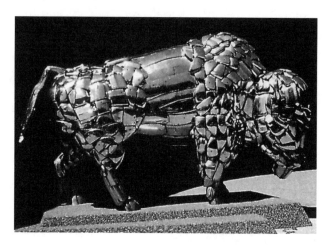

Artists are increasingly taken with the iconic power of the bison image. This sculpture plays with the contrast between chrome-plated auto bumpers and the majesty of the natural animal. Chrome on the Range *by Lou Wille is a public art piece in Grand Junction, Colorado. Photo courtesy Grand Junction Tourist & Convention Bureau.*

New Times, New Terms

In the long run, the future role of bison in America will turn on the usual political situation: if the public wants a change of policy and is willing to foot the bill for it, and if national leaders see something of political value to be gained by it, change may happen. Such political change is always slow, painful, and expensive. The long, difficult job of research, public education, and opinion shifting must be carried out by scientists, writers, educators, environmentalists, and those ubiquitous NGOs, or nongovernmental organizations, that provide most of the impetus for innovation and improvement in the world today. Then the hardheaded political operators will see that different kinds of money can be made, new votes secured, and new alliances shored up. So it will surely be with the ranching culture. We can even foresee a day when ranchers who now loathe coyotes come to understand that they are a species somewhat like humans—clever opportunists with a certain claim on existence. (Coyotes even keep down for us the population of the mice that carry the fatal hantavirus.) We can foresee, too, a time when the U.S. Department of Agriculture will educate its county agents not only about bison, so that they can in turn educate farmers and ranchers, but also about wind power—an inexhaustible resource that, as we saw in the last chapter, will someday provide a much-needed new source of income to Plains landowners.

Myths grow and hold their power by emotive words as well as by images. When an old myth weakens and the words associated with it no longer connect with powerful elements in people's experience, new words (and images) come to displace them. So it will be, in time, with the term "cowboy," but the right new name has not yet appeared. Ranch hands working with bison are occasionally called "buffs," but this term seems unlikely to stick—it is confusing because bison themselves have sometimes been called buffs, and it certainly lacks mythic associations. "Bison rangers" would describe people working on public lands, but the term is not appropriate for ranch workers; nor would we want to appropriate the term the Canadian government used in 1911 when it hired people to help increase bison populations: "game guardians." Perhaps "buffalo hands" comes close to what is needed: a name for strong men and women who are comfortable on the land and love its native creatures, are willing to face the loneliness of vast open spaces, are accustomed to harsh weather and heavy physical work, and are resourceful enough to deal with the practical problems that freedom-loving beasts and complex ecosystems will pose over the years. Since our language also is wild—grammarians only imagine they control it—in time the name we need will probably evolve. Then songwriters will use it to lament sorrow and heartbreak on the range and, perhaps, to suggest what it is like to feel truly at home there—not as a dominator and controller of all other species but as their faithful companion.

Maps and Reality

Like most of the United States, the Great Plains are politically subdivided into states and counties whose boundaries were fixed without much attention to landscape features. A map of the Plains shows a lot of straight lines; like the flatter country to the east, the area was level enough to be a surveyor's paradise. During the settlement years, a rigid Euclidean grid of "township and range" divisions was laid down over half a continent. But in nature, divisions of the land are created by mountain ridges or hill ranges, which form the boundaries of drainages where plant life and animal life form consistent communities. To nature, rivers and streams are not borders but the central axes of watersheds, like the veins of a leaf, which their patterns so magically resemble. A river basin exerts a powerful unifying effect. In older societies, and also in new bioregional thinking, such unities are respected—because sooner or later human communities that endure must honor and reflect the underlying natural order.

Thus, one consequence of beginning to see large parts of the Plains as fundamentally bison country would be that county divisions would seem in many ways irrelevant, like the county lines that still, on the map, cross national forests or parks. (To take just one example, The Nature Conservancy's 57,000-acre bison preserve in the Niobrara River valley in northern Nebraska occupies parts of three different counties.) Bison are like wind; they tend to move by their own laws. In time, the arbitrary divisions we have applied to the land will need to be reworked on a different scale. The whole Niobrara valley comprises parts of half a dozen counties, yet it is a breathtakingly beautiful ecological whole. Someday the wholeness of such valleys must be recognized in the human institutions they support. This would help people in the new units to make decisions that fit the landscape, in a literal as well as ecologically sound way.

In bison territory, as we have seen, the populations of many rural counties have been shrinking since the 1920s. These counties have very slender financial resources, yet they must try to maintain the fundamental services of local government: police protection, civil and criminal courts, emergency medical care, property ownership records, and some supervision of education. Even in California and other rich states, some rural counties totter along on the verge of bankruptcy, bailed out occasionally by the state. In a Plains county numbering only a thousand or so souls, it is extremely difficult to find the money to manage the basic necessities, but several counties combined might be able to get by more easily. Some county-seat towns are doing pretty well, but many are not. There will come a time when county consolidation and reorganization, as well as ad hoc cooperation, will be necessary.

In 1994 the U.S. Postal Service issued a plate of wildlife stamps, one featuring bison.

Institutions, in the long run, need to fit the land. The evenly spread web of yeoman farmers that settled the country east of the Plains was made possible by the combined flatness and fertility of the land. County lines made little difference; one county was much like another, except where ethnic settlement patterns set different cultural norms. In bison country, where human settlements are now and will remain scattered and small, towns will tend to survive along transportation corridors and in particularly desirable locations, which tend to be near water. A few people will probably still want to live in isolated houses, but since the work of bison fostering and harvesting is extremely mobile, most people active in it will probably live in the towns, where a lot of ranch and farm workers already live, since they drive to work. Similarly, some people working on wind farms may wish to live near the installations, but these are spread over a wide area, so living in town would often be just as practical and, for some, at least, more enjoyable. On the whole, an economy of bison and wind power should support more economically viable and livelier towns than cattle ranching does.

It seems to be the nature of towns and cities that in any given region, one town grows to commercial and cultural dominance. In bison country, we would expect these larger towns to be the seats of the supercounties of the future, as well as of banks, offices of federal agencies, institutions of higher education, medical centers, television and radio stations, law offices, and local newspapers. These towns would have good access to transportation, numerous wholesale establishments, a large variety of stores, and in some cases a bison slaughterhouse and freezer plant. Instead of merely refusing to die, they could thrive.

O give me a home
Where the buffalo roam
Where the deer and the antelope play
Where seldom is heard
A discouraging word
And the skies are not cloudy all day.
—TRADITIONAL

Conclusion They Will Come

Thinking seriously about bison means thinking about our place here on earth as well as the place of bison. If we decide that it is fitting for these noble beasts to share our future, and make room for them on the continent again, we will be a different people. It is worth entertaining the possibility that we will be a more humble, less driven, less exploitative people, with a livelier sense of connection to the wild in ourselves as well as in bison.

Meanwhile, what we need now and what the bison and their companion grazers need is a fundamental reorganization of grazing on the Plains of the kind outlined in this book. Any alteration in land use, especially in the West, can be disturbing. But the only real certainty is that things change, and our ways of occupying the American landscape will inevitably change too. When we visit bison herds, study bison ways, defend bison needs, tell our friends and family about bison, support bison restoration, and even eat bison, we are participating in a great cultural transformation.

As philosophers remind us, ecological principles are ultimately spiritual and cultural. They are axiomatic, just as economic principles are: both rest on unprovable assumptions. In this they are like the fundamental beliefs of all cultures that have risen and fallen before us—they rest on structures of social agreement, and they are subject to revision. There is no way to "prove" that a healthy and sustainable bioregion is more valuable than a few years of five-cents-a-pound-cheaper hamburger, or vice versa. Only on the basis of what our values really are can we resolve such choices. Like all humans before us, we must decide what is proper, what is right—not merely what is expedient. Such decisions can be uncomfortable. It would be much easier if we could simply let the economic bottom line be our guide. But mere numbers can never define a satisfactory relationship with the earth or with the universe. To know what we should do about bison, we must consult our hearts.

As I was completing this book, news arrived of a bison blessed event: the birth of a rare white female calf. Two months after Alex White Plume at the Pine Ridge Reservation told me that his tribe's elders were expecting the return of a sacred white bison in the near future, it came to pass—and in his lifetime, as he had hoped. According to some Indians, a white female calf is to be expected only every two thousand years, and her birth heralds the beginning of an epoch of peace and reconciliation among all peoples.

The calf was given the name Miracle, and when word of her arrival got out, thousands of people—more whites than Indians—began descending on the modest forty-acre ranch in southern Wisconsin where a ranching couple, Dave and Valerie Heider, keep fourteen bison. Newspapers ran stories. On national television, Miracle gamboled around her mother and exchanged grunts, flipped her tail, lay down, stood up, and sprinted daringly across the pasture.

Intense interest in Miracle brought Indians from many tribes to the Heider ranch: Oneida, Cherokee, and other eastern tribes as well as Sioux. A Lakota elder among them named Looks for Buffalo said that he had been having premonitions about the event. "It was born to a white family," he commented, "as an omen to the white people. They must pay attention to what they are losing. When they want to know something, they ask a machine. They have lost touch with Mother Earth." Indian visitors hung offerings of sage, turquoise, tobacco, and feathers on the fence. They talked about rebirth; they prayed and chanted and drummed. The Heiders originally had some difficulty understanding what all the fuss was about, but they soon began to take the event seriously. With the help of a Chippewa woman from Milwaukee, they established a trust fund for Miracle's care.

After some months, Miracle began to turn brownish and it now appears, say the Heiders, that she will mature as a bison of normal coloration. This fact has not, however, diminished her sacred status to Native Americans in the slightest; as they see it, what is crucial is that she was born female and white. (She is not an albino; albinos are fairly common among bison and many other animals.) Some elders even suggest that she may change color again—going back to white, or to others of the four sacred colors. In any case, eight months after her birth she was in fine health, and had had some 40,000 visitors.

In the television program, Miracle peered curiously at the visitors. As she frisked about, they watched her with serious, concerned expressions. I think that in some mysterious way they may have felt more optimistic about the world. And hope is not a commodity in oversupply in contemporary life. We need all the help we can get.

Now picture this: It is a sunlit day on the Great Plains in the mid-twenty-first century, and the flower-bedecked native grasses wave in the wind like a green sea. Thousands of dark bison shapes move steadily through the grass. Their grazing groups veer a little around the towers of wind machines scattered across the rolling terrain. The great blades spin gracefully, far above the ground. In the distance we can make out the white-painted houses of a small town, complete with church steeple. Among the healthy small businesses on the town's main street are some connected with bison raising, some with tourism, some with wind-energy production.

This is a portrait of hope, and it is not beyond our reach. This future accepts that its fate rests on the eternal ecological verities of the Plains—grass, sustainably utilizable only through bison and their companion grazers, and wind, sometimes felt to be a curse of Plains life, now part of its salvation.

We have little experience in coexisting with an animal that is as useful to humans as the bison and yet still wild. Our usual concepts of "wild" and "domestic" need stretching; they no longer fit ecological reality. We can learn to trust in the sturdy self-sufficiency of bison. They ask only to live as bison, roaming and free. Through being attentive to their spirit and receptive to their needs, we can envision at last a new ecologically and economically stable inhabitation of the rural Plains.

Bison belong on the American landscape. They will help sustain us if we sustain them. If we make room for them, they will come.

Notes

Chapter 1

P. 13: dominance orders. V. Reinhardt, "Social Behavior in a Confined Bison Herd," *Behavior*, 92 (3): 209–226. This paper is full of good, close observations.

P. 13: tail position. Milo J. Schult and Arnold O. Haugen, *Where Buffalo Roam* (1979). Badlands Natural History Association, Interior, SD 57750.

P. 17: Powell quote. Wes Jackson, *New Roots for Agriculture* (San Francisco: Friends of the Earth, 1980), 72.

P. 20: biological productivity. Douglas H. Chadwick, "Roots of the Sky," *National Geographic*, October 1993, 116.

P. 20: Jacobs quote. Lynn Jacobs,*Waste of the West: Public Lands Ranching* (1991), 47–48. Free Our Public Lands, Box 5784, Tucson, AZ 85703.

P. 20: positive effects of grazing. T. R. Seastedt, "Maximization of primary and secondary productivity by grazers," *American Naturalist* 126: 559–563 (1985).

P. 21: humus. Paul R. Ehrlich and Anne H. Ehrlich, "The Value of Biodiversity," *Ambio*, May 1992, 22.

P. 21: rainfall. Roland Dallas, "The agricultural collapse of the arid Midwest," *Geographical Magazine*, October 1990, 16.

P. 22: Knowles quote. Craig J. Knowles, "Beyond Beef—Back to Bison," report prepared for the Northern Cheyenne tribe.

P. 22: "scintillating interdependence." Allan Savory, *Holistic Resource Management* (Washington, DC: Island Press, 1988), 204.

P. 24: grasses. Jacobs, *Waste of the West,* 44.

P. 24: patch dynamics. Al Steuter et al., "A Synthesis Approach to Research and Management Planning," *Natural Areas Journal*, 10 (2): 61–68 (1990). See also Nichole M. Dankey and Kent E. Pfeiffer, "Field Testing a Bison-Fire Interaction Model on Sand Hills Prairie," in *Environmental and Natural Resources of the Niobrara River Basin* (symposium), 14–15 October 1993.

P. 25: lightning-induced fires. Al Steuter, Letter in *Conservation Biology*, June 1991, 136–137.

P. 25: rained-out fires. Ibid., 141.

P. 25: bison versus cattle. Glenn E. Plumb and Jerrold L. Dodd, "Foraging Ecology of Bison and Cattle on a Mixed Prairie: Implications for Natural Area Management," *Ecological Applications* 3 (4): 639 (1993).

P. 26: comparison of productivity. Yvonne Baskin, "Ecologists Dare to Ask: How Much Does Diversity Matter?" *Science,* 8 April 1994, 202.

P. 28: bison grazing. *The Bison Breeder's Handbook* (1993), 69–70. American/National Bison Association, Box 16660, Denver, CO 80216.

P. 30: Russell quote. Sharman Apt Russell, *Kill the Cowboy: A Battle of Mythology in the New West* (Boston: Addison-Wesley, 1993), 21.

P. 31: protein and energy intake. Plumb and Dodd, "Foraging Ecology of Bison and Cattle," 631–643.

Notes

P. 31: efficiency of bison digestion. Thomas J. DeLiberto and Philip J. Urness, "Comparative Digestive Physiology of American Bison and Hereford Cattle," in *Proceedings of the North American Public Herds Bison Symposium,* 1993.

P. 33: population limits. A good discussion of these matters can be found in Douglas B. Bamforth, *Ecology and Human Organization on the Great Plains* (New York: Plenum Press, 1988), 7–8.

P. 33: buffalo-bellow and other edible plants. William Least Heat-Moon, *PrairyErth* (Boston: Houghton Mifflin, 1991), 242.

P. 34: decline of herds. Richard White, *"It's Your Misfortune and None of My Own": A New History of the American West* (Norman: University of Oklahoma Press, 1991), 217–218.

P. 35: Frazier quote. Ian Frazier, *Great Plains* (New York: Farrar, Straus, and Giroux, 1989).

CHAPTER 2

Pp. 37–38: first buffalo hunting excerpt. James Willard Schultz, *Blackfeet and Buffalo: Memories of Life among the Indians* (Norman: University of Oklahoma Press, 1962), 53–54.

Pp. 38–39: second buffalo hunting excerpt. Mari Sandoz, *The Buffalo Hunters: The Story of the Hide Men* (New York: Hastings House, 1954), 245.

P. 39: protection laws. For a thorough survey of this and other aspects of bison history, see David A. Dary, *The Buffalo Book: The Full Saga of the American Animal* (Athens: Ohio University Press, 1974, 1989), 125.

P. 39: Captain Moses Harris. Ibid., 130–31, 133.

P. 39: White quote. Richard White, *"It's Your Misfortune and None of My Own": A New History of the American West* (Norman: University of Oklahoma Press, 1991), 219.

P. 40: poem. Displayed in Visitor Center of Badlands National Park.

P. 40: early sodbusters. Mari Sandoz, *Old Jules* (New York: Hastings House, 1935). Sandoz, *The Buffalo Hunters.*

P. 41: White quote. Richard White, *"It's Your Misfortune,"* 216.

P. 42: Sandoz quote: Sandoz, *Old Jules,* 110–111.

P. 44: statistics on farm ownership. Gene Wunderlich, "U.S. Farmland Ownership: A Century of Change," in *Agricultural Economy, 1993* (Washington, DC: U.S. Department of Agriculture). The information was compiled through the Economic Research Service's Census of Agriculture data, 1987—the latest information available.

P. 46: Popper quote. Frank Popper, "Ownership: The Hidden Factor in Land-Use Regulation," in R. Andrews, ed., *Land in America* (Lexington, Kentucky, 1979), 131.

P. 48: agricultural occupations. At one time, a massive majority of Americans farmed. In 1993, we had only 1,232,000 farm operators and managers, 2,054,000 people in related occupations, and 866,000 farm workers. *U.S. Statistical Abstracts.*

P. 48: capture of agencies. See, for example, Gabriel Kolko, *Railroads and Regulation, 1877–1916* (Princeton, NJ: Princeton University Press, 1965).

P. 49: support programs. Dan Goodgame, "Reining in the Rich," *Time,* 19 December 1994, 38.

P. 49: checks. Andrew Nikoforuk, "Where the Buffalo Roam," *Harrowsmith Country Life,* July–August 1993, 29.

P. 49: North Dakota farm income. William M. Welch, "For farmers, seeds of concern," *USA Today,* 27 February 1995, 5A.

P. 50: death threats. For some recent cases, see *Inner Voice,* September 1994. Antienvironmentalist terrorism is particularly on the rise in connection with timber issues.

P. 50: range degradation. David Pimentel et al., "Environmental and Economic Costs of Soil Erosion and Conservation Benefits," *Science,* 24 February 1995, 1117.

P. 51: a billion dollars per year. Lynn Jacobs, *Waste of the West: Public Lands Ranching* (1991). Free Our Public Lands, Box 5784, Tucson, AZ 85703.

P. 52: $3,500 per rancher. Jacobs, *Waste of the West,* 375, quoting Commission on Government Operations, Federal Grazing Program, 1986.

P. 53: tax loopholes. Jacobs, *Waste of the West,* 380–400.

P. 54: poisoning of predators. Galen Buterbaugh, regional director, U.S. Fish and Wildlife Service, cited in *Waste, Fraud, and Abuse in the U.S. Animal Damage Control Program,* 17. New West Research, Box 401, Santa Fe, NM 87504.

P. 54: nonpredator losses. U.S. Department of Agriculture, Agricultural Statistics Board, National Agricultural Statistics Service, May 1992.

P. 54: ADC activities. For an analysis of ADC's budget, see Randal O'Toole, *Audit of the U.S.D.A. Animal Damage Control Program.* CHEC Research Paper no.31, April 1994. Cascade Holistic Economic Consultants, 14417 S.E. Laurie, Oak Grove, OR 97267.

P. 56: ecological roots. For an interesting attempt to foresee processes of social breakdown, see Robert D. Kaplan, "The Coming Anarchy," *The Atlantic,* February 1994.

P. 57: diminishing grain availability. Worldwatch Institute: *State of the World, 1993* (New York: Norton, 1993); Lester Brown: *Vital Signs, 1994* (New York: Norton, 1994).

P. 57: food riots. For a farm-based perspective, see Wes Jackson, *New Roots for Agriculture* (San Francisco: Friends of the Earth, 1980), 148.

CHAPTER 3

P. 66: Sandoz quote. Mari Sandoz, *The Buffalo Hunters: The Story of the Hide Men* (New York: Hastings House, 1954), xi.

P. 67: Buffalo woman. Paul Goble, *Buffalo Woman* (New York: Macmillan, 1984).

P. 67: Lame Deer quotes. John Fire/Lame Deer and Richard Erdoes, *Lame Deer, Seeker of Visions* (New York: Simon and Schuster, 1972), 120.

P. 77: sustainable management by tribes. Winona LaDuke, "The Dilemma of Indian Forestry," *Earth Island Institute Journal,* Summer 1994, 37.

P. 80: DuBray quotes. *Proceedings of the North American Public Bison Herds Symposium,* 1993.

P. 84: movements of tribes. Ian Frazier, *Great Plains* (New York: Farrar, Straus, and Giroux, 1989), 50–51.

P. 85: ecosystem-level protection. William K. Stevens, "Entire Ecosystems on Endangered List," *San Francisco Chronicle*, 14 February 1995, A2.

CHAPTER 4

P. 88: jobs study. This study was done at the Atlanta regional office of the Forest Service, according to an inside account that surfaced through Lighthawk, an organization of environmentalist pilots, but it was "disappeared" at the end of the Bush regime. Similar studies have been done in the Pacific Northwest.

P. 88: ITBC plan. Described in a press release, 5 September 1994.

P. 89: injections. *Proceedings of the North American Public Bison Herds Symposium*, 1993, 165.

P. 89: bison herd information. The foregoing and following information is basically drawn from *Proceedings*, 1993.

P. 102: refuge management. John Fedkiw, *The Evolving Use and Management of the Nation's Forests, Grasslands, Croplands, and Related Resources*, U.S.D.A. Forest Service Publication no. RM-175, September 1989, 38, 44.

P. 104: service on the grasslands. Terry West, "USDA management of the national grasslands," *Agricultural History*, Spring 1990, 86.

P. 105: Forest Service and BLM positions. Telephone conversations with Williamson and Segrist.

P. 110: Plumb quote. *Proceedings*, 76–77.

CHAPTER 5

P. 115: Savory's ideas. Allan Savory, *Holistic Resource Management* (Washington, DC: Island Press, 1988).

P. 120: Dana Jones. *Seattle Post-Intelligencer*, 11 October 1993, C1, and telephone conversation.

P. 124: Turner quote. *US News & World Report*, 14 November 1994, 108.

P. 129: *The Bison Breeder's Handbook* (1993). National Bison Association, Box 16660, Denver, CO 80216.

P. 134: diseases. Alfred W. Crosby, *Ecological Imperialism: The Biological Expansion of Europe 900–1900*. (Cambridge: Cambridge University Press, 1986).

P. 135: Davis paper. Donald S. Davis, "Brucella abortus in Captive Bison. I. Serology, Bacteriology, Pathogenesis, and Transmission to Cattle," *Journal of Wildlife Diseases* 26 (3): 360–371 (1990).

P. 136: Davis quote. Donald S. Davis, "Brucella abortus in Captive Bison: II. Evaluation of Strain 19 Vaccination of Pregnant Cows," *Journal of Wildlife Diseases* 27 (2): 258–264; this from 262–263 (1991).

P. 136: lowering brucellosis rates. Markus J. Peterson et al., "Bison-brucellosis management: simulation of alternative strategies," *Journal of Wildlife Management*, April 1991, 205.

P. 137: Houck bison brucellosis rate. Dale Lewis, *Roy Houck: Buffalo Man* (1992), 32–36. Buffalo Press, HC 33, Box 42, Fort Pierre, SD 57532.

P. 142: Jim Shaw quote. In "Buffalo: Back Home on the Range," *National Geographic,* November 1994, 80.

PART III INTRODUCTION

P. 146: biophobia. David Orr, " The Coming Biophilia Revolution," in *The Biophilia Hypothesis* (Washington, DC: Island Press, 1994).

CHAPTER 6

P. 150: George Wuerthner quote. *Wild Earth,* Fall 1993, 73.

P. 152: subsidies worth more than land. Daniel S. Licht, "The Great Plains: America's Best Chance for Ecosystem Restoration, Part 1," *Wild Earth,* Summer 1994, 47f.

P. 153: land values. Ibid. Licht cites U.S.D.A., *Agricultural Statistics,* 1992, 359, 392.

P. 154: "Wildlands Proposal." *Wild Earth,* special issue, 1993.

P. 155: corridors. Harvey Locke, "Yellowstone to Yukon," *Wild Earth,* Winter 1993–1994, 72.

P. 160: fence story. Dale Lewis, *Roy Houck: Buffalo Man* (1992), 141. Buffalo Press, HC 33, Box 42, Fort Pierre, SD 57532.

P. 165: Yellowstone accident statistics. All information in this section is from Yellowstone Park police records.

P. 168: "Buffalo Crossing" road sign. Copies of this sign are available from Badgerworks, Box 1275, Whitefish, MT 59937.

P. 169: elephant bridges. Bruce G. Marcot, *Conservation of Forests of India: An Ecologist's Tour,* U.S.D.A. Forest Service, Pacific Northwest Research Station, January 1993, 26.

P. 169: road closings. Oregon Department of Fisheries and Wildlife, cited in Katie Scarborough, "Developing Roads Scholars," *Wild Earth,* Summer 1994, 20.

CHAPTER 7

P. 171: McDonough quote. (William McDonough is an architect.) "Design, Ecology, Ethics, and the Making of Things," centennial sermon for the Cathedral of St. John the Divine, New York City, 7 February 1993.

P. 171: erosion. For a recent review, see David Pimentel et al., "Environmental and Economic Costs of Soil Erosion and Conservation Benefits," *Science,* 24 February 1995, 1117.

P. 174: "living machines" and"zero-emissions" clusters. Fritjof Capra and Gunter Pauli, eds., *Steering Business Toward Sustainability* (Tokyo: United Nations University Press, 1995). In this book John Todd describes his living machines, which originated as a means of treating sewage and are already being deployed in numerous locations.

P. 176: social traps. Gretchen C. Daily and Paul Ehrlich, "Population, Sustainability, and Earth's Carrying Capacity," *BioScience,* November 1992, 767. For a thorough and penetrating discussion of discount rates and their social effects, see Colin Price, *Time, Discounting and Value* (Oxford: Blackwell, 1993).

P. 177: Barsness quote. Larry Barsness, *The Bison in Art* (Flagstaff, AZ: Northland Press, 1977), 6.

P. 177: "primitive" life. For the most entertaining introduction to this subject, see Marshall Sahlins, *Stone Age Economics* (Chicago: Aldine, 1972, especially chap. 1.

P. 178: productivity of gazelle. John Heminway, "Cashing In on God's Cattle," in *No Man's Land: The Last of White Africa* (New York: Dutton, 1983).

P. 178: Jacobs quote. Lynn Jacobs, *Waste of the West: Public Lands Ranching* (1991), 110. Free Our Public Lands, Box 5784, Tucson, AZ 85703.

P. 180: Jackson quote. Wes Jackson, *Altars of Unhewn Stone: Science and the Earth* (San Francisco: North Point Press, 1987), 158.

P. 181: watery grave. Jackson, Ibid., 156.

P. 183: Jackson quote. Ibid., 135.

CHAPTER 8

P. 187: cooking suggestions. *University of California Wellness Letter,* November 1993, 7.

P. 187: Snyder quote. Gary Snyder, *The Practice of the Wild* (San Francisco: North Point Press, 1990), 184.

P. 189: Quammen quote. David Quammen, *Natural Acts* (New York: Schocken, 1985), 136.

P. 193: supermarket chains. "The Plains truth on buffalo: beef lovers find it a healthy choice," *Chicago Tribune,* 12 December 1993.

P. 194: National Bison Association. Address: Box 16660, Denver, CO 80216. Telephone: (303) 292-2833.

P. 195: cholesterol. *University of California Wellness Letter,* August 1994.

P. 195: fat measurements. M. J. Marchello et al., "Nutrient Composition of Raw and Cooked Bison bison [the official scientific name of the species]," *Journal of Food Composition and Analysis* 2, 177–185 (1989), 179, table 3. Similar work by J. C. Meiske et al. for the Minnesota Extension Service, in Publication no. AG-FS-3688, 1989, gives fat percentages for bison as 2.7 percent, for Herefords as 5.3 percent, and for Brahmans at 3.4 percent; the "total fat trim" was only 13.3 percent for bison, whereas it was 22.2 percent for Herefords and 21.3 percent for Brahmans.

P. 197: quality after storage. S. M. Leonard and D. K. Larick, "Effect of Vacuum-Packaged Frozen Storage, after Cooking, on the Phospholipids of Hereford and Bison," *Meat Science* 28 (199): 299–311.

P. 197: major ad campaign. *Adweek's Marketing Week,* 3 February 1992, 14.

P. 198: bacterial resistance to antibiotics. Brian B. Spratt. "Resistance to Antibiotics Mediated by Target Alterations." *Science,* 15 April 1994, 392.

CHAPTER 9

P. 201: Buffalo homeland/commons. Anne Matthews, "The Poppers and the Plains," *New York Times Magazine,* 24 June 1990, 24.

P. 202: best-laid plans. See Constance Perin, *With Man in Mind* (Cambridge: MIT Press, 1970), for an inside view of the process. Perin served as editor of the *Journal of the American Institute of Planners.*

P. 202: rainfall and soil moisture. Intergovernmental Panel on Climate Change, World Meteorological Organization.

P. 203: Tallgrass Prairie National Park. See William Least Heat-Moon, *PrairyErth* (Boston: Houghton Mifflin, 1991).

P. 203: New York Times reporter. Anne Matthews, *Where the Buffalo Roam: The Storm Over the Revolutionary Plan to Restore America's Great Plains* (New York: Grove Press, 1992).

P. 204: return of internal frontier. Frank and Deborah Popper, "Yo, Pioneers!" *Washington Post*, 5 September 1993, C5.

P. 204: land heritage. Frank Popper and Deborah Popper, "The Return of the Frontier," *Columbia*, Summer 1991.

P. 204: delinquent loans. Roland Dallas, "The agricultural collapse of the arid Midwest," *Geographical Magazine*, October 1990, 16.

P. 205: loss of water. Frank J. Popper, "The Strange Case of the American Frontier," *Yale Review*, Fall 1986.

P. 207: Nebraska telecommunications. Bill Richards, "Many Rural Regions Are Growing Again; A Reason: Technology," *Wall Street Journal*, 21 November 1994, 1.

P. 208: disaster area. Stephen E. White, "Ogallala Oases: Water Use, Population Redistribution, and Policy Implications in the High Plains of Western Kansas, 1980–1990," *Annals of the Association of American Geographers*, 84 (1): 29–45 (1994).

P. 209: more urban and more frontier. "'Progress of the Nation': The Settlement History of the Enduring American Frontier," *Western Historical Quarterly*, Autumn 1995.

P. 211: 231 residents. Dayton Duncan, "Westward NO," *Boston Globe*, 10 June 1990.

P. 211: tourism growth. Derek Denniston, *High Priorities: Conserving Mountain Ecosystems and Cultures* (Washington, DC: Worldwatch Institute, 1995), 37.

P. 211: Ferguson quote. Denzel Ferguson, *Sacred Cows at the Public Trough* (Bend, OR: Maverick Publications, 1983).

P. 215: "The Tragedy of the Commons." Garrett Hardin, "The Tragedy of the Commons," *Science*, vol. 162, 1243.

P. 216: magisterial study. J. M. Neeson, *Commoners: Common Right, Enclosure, and Social Change in England, 1700–1900* (Cambridge: Cambridge University Press, 1993).

P. 216: rhyme. Quoted in *Whose Common Future?*, ed. by the editors of *The Ecologist* (London: New Society, 1993). *The Ecologist* consistently follows commons issues, especially from the viewpoints of indigenous peoples, whose commons (in forestlands and elsewhere) are still being appropriated.

P. 216: direct-action tactic. *The Ecologist*, January–February 1994.

P. 217: Snyder quote. Gary Snyder, "The Place, the Region, and the Commons," in *The Practice of the Wild* (San Francisco: North Point Press, 1990).

P. 218: well drilling. For a fascinating analysis of the limitations of property ideas, see Theodore Steinberg, *Slide Mountain, or the Folly of Owning Nature* (Berkeley and Los Angeles: University of California Press, 1995).

CHAPTER 10

P. 223: future energy supplies. Philip Abelson, "Supplies of Oil and Natural Gas," *Science*, 21 October 1994, 347.

P. 224: nation's energy needs. Lester Brown, *Vital Signs 1993* (New York: Norton, 1993), 48.

P. 225: land's surface. *Science*, 3 September 1993, 1255, estimates 5 percent, but from aerial observation, I share energy expert John Berger's estimate of 2 percent or even less (personal communication).

P. 225: 20 percent of the world's energy. *Powering the Future* (Washington, DC: Worldwatch Institute, 1994) 26, 27.

P. 227: renewable technologies abroad. Curtis Moore and Alan Miller, *Green Gold: Japan, Germany, the U.S., and the Race for Environmental Technology* (Boston: Beacon Press, 1994) 124.

P. 228: nuclear subsidies. Phillip A. Greenberg, "Dreams Die Hard." *Sierra*, November–December, 1993, 38.

P. 228: prospective costs of wind power. Philip H. Abelson, "Power from Wind Turbines," *Science*, 3 September 1993.

P. 228: wind versus gas. *Coalition Energy News,* Summer 1994, P. 7.

P. 228: photovoltaic payback. Alexandra von Meier, "Manufacturing Energy Requirements and Energy Payback of Crystalline and Amorphous Silicon PV Modules" (Berkeley: University of California, Energy and Resources Group, 1993).

P. 229: peak-period power. *Powering the Midwest: Renewable Electricity for the Economy and the Environment* (Cambridge, MA: Union of Concerned Scientists, 1993), 68.

P. 229: jobs. New York State Energy Office, 1992.

P. 229: oil dependency. Robert K. Watson, *Looking for Oil in All the Wrong Places: Facts About Oil, Natural Gas, and Efficiency Resources* (New York: Natural Resources Defense Council, 1991).

P. 230: military subsidies to oil industry. Amory Lovins, "Make Fuel Efficiency Our Gulf Strategy," *New York Times*, 3 December 1990, op. ed. page.

P. 231: outflow of dollars. *Powering the Midwest*, 7.

P. 231: royalty income. Ibid., 26, 29, 104.

P. 233: irrigation farming versus bison raising. Dale Lewis, *Roy Houck: Buffalo Man* (1992), 105. Buffalo Press, HC 33, Box 42, Fort Pierre, SD 57532.

P. 237: energy dependency. Energy Information Administration, U.S. Department of Energy, *Annual Energy Outlook 1992 with Projections to 2010* (Washington, DC: U.S. Department of Energy, 1992), 20.

P. 238: fixed-vane system. George Wagner, Wind Harvest Company, personal communication.

CHAPTER 11

P. 242: "cowboy welfare program." Like "welfare ranching," the term is common; for a recent example, see the *San Francisco Chronicle*, 23 December 1994.

P. 244: ranchers' incomes. "Ranchers Say Grazing Fee Will Ruin Them." *San Francisco Chronicle,* 3 November 1993, A1.

P. 247: domestication. "Zebras and the Anna Karenina Principle," *Natural History,* September 1994, 4.

P. 248: Baca's questions. Joan Hamilton, "Tough Talk from the Feds," *Sierra,* January–February 1994, 38.

P. 248: mining-law reform. *San Francisco Chronicle,* 4 February 1994, A6, and 30 September 1994.

P. 249: Roy Rogers. Roy Rogers and Dale Evans, *Happy Trails: Our Life Story* (New York: Simon and Schuster, 1994).

P. 249: Russell quote. Sharman Apt Russell, *Kill the Cowboy: A Battle of Mythology in the Old West* (Boston: Addison-Wesley, 1993), 3.

P. 250: permittees. Lynn Jacobs, *Waste of the West: Public Lands Grazing* (1991), 26. Free Our Public Lands, Box 5784, Tucson, AZ 85703.

P. 254: rodeo life. A recent book about the realities of rodeo life is Dirk Johnson, *Biting the Dust* (New York: Simon and Schuster, 1994).

CONCLUSION

P. 262: white bison calf. The birth date was 20 August 1994. The Heider ranch, on which she was born, is near Janesville, Wisconsin.

P. 262: Mother Earth quote. *Los Angeles Times,* 11 September 1994, E9.

Recipes

The following recipes are intended only to introduce you to the cooking of bison. For more detailed suggestions, you might wish to obtain the National Bison Association's Bison Cookbook—$1.50 *plus postage from the N.B.A., Box 16660, Denver, CO 80216.*

BISON ROAST

1 boned bison top sirloin or cross-rib roast (about 5–8 lb.)
  (If you buy the bison frozen, allow two days for this size roast
  to defrost in the refrigerator.)
1 paper or plastic oven roasting bag

marinade:
2 tbs. honey
2 tbs. olive oil
1 tbs. soy sauce
1 tbs. Dijon mustard
2½ tbs. mustard seed
8 thin slices fresh ginger

gravy:
2 cups dry sherry
2 cups beef broth
½ cup thinly sliced green onions

Rinse the meat with cool water and dry. Trim off whatever small remnants of visible fat you find. Some people also remove, with a very sharp knife, the silver-colored membrane found over and inside some of the roast, though this becomes perfectly edible after cooking. (Be sure to plan ahead for defrosting and letting the roast marinate—for up to three days.) You may also wish to make some incisions in the roast and insert garlic cloves.

Prepare the marinade by crushing the mustard seeds with a mortar and pestle or by grinding them briefly in a blender; save 1½ teaspoonful for the gravy. Mix with the other ingredients and coat the roast thoroughly—this will later help to retain moisture. The easiest way to coat the roast is to put it in a plastic bag and pour the marinade over it, then turn it repeatedly until you get good coverage. (You can do this the day before you cook the roast if you allow enough time for defrosting.)

Bison can be roasted on a rack like a beef roast. A roasting bag is desirable to avoid moisture loss; paper bags give slightly better flavor than plastic. Insert a meat thermometer through a half-inch slit in the bag into the center of the roast. Cook at 275°F until the thermometer reads 130°F. This normally takes 1½ to 2 hours. Do not overcook;

this is the greatest hazard in cooking bison! Carefully controlled scientific tests prove that as oven temperature and cooking time increase, taste scores for texture, juiciness, and tenderness decrease.

Let the cooked roast rest for fifteen minutes before slicing, while you prepare the gravy. Bring the ingredients to a boil on high heat and cook uncovered, to reduce, for about eight minutes. Stir in the sliced green onion, and serve in a bowl or gravy boat.

Slice the roast thinly and arrange on a serving plate; add salt and pepper or let your guests do so if they wish.

BISON STEW

3 lb. bison stew meat
2 cups finely chopped onion
2 cloves garlic, chopped
2 bay leaves
½ cup flour
⅓ cup salad oil
3 cups red wine
2 cups water
1 can tomato paste

Put the meat, onion, garlic, and bay leaves in a shallow baking pan; if you wish, sprinkle with salt and pepper. Bake uncovered in a hot (425°F) oven for ten minutes; reduce to slow (300°F) and continue for about thirty minutes. Make a sauce with the flour, oil, wine, water, and tomato paste. Pour over the meat, cover, and bake in a slow oven about 1½ hours or until the meat is very tender but not dry. Serve over rice or noodles.

NEW MEXICO BISON CHILE

5 lb. coarsely ground bison meat
5 ancho chiles, soaked and pureed
4 yellow onions, chopped
3 green bell peppers, chopped
4 jalapeño peppers, chopped
5 lb. tomatoes
3 chipotle chiles, soaked and pureed
¼ cup roasted cumin seeds, ground
½ cup Chimayo or other chile powder, toasted

Brown the bison in a heavy pan—a touch of oil will probably be needed, unless some fat is present in the meat. Add the vegetables and cook for five minutes. Add the spices and just enough liquid to cover. Simmer for one hour. Add salt and pepper to taste.

Acknowledgments

Christine Leefeldt not only came up with the original idea for the book but also collaborated on many aspects of its preparation, from field research through the manuscript's several rewrites.

I am deeply appreciative of the people named in the text who graciously consented to be interviewed and generously shared their information and thoughts. I am also grateful to the researchers and writers whose work is discussed or quoted in the text, especially Frank and Deborah Popper, who also supplied many productive research leads. The real value of any book comes, implicitly or explicitly, from its being a collaborative conversation among many minds.

I have benefited from the support of numerous talented friends. Malcolm Margolin, incomparable publishing comrade, helped me reorganize the text, generally saved me from myself, and helped shape the book's format. Marigay Graña read an early version of the manuscript and provided sound advice. John Berger contributed authoritative guidance for the wind-power chapter. Catherine Moss and Barry Pilger gave informed critical reactions to the manuscript. Richard Kahlenberg and Michael Phillips, longtime fellow conspirators, lent their usual bolstering. William Woodcock, who comes from bison country, gave inspiration and useful research suggestions. Karen Branson's flair for the clear presentation of ideas helped me focus mine. Bob Newhall and Joan Kresich sent me to intriguing historical sources.

The cover painting and the drawings that open each chapter are by Carl Dennis Buell. The drawings of grasses are the work of Bellamy Parks Jansen, and are reproduced by permission from James Stubbendieck, Stephan L. Hatch, and Charles H. Butterfield, *North American Range Plants*, 4th ed. (Lincoln: University of Nebraska Press, 1992). I am grateful to the skilled and patient photographers whose credits appear in the captions. (I took all uncredited photographs.) The National Geographic Society gave permission to reproduce their carefully researched map of bison ranges and herds.

Hans Callenbach skillfully designed and laid out the book; I am delighted to have been the beneficiary of his talents in this father-son collaboration. Barbara Dean, Barbara Youngblood, Pat Harris, Bill LaDue, and others on the Island Press staff enthusiastically saw the book through to publication.

Librarians at the Berkeley Public Library and the libraries of the University of California, Berkeley, proved unfailingly helpful, as librarians always do. Many museum staff people and many park and government agency employees provided information or aided me in finding it. I also received valuable aid from people not named in the text who provided background, clues, or encouragement; they include J. Baird Callicott, Elio and Diane DePisa, Barry Miller and Janice Moulton, Richard Register, Sonya Richardson, Patricia Ryan, Andy Stahl, David Tilman, Ken Throlson, and Linda Wallace.

Despite the assistance I received from all the people mentioned here, any errors in the book are my sole responsibility.

I would like to add that I am also grateful to the bison themselves. Their tenacity against great odds in the past and their present strength and grace moved me far more than I anticipated when I first began this project.

Index

Accidents with bison, 166-68
"Adopt-an-allotment" programs, 50
Alliance for a Paving Moratorium, 169
American Bison Association, 118
Animal Damage Control, 54-55
Animal rights movement, 188
Anishinabe (Ojibwe), 77
Antelope Island State Park, 89, 98
Antibiotics, 195, 197-98
Arikara, 32
Aristotle, 241

Babbitt, Bruce, 248
Baca, Jim, 247-48
Badlands National Park, 95, 110
Barsness, Larry, 177
Beef consumption, 185, 189
Bender, Marty, 182
Bereuter, Doug, 98
Beyond Beef, 186
Biodiversity, 26, 149
Biomass energy, 230, 236-37
Biophobia, 146
Bioregionalism, 256
Bison: basic groups, 11; "buffalo"
    name, 3; calving, 15; coexistence
    with, 16; conflicts with cars, 163;
    conflicts with humans, 158; cook-
    ing, 194; cuts of, 193; digestion, 30;
    distribution of meat, 193; domi-
    nance patterns, 163; early hunters,
    34, 40; ecological virtues, 6, 25;
    European, 119; "exotic animals" to
    U.S.D.A., 102; feedlots, 128-29; fur,
    13; genetics, 142; government stew-
    ardship potential for, 109; grazing
    movements, 11-12; handling, 254;
hunts, 70, 142; Indian reservations,
65-86; loafing, 17; "management,"
118; marbling in, 128; mating
season, 14; migrations, 11; military
land, 100; national animal status
(proposed), 2, 241; noises, 13; public lands, 87-114; original range,
18; predation on, 89, 91; productivity of, 178; ranches, 115-43; reserves
for, 243; restoration of, 243, 246;
roaming, 26; rubbing, 96, 238;
sacred white, 77-78, 262; senses, 13;
shipping of, 194; slaughtering, 74,
192; storage of meat, 194; tails, 13;
tourism based on, 139-42, 202;
wallowing, 181; zoos, 113

Black-footed ferret, 151
Blue Mounds State Park, 99
Bronx Zoo, 36, 113
Brucellosis, 134-39
Buddhism, 189
Buffalo: see bison
Buffalo Gap National Grassland, 26
Buffalo jumps, 31, 83
Buffalo Woman, 67, 68
Bureau of Land Management, 52, 87,
    101, 157, 242-43
Byer, Tim, 107-8

Canadian bison, 100
Carleton, Phil, 114
Catalina Island herd, 112-13, 239
Cattle impacts on earth, 178
Catton, William, 57
Cheyenne River Sioux Reservation,
    72, 75, 82
Cholesterol, 194-96

Classification and Multiple Use Act,
    108
Coal, 43, 105-7, 173
Cody, "Buffalo Bill," 37
Commons: efficiency of, 219;
    history of, 214-17; prospects of, 214;
    "tragedy" of, 215-16
Congress, 104, 153, 157, 236, 241, 243
Conservation Reserve Program,
    152-54
Corbett, Jim, 253
Counties, future of, 256-58
Cowboy culture, 248-54
Crazy Horse monument, 214
Crow, 72
Custer State Park, 92, 122, 131,
    136, 139, 166

Daily, Gretchen C., 176
Dances with Wolves, 70, 123, 160, 191,
    197, 212
Danz, Harold, 186
Davis, Donald S., 135-38
Deep ecology, 73
Degradation of ranch land, 245
Delinquent farm loans, 204
Deloria, Vine Jr., 202
Demography, 204
Denver Buffalo Company, 60, 186, 197
Denver Zoo, 114
Depopulation of rural lands, 46
Diamond, Jared, 246
Diet and health, 186
Diversity of grassland species, 26
Domestication, 246
Drug dosing of livestock, 198
DuBray, Fred, 72, 80-82, 84
Dude ranches, 213
Durham Ranch, 119-20, 128, 161
Dust Bowl, 41-43, 199

Ecosystem (defined), 4
Ecotourism, 212
Ehrlich, Paul, 213
Electric vehicles, 237-38
Elk, 9, 91, 106, 109, 138, 143, 178, 253
Erosion, 21, 172, 202

Farm Bill of 1990, 180
Farm Bureau, 45
Fat: in bison, 194-96; in diet, 185, 195
Federal Lands Policy and
    Management Act, 108
Fences, 62, 160-62, 184
Ferguson, Denzel, 211
Fiber optics, 207
Fire, 22, 24-25, 29, 107, 112
Fish consumption, 185
Flocchini, John, 119-20, 129, 131-32,
    161-62
Flywheels for energy storage, 226, 237
Food Security Act, 102
Forest Service, 52, 103-4, 107, 157-58,
    169, 242-43, 248
Fort Berthold Indian Reservation, 95
Fort Niobrara National Wildlife
    Refuge, 89, 96
Fort Wingate, 100
Fossil fuels, 222, 235
Frazier, Ian, 55

GATT, 47
Garreau, Joel, 200
Gathering and hunting societies, 177
Gates, C. Cormack, 137
Goble, Paul, 68
Gold Trophy Bison Show, 133
Government land acquisition,
    156, 208
Government ownership of land, 62
Grand Teton National Park, 91, 136
Grasses, root systems of, 23

Grassland ecology, 22-26
Grasslands National Park (proposed), 97
Grazing Act, 103
Grazing associations, 108, 176
Grazing fees and permits, 50, 52, 242, 253
Griffith, Bud, 124-25

Hamilton, Bob, 111
Hardin, Garrett, 201, 215-18
Harris, Captain Moses, 39
Haugen, Arnold O., 13-14
Heat-Moon, William Least, 34, 203
Heckert, Mark, 71-79, 103-4
Heider, Dave and Valerie, 262
Hinduism, 188
Hobby ranchers, 121
Holistic resource management, 115
Homesteaders, 41
Hormones, 195, 197
Houck, Roy, 122-23, 137
House Rock Valley, 99
Hunting, 70, 142
Hydropower, 229, 232, 236

Indian artifacts made from bison, 21
Indian diet, 33-34
Indian reservation bison, 65-86, 243
Indian women and bison, 78
Indians: and bison, 31, 59, 65-86, 212, 243; and ecology, 79; and wind power, 232
Interest and discount rates, 174-75
InterTribal Bison Cooperative, 70-79, 88

Jackson, Wes, 17, 57, 180-84
Jones, Dana, 120

Kansas Water Office, 205
Knowles, Craig, 22, 74-76
Kosher rules, 188

Lakota Sioux, 65, 77
Lame Deer, 67
Land availability for bison, 152
Land Institute, The, 180-84
Land values less than subsidies, 153
Landownership, 44
Lang, Robert E., 208
Licht, Daniel, 152-54
Little Elk, Edna, 78
"Living machines," 174
Longhorns, 176, 183
Looks for Buffalo, 262
Lott, Dale, 163
Lower Brule Sioux, 72
Lyman, Howard, 186

Mandan, 32
Maps, 256
Marchello, Martin, 185
McDonough, William, 171
Meagher, Mary, 137, 163
Menominee, 77
Meyer, Margaret, 137-39
Miller, Russ, 125
Mining, 105, 171
"Miracle," white bison calf, 262
Multiple Use Sustained Yield Act, 103

NAFTA, 47
National Bison Association, 118, 123
National Bison Range, 10, 92, 131, 136, 239
National Park Service, 98, 243
National forests, 87, 101
National grasslands, 87, 101
Native American Bison Refuge (proposed), 85
Native Americans and bison, 31, 59, 65-86, 212, 243
Native grasses, 22, 24, 26, 246, 263

Index

Natural gas, 229, 235, 237
Nature Conservancy, 22, 24, 59, 61, 99, 111, 162, 243, 256
"Negawatts," 229
Net-energy-negative agriculture, 172
Nikoforuk, Andrew, 49
Niobrara River valley, 97, 256
Nonprofit bison herds, 110
Norland, Jack, 28-9
Northern Arapahoe, 72
Northern Ute, 72
Noss, Reed, 154

Ogallala aquifer, 171, 199, 205
Oglala Sioux Reservation, 68
Oil, 44; as basis for agriculture, 172
Orr, David, 146

Patch dynamics, 24
Pawnee, 32, 55, 65
Perennial polycultures, 180, 184
Perot, H. Ross, 54
Pimentel, David, 172
Pine Ridge Reservation, 68, 213
Pishkun, 31, 83
Plains vs. prairies, 19
Plumb, Glenn, 110
Political change process, 255
Popper, Frank and Deborah, 199-215
Poultry consumption, 185
Prairie dogs, 71, 107
Productivity, 46, 171
Pronghorn, 9, 96
Public lands for bison, 101, 242-43

Quade, Monte and Colleen, 190-91, 196
Quammen, David, 189

Rainfall, 21
Ranchers, hiring to restore bison, 244-46
Ranching economy, tax base of, 244
Ranching strategies, 133
Red Cloud, 79
Renewable energy, 222
Reversion of land to Indians, 82, 84, 248
Rodeo, 253-54
Rölvaag, O. E., 41, 223
Roosevelt, Theodore, 214
Rotational grazing, 130
Rural electrification, 234
Russell, Sharman Apt, 30, 249, 252-53

Sahlins, Marshall, 177
San Francisco Zoo, 113-14
Sand Hills (Nebraska), 97
Sandoz, Mari, 40, 65
Savory, Allan, 27-29, 115-18, 131, 252
Schult, Milo, 13-14
Scott, Robert, 201
Secrist, Glenn, 108-9
Selective breeding, 130, 142
Settlement of Plains, 210
Sharecropping, 45
Shaw, Jim, 142
Sheridan, General Philip, 39, 80
Sherman, Richard, 77
Snyder, Gary, 146, 187, 217-18
Social traps, 176
Soil organisms, 20
Solar ages, 6
Solar energy, 236
Southern Ute, 72
Steuter, Al, 24
Subsidies, 48-50, 153, 227, 237, 243-46
Sullys Hill National Wildlife Refuge, 99
Sunshine Farm, 182
Sustainability, 4, 173-74, 219, 222, 228

Tallgrass Prairie National Park
(proposed), 203, 243
Tallgrass prairie preserve (proposed),
154
Talmudic law, 188
Taos Pueblo herd, 72
Tax loopholes, 53
Tennessee Valley Authority, 100, 200
Terry Bison Ranch, 126-28, 131, 139-42
Theodore Roosevelt National
Memorial Park, 95
Thiel, Dan and Ron, 126-27, 129
Thunder Basin National Grassland,
105
Thundering Herd Buffalo Products,
60
Tibbits, Tommy, 213
Tourism, bison-based, 202, 211
Tribal land base, 82
Turner, Frederick Jackson, 35, 199
Turner, Ted, 59, 123-26, 179

Union of Concerned Scientists, 233
U.S. Department of Agriculture, 61,
75, 157, 180
U.S. Fish and Wildlife Service, 98

Vegetarians, 188

Walker, Ron, 92
Walking Coyote, Samuel, 92
Wallach, Burt, 200

White bison, sacred, 77, 262
White, Richard, 39, 41
White, Stephen E., 208-9
White Plume, Alex, 68-70, 262
Wichita Mountains National Wildlife
Refuge, 98
"Wild" vs. "domestic," 263
Wildlands Proposal, 154-55
Wildlife biologists, 104
Wildlife corridors, 155
Wildlife refuges, 98, 109
Williams, Pat, 51
Williamson, Robert, 103-4
Wilson, Edward O., 7
Wind Cave National Park, 93-94
Wind farms, 257; maintenance of, 225;
royalties on, 231-32
Wind power: abroad, 225; bird losses
to, 238; California, 226; compat-
ibility with bison, 229, 232; costs,
228; transmission lines, 233, 236
Windmills, traditional, 221
Wolves, 12, 89, 253
Wood Buffalo National Park, 100
Wounded Knee, 214
Wright Brothers, 183
Wuerthner, George, 150

Yellowstone National Park, 2, 28,
59, 60, 88, 91, 131, 139, 155, 158-59,
164-67, 211

About Island Press

Island Press is the only nonprofit organization in the United States whose principal purpose is the publication of books on environmental issues and natural resource management. We provide solutions-oriented information to professionals, public officials, business and community leaders, and concerned citizens who are shaping responses to environmental problems.

In 1994, Island Press celebrated its tenth anniversary as the leading provider of timely and practical books that take a multidisciplinary approach to critical environmental concerns. Our growing list of titles reflects our commitment to bringing the best of an expanding body of literature to the environmental community throughout North America and the world.

Support for Island Press is provided by The Geraldine R. Dodge Foundation, The Energy Foundation, The Ford Foundation, William and Flora Hewlett Foundation, The John D. and Catherine T. MacArthur Foundation, The Andrew W. Mellon Foundation, The Joyce Mertz-Gilmore Foundation, The New-Land Foundation, The Pew Charitable Trusts, The Rockefeller Brothers Fund, The Tides Foundation, Turner Foundation, Inc., The Rockefeller Philanthropic Collaborative, Inc., and individual donors.

Island Press Board of Directors